Hinduism

Hinduism: A Contemporary Philosophical Investigation explores Hinduism and the distinction between the secular and religious on a global scale. According to Ranganathan, a careful philosophical study of Hinduism reveals it as the microcosm of philosophical disagreements with Indian resources, across a variety of topics, including: ethics, logic, the philosophy of thought, epistemology, moral standing, metaphysics, and politics. This analysis offers an original and fresh diagnosis of studying Hinduism, colonialism, and a global rise of hypernationalism, as well as the frequent acrimony between scholars and practitioners of Hindu traditions.

This text is appropriate for use in undergraduate and graduate courses on Hinduism, and Indian philosophy, and can be used as an advanced introduction to the problems of philosophy with South Asian resources.

Shyam Ranganathan is a Faculty Member of the Department of Philosophy, and a Research Associate at the York Center for Asian Research, York University, Toronto, Canada.

Investigating Philosophy of Religion

Series editors: Chad Meister, Bethel College, and Charles Taliaferro, St. Olaf College

This is a series of interfaith texts that philosophically engage with the major world religions in light of central issues they are currently facing. Each work is an original contribution by a leading scholar from that religious tradition and incorporates the latest developments in scholarship in the field. The texts are written for students, scholars, and all those who want a fairly detailed but concise overview of the central issues in contemporary philosophy of religion from the perspective of the major world religions.

Judaism
A Contemporary Philosophical Investigation
Lenn E. Goodman

Buddhism
A Contemporary Philosophical Investigation
David Burton

Islam
A Contemporary Philosophical Investigation
Imran Aijaz

Naturalism and Religion
A Contemporary Philosophical Investigation
Graham Oppy

For more information about this series, please visit: www.routledge.com/Investigating-Philosophy-of-Religion/book-series/IPR

Hinduism

A Contemporary Philosophical Investigation

Shyam Ranganathan

Routledge
Taylor & Francis Group
LONDON AND NEW YORK

First published 2018
by Routledge
2 Park Square, Milton Park, Abingdon, Oxon OX14 4RN

and by Routledge
711 Third Avenue, New York, NY 10017

Routledge is an imprint of the Taylor & Francis Group, an informa business

British Library Cataloguing-in-Publication Data
A catalogue record for this book is available from the British Library

Library of Congress Cataloging-in-Publication Data
A catalog record has been requested for this book

ISBN: 978-1-138-90909-0 (hbk)
ISBN: 978-1-138-90910-6 (pbk)
ISBN: 978-1-315-69416-0 (ebk)

Typeset in Times New Roman
by Swales & Willis Ltd, Exeter, Devon, UK

Contents

Preface

This is a book on Hinduism, the religion—not parts of Hinduism, or traditions within Hinduism. Once we know that Hinduism is not characterizable by some basic doctrine or perspective, then talking synoptically about the religion without oversimplification or overgeneralizations is as easy as accounting for it by disagreement, which is inclusive. Nevertheless, it still takes some learning about the diversity of options in Hinduism to say something about such disagreements. My formal schooling in these matters ended when I graduated with an MA in South Asian Studies from the University of Toronto in 2002. Leonard C.D.C. Priestley, Narendra K. Wagle and the late Joseph O'Connell all played an instrumental role in my introduction to Indology and Religious Studies. But my continued education in this area was facilitated by becoming a member (and increasingly, fly on the wall) of two online communities of scholars: L-RISA (the listserve for Religion In South Asia, of the American Academy of Religion) and the INDOLOGY discussion forum. If you are reading this preface after finishing this book, you might be surprised at my gratitude. I argue that much of what passes for scholarship on Indian philosophy and Hinduism is confused on multiple levels, yet I'm quite sure that I would not have come to these conclusions without the generosity of scholars willing to talk about their research. Week after week, just as I would start to form some delusional sense of having a handle on Hinduism and Indian philosophy, some discussion would alight on these lists, only for my naivety to be mercifully burst.

By the time I completed my graduate studies in South Asian Studies, I was exhausted. A two-year degree (one year longer than the usual as I had to catch up for a lack of undergraduate preparation) turned into five years—almost a second doctorate. It was inexplicable to me that a whole community of scholars found it a more likely explanation that Indian thinkers whimsically and capriciously, for no apparent reason, used one word "dharma" for so many disconnected topics—instead of the simpler, parsimonious answer that they were just disagreeing about ethical theory. For a long time I tried to pursue the question by arguments in favor of my position. This resulted in my first book, *Ethics and the History of Indian Philosophy*. There I argued two points: (a) "dharma" is the word that Indians used to discuss morality or ethics and it has no second meaning; (b) if one wishes to locate an ethical concern, find the topics that people are touchy about. No sooner had I completed it, that I started to regret it. This game of providing an account of the facts different from the standard account has no end game for the methodology of explanation by way of what one takes to be true is incurably subjective. Really, we need to take the issue up a level—to the question of appropriate methodologies for what counts as understanding and rational explanation. But this conversation is difficult to have in Indology for two reasons. So many scholars here want to be in the position of explaining to their students what Hinduism is, or other Indian religions are, or what Hindus or Indians believe, and this creates a context where there has to be some account of the facts that constitutes the curriculum. It was in this haze that I found myself arguing that if scholars of India really want to know where to find all the Indian ethics, just look at what people are touchy about, and what they are inclined to get annoyed at, if you do not take it seriously. In Chapter 5 of this book, I have a better explanation now for this phenomenon—it's really what ethics looks like in a *W*esternized world, where thought is conflated with belief. But the earlier view that ethics is simply that touchiness is wrong, and yet in keeping with the empirical bent of work in Indology. The second reason that methodological questions of understanding are not easily raised in Indology and South Asian Studies is that scholars here are (with rare exceptions) not philosophers critically engaging in finding solutions to problems of translation or cross-cultural understanding, but passive consumers of philosophical theory generated by the *W*est—the tradition that entails that interpretation is the basic mode of explanation. This is evidenced by the widespread tendency of scholars in this field thinking that research into things Indian has to address hermeneutic (interpretive) questions. So when folks in this field reach out to philosophers for some guidance on questions of cross-cultural understanding, what they end up reading cements an insularity of interpretation. In this context, it is easier to have a discussion about the correct account of Hindu or Indian perspectives, than a conversation about whether an account of a perspective is the appropriate target of inquiry. If we interpret, we treat perspectives as the means and ends of explanation. If we explicate, we take it that disagreements, not perspectives, are the means and ends of explanation.

At this point (2002–2007) I resumed studies in philosophy, ostensibly not on South Asia. Thankfully, my advisor, Robert Myers, and readers Henry Jackman and Stuart Shankar (now my colleagues) created an environment where I could pursue very basic questions in recent Analytic (and Continental) philosophy on issues such as the nature of propositions, philosophy of language, metaethics, moral theory—and translation. Yet, contrary to the usual stereotypes of Analytic philosophers, I found them to be more open to the possibilities of systematic and pervasive moral philosophical disagreement in the Indian tradition than scholars who profess an interest in South Asia. This is not to say that these philosophers always agreed with me. But here, in philosophy, disagreement was a way to further the conversation. Disagreement in contrast seemed to end conversations when I was pursuing work in South Asian Studies. So I turn out to be a relatively unsympathetic ear now to folks wanting to bash Analytic philosophers for being small-minded—a dig I often hear from grad students and sometimes to my surprise from colleagues, who take themselves to be on the side of diversity in philosophy. As one such philosopher, I disagree.

One of the peculiar outcomes of my return to philosophy was that I came to see that the kinds of problems that plague the study of things Indian are completely rooted and traceable to historically influential and dominant accounts of thought in what I call the *W*est. I probably would not have noticed this had I not tried to address the question of the apparent missing ethics from the Indian tradition, followed by a more abstract exploration of moral discourse translation as my PhD dissertation. But through this all, my own identity as a Hindu started to come apart.

Growing up Hindu, if one is not delusional and if one is well informed, involves several incremental steps towards the realization that Hindus have basically nothing distinctive in common, except for their disagreements. At first, one's identity as a Hindu seems inescapable because it's a matter of family and heritage, and then it becomes apparently inescapable for it's unclear how one can opt out of it: any position one chooses to adopt could be Hindu. Delusion creeps in by interpretation: if you have to explain Hinduism by way of what you take to be true, then you simply organize the data in accordance with your beliefs, and you will be quite immune to the evidence. But I fear I was born explicating—something that made me rather difficult to get along with, I'm sure. All of this meant that I would be a better fit for what goes on in philosophy. Yet, simply burrowing in philosophy would not really free me from certain problems.

First, being Hindu in a 'secular' world is a most bizarre experience: it is in effect to be committed to the project of open and radical disagreement, but to be interpreted as endorsing an ancient belief system. This is a problem for there is no way out: if I were to deny that I am a Hindu, I deny this practice of free thinking characteristic of Hinduism. But if I affirm being Hindu, then I would be interpreted as having some characteristically Hindu worldview. If I were to hence advertise that my work as a philosopher draws on ideas and texts from the Hindu tradition, I would be labeled as doing something non-standard, religious, and not secular. That in and of itself would render it not attractive to journals or publishers interested in focusing on secular research—even though the more Hindu, the more secular and open to disagreement. By the same token such work does not fit the mold of what counts as conventional publications in Indian philosophy or Hindu studies. Specialists in this field often see themselves as representing the beliefs of Indians and Hindus (historical and contemporary) and departments that look to hire people for a position on Indian philosophy typically want the same. Pointing out that good work in these areas involves rejecting a focus on belief not only seems insensitive to Indian and Hindu belief, but also often undermines the motivation for hiring in such positions: to have someone doxographically represent imagined Indians and Hindus in the interest of diversity.

Second, all of the problems I found in Indology did not disappear because I decided to focus on philosophy. For it is the *W*est's intellectual tradition that dominates what we read and count as classical contributions to research in philosophy as pursued in many parts of the world that really accounts for the problems of understanding diversity.

It was in my post-dissertation transition, as I was pursuing teaching at my *alma mater*, York, that Chakravarthi Ram-Prasad invited me to edit the *Bloomsbury Research Handbook of Indian Ethics* (2017), in part because of my earlier work on the topic. I thank him for bringing me back to Indian Ethics and for supporting my research. All the scholars who contributed to that volume added texture and detail to my sense of the historical possibilities of Hinduism—and they put up with my tendency to make explication a methodological priority. To this end, I would like to thank: A. Raghuramaraju, Ashwani Peetush, Dagmar Wujastyk, Edeltraud Harzer, Francis X. Clooney, Jake Davis, Jayandra Soni, Kisor Chakrabarti, and William Edelglass. I would also like to thank A. Raghuramaraju for inviting me to design the first year MA course on Indian Ethics as part of the Government of India's efforts to render graduate education materials freely available online (e-PG *Pathshala*). Writing several lessons for this project served to bring home that salient options in the Hindu tradition are merely options of moral theory.

While I began to work on the first of these projects (in 2013), Chad Meister emailed me for himself and Charles Taliaferro, to invite me to contribute to the *Investigating Philosophy of Religion* series, of which this book is a part. It was with great trepidation that I considered the invitation and wrote up a proposal. My reason for the trepidation is that in order to talk about Hinduism, properly, one has to talk about the conditions under which the open-ended intellectual exploration of an entire subcontinent of people became a religion, and that discussion widens the scope from what we would nominally expect from an account of a religion—even a philosophical account. To my great surprise, and later befuddled joy, Chad and Charles stood by my proposal, and were extremely supportive as they reviewed it and the subsequent manuscript, and as Routledge had the latter externally reviewed. I thank them for their support. In this process too, I owe a debt of gratitude to the anonymous reviewers for their helpful comments. It was at the prompting of the external reviewer of the completed manuscript that I brought into discussion the work of fellow *Indian Philosophy Blog* contributor, Jonathan Edelmann, in Chapter 4, and drew out other distinguishing features of a representative Hinduism (Hinduism that represents the disagreements of Hindus). Also of note here is the role that the publisher at Acumen Press, Tristan Palmer, played in supporting this project early on. Tristan oversaw the review of the first proposal for the manuscript, providing valuable feedback and seeing it through this early stage. I would like to thank Chad, Charles and Tristan for endorsing the potential in this book early on.

Through much of this I had wonderful and supportive interactions with fellow *Indian Philosophy Blog* contributors, such as Andrew Nicholson, Andrew Ollet, Jonathan Edelmann, and Malcolm Keating. The blog founders, Amod Lele, Elisa Freschi, and Matthew Dasti, also deserve thanks for creating this very useful forum in addition to being great online interlocutors.

My York colleagues have been exceptional in supporting me in all of my research and teaching interests. In the now old and status quo world of precarious academic work, they supported me as I competed for and won via an open competition a contractually limited position as Assistant Professor of Moral and

Political Philosophy (which lasted four years), and later as I applied for conversion to the full-time faculty. It was during my stint as a genuine professor, when I had my own office, and even a research assistant, that I began many of my recent projects, including this book. I also would like to thank York University and the Canadian Union of Public Employees Local 3903 for awarding me a one-year research leave for 2017–2018. I had finished the draft of the manuscript for review prior to this leave, but the time has helped with the review and revisions.

In addition I would like to thank colleagues and friends far and wide, some of whom I interact with more occasionally over email but whose responses to questions and interactions have supported me in my research. This list includes: Adheesh Sathaye, Adrienne Martin, Ajay Rao, Alice Maclachlan, Amy Allocco, Antoine Panaioti, Benjamin Kelly, Bianca Torchia, Bindu Puri, Brandon Tinklenberg, Brian Black, Brian Huss, Caleb Dewey, Chandan Narayan, Claudine Verheggen, Clinton Debogorski, Dennis Vasilis Papadopoulos, Daniel Barron, David Slakter, Dermot Killingley, Evan Thompson, Gordon Davis, Ian Whicher, Ithamar Theodor, J. Piers Rawling, Jeffery Long, Josh Moufawad-Paul, Joshua R. Farris, Jyotirmaya Sharma, Jyoti and Rajat from SynTalk, Kristen Andrews, Lauren Edwards, Luis Cordeiro Rodrigues, Martin Gansten, Mengxiao Huang, Muhammad Ali Khalidi, Nathaniel Roberts, Nell S. Hawley, Philip Harland, Philip Wilson, Purushottama Bilimoria, Regina Rini, Richard Gombrich, Sudhakshina Rangaswami, Susanne Kathrin Beiweis, Tim Beaumont, Tom Angier, Vasudha Narayanan, and Vishwa Adluri.

My students—the wonderfully diverse body of students at York, which reflects Toronto—have been crucial in helping me clarify the varying issues that I write about in this book. In the varied classes I teach, whether it is ethical theory, philosophy of language, or Asian philosophy, I have been struck not only by their willingness to learn about philosophy that is radically new to them but their willingness to benefit from it, not as a mere intellectual curiosity, but as practical solutions to ongoing problems.

I would like to thank the team at Routledge, starting with Sarah Gore, whose patience in seeing this project past the finish line has made the entire process easy. Thanks also to Eve Mayer and Rebecca Shillabeer who helped move the project along in the commissioning stages. And thanks to Rosie Stewart at Swales & Willis and freelance copy-editor Jonathan Hoare.

I owe a special debt of gratitude to my parents, Saroja and Narasimhan Ranganathan, and my larger family. My parents and my larger family are my first teachers on the topic of Hinduism. I would like to thank my wife, Andrea Yandreski, and our human son, Keshava, and our border collie daughter Jyoti, for their company, love, and support. While I was born with being Hindu as something inescapable, they showed me what it looks like to be Hindu on purpose—it's similar to being born Hindu with the feeling of inescapability, but more fun, beautiful, and inspirational. Disagreement and diversity is inescapable but it is also fun, beautiful, and liberating—when we choose it on purpose.

1 Introduction

Our topic: Hinduism the religion

This book is a philosophical investigation into Hinduism. This is not the same as a review of Indian philosophies (cf. Dasgupta 1975; Hiriyanna 1995; Mohanty 2000, 1992; Matilal and Ganeri 2002; Ganeri 2001, 2007; Ram-Prasad 2001, 2007; Bartley 2011) that are called Hindu, nor is it an empirical review of Hindu practices and beliefs (Knott 1998; Doniger 2010, 2014; Narayanan 2010, 2004; Hawley and Narayanan 2006). Works on these topics are certainly worth reading—but that is not our topic. In order to embark on these investigations we need some grasp of the category *HINDUISM* that would allow us to distinguish Hindu philosophies from non-Hindu philosophies, and Hindu practices and beliefs from non-Hindu practices and beliefs. Answering the question of what Hinduism as a category amounts to—an analysis of the concept of *HINDUISM*—is the proper topic for a philosophical investigation of Hinduism. It might seem that once we have such an analysis, we will be in a position to study philosophies that are Hindu, or practices and beliefs that are Hindu. Yet, *HINDUISM*, the category is open-ended. An adequate appreciation of its logical properties not only underdetermines what philosophies, practices or beliefs are Hindu, but by extension it will underdetermine what counts as a religion. This is because Hinduism, properly understood, is the microcosm of philosophy itself, with a South Asian twist. The possibilities of Hinduism are the possibilities of philosophy. Everything from realism to antirealism on questions of metaphysics, epistemology, and ethics, are to be found within the options of Hinduism. Even the question of whether the gods are real or there is an afterlife is a disagreement firmly within the boundaries of Hinduism: one can be an atheist and a Hindu for instance (Bilimoria 1990, 1989).

My goal in this book is to move away from thinking about Hinduism in terms of beliefs that Hindus have. The idea that there are some basic beliefs that characterize Hinduism is implausible as is the idea that there are some basic practices that are definitively or essentially Hindu (Ranganathan 2016). Rather in appreciating that Hinduism is the microcosm of philosophy itself, we should identify representative ideas from the Indian tradition that stand for the project of philosophy itself—ideas that model differing topics and their disagreements within philosophy. These Hindu representations of philosophy will allow us to say something synoptic about Hinduism without committing to implausible claims about what all Hindus believe or what all things Hindu endorse. The philosophical topics I will cover include: (meta) philosophy, moral theory, logic, propositional content, epistemology, moral standing, metaphysics, and politics. These Hindu representations of specific topics within philosophy will also constitute synoptic Hindu responses to major areas of philosophy. These responses are what Hindus converge on while they disagree in the respective areas. If these Hindu ideas really do represent Hinduism as the microcosm of philosophy, and if truth reveals what it represents, these representative ideas are true of philosophy—or perhaps more plainly, philosophically true.

My reasons for approaching Hinduism philosophically are not merely a matter of my interests as a philosopher. I think that this approach is representative of what is objective about Hinduism. In other words, it is an unbiased account of Hinduism that reveals Hinduism as an object of investigation. In identifying Hinduism as the microcosm of philosophy with a South Asian twist we appreciate that to the extent that Hindus have views about how and what things exist, how we can know about them, and how to mediate differences of opinion, they have philosophical views about metaphysics, epistemology, and logic.

To the extent that Hindus have positions on what to choose, how to behave, and what to aim for, they have positions in moral and political philosophy. Practices, rituals and festivals that Hindus endorse and participate in are part of their moral and political theories in practice. Certainly these practices could be described and studied social-scientifically and independently of philosophical reasons that constitute supporting Hindu outlooks, but that would be to divorce the practices of Hindus from their reasons. The only motivation for engaging in a non-philosophical study of Indian ritual and practice is a commitment to an Orientalist narrative that depicts Indians as creatures of tradition and habit with no reasons for their choices (cf. Said 1978; Inden 1990). Certainly we could engage in this kind of scholarship but we would be responsible for divorcing these Hindu practices from their supporting philosophy. If the practices thereby appeared extra-philosophical, that would be a function of our research methodology—we would have no reason to believe that our resulting representations of Hindu practice are accurate.

To the extent that Hindus have views about what all Hindus should endorse, they have second-order philosophical views: metaphilosophical views. But as is commonly observed (cf. *Philosophical Investigations* I.121), there is not a huge difference between a metaphilosophical view and a philosophical view as any substantive philosophical option is a view about what is true for all options. To the extent that what keeps Hinduism together is philosophical disagreement—a disagreement about what is philosophically true for all philosophical options—then all Hindu positions are metaphilosophical.

In appreciating that it is the philosophical debates of South Asia that keep Hinduism together, we note that there is neither need nor necessity to identify something that all Hindus endorse in order to make sense of Hinduism. This insight sheds a critical light on *comprehensive* accounts of Hinduism: accounts of Hinduism that identify Hinduism with some foundational philosophical commitment. Often, comprehensive views of Hinduism are expressed under the idea that there is a historical unity in Hinduism—or the opposite, that Hindus are ecumenical in believing that all paths lead to the same god. The number of comprehensive accounts of Hinduism abound.[1] They arise naturally from Hindus disagreeing, metaphilosophically, about what Hindus should endorse: everyone who has a philosophical view about what Hindus should endorse has one such view. The difference between the *representative ideas of Hinduism* that I will identify and *models of Comprehensive Hinduism* is that the representative ideas do not entail what Hindus have to endorse in order to be a Hindu. Rather they represent Hinduism as a philosophical disagreement so in some respect they depend upon an open-ended diversity of dissenting views to constitute the objectivity of Hinduism. Most importantly, the dissenting views do not have to be tolerant or instantiate the openness of Hinduism just as in philosophy, dissenting views within a philosophical debate do not have to display the virtues of criticism and reason that characterizes philosophy to be part of the philosophical debate. The virtues of the debate are not necessarily reducible to the contributions to the debate, but the openness of the debate itself. Representative Hinduism accommodates all versions of Hinduism: the good, the bad, and the ugly. It accurately reveals the object: Hinduism. We shall see, it is able to deliver philosophical guidance because it does not deny the reality of diverse contributions to Hinduism.

Comprehensive versions of Hinduism in contrast might either *define* "Hinduism" in terms of some doctrine or practice (for instance, one might think that to be a Hindu one must be devoted to Hindu gods, or some subset of Hindu gods), or they might *stipulate* what Hindus should believe to be good Hindus (one might think that to be a good Hindu is to worship a specific god and not all gods). *Definitional* versions of *Comprehensive* Hinduism are all implausible as accounts of Hinduism. To make a case for any comprehensive doctrine as definitive of Hinduism involves a tremendous amount of cherry picking and sample bias. Philosophers can have far more sympathy for *Stipulative* accounts of Comprehensive Hinduism that make a case for what would be advisable for followers of Hinduism to endorse in so far as such positions arise out of philosophical reflection. But they would be mistaken as a synopsis of Hinduism—unless they are based on representational Hinduism. We can and should think about the minimal philosophical commitments that are *entailed* by philosophical disagreements because these are philosophically true as representations or revelations of philosophical disagreement. They *reveal* the disagreement as they are consistent with them having been entailed by them. These would be synoptic of Hinduism but of philosophy as well, and worth taking seriously for these reasons.

Myths of the substance of religion

Appreciating what Hinduism is as a religion requires doing away with several myths about:

- religion as a phenomena on the periphery of philosophy,
- the irrelevance of politics and colonialism to what counts as a religion,
- (but also) what the philosophy of religion has to look like when faced with the reality of religion as a global phenomenon.

Eurocentrism

The usual myths about religion as a phenomenon at the boundaries of philosophy goes hand in hand with the usual myth that the philosophy of religion is primarily concerned with details of theism. Philosophy is a critical disagreement between every and all manner of theories and to the extent that theism is depicted as the basic substance of religion, it seems like religion stands outside of the debates of philosophy. One must be a believer to be religious it seems. We get this impression of religion by focusing on religious options on the doorstep of Europe—Judaism, Christianity, and Islam. That religion is about theism is put to rest when we consider religion on a global scale, and what we find is that the diversity and range of options across religions is no different than the diversity of options across philosophy. As Victoria Harrison (2006) has noted, in a multicultural world, we have to look to pragmatic considerations to inform our understanding of religion as there is no essence to religion, if we take in all the evidence. Hinduism is paradigmatic of the reality that there is nothing in philosophy that is left over when we look at the reality of religion. The global reality of philosophical diversity is the philosophical reality of Hinduism. Hinduism is the world's philosophical diversity in miniature with a *masala* twist. But this puts a fair bit of stress on the idea that religion is a phenomenon on the boundaries of philosophy. It also brings to light the elephant in the room:

- The only people's whose philosophy is not religious or constitutive of a religion are European peoples and their philosophy.

This observation pertains to a more contemporary world, of the Common Era, where "religion" has no obvious essence. This observation was not true in the ancient world if we read back our idea of religion into the Roman perspective. Our term "religion" comes from the Latin *religio* and is originally part of the bureaucratic framework of the ancient Romans. They would use "religio" for any duty to the divine (pagan or other) and contrasted with *superstitio*, which overlaps with our "superstition." The latter was a term of abuse while the former is not. This distinction mirrors in some way our distinction between a religion and a cult.[2] But what is noteworthy about European and human history is that anything that might have been a religion of European descent and pedigree was wiped out in practice and absorbed into the cultural history of Europe. Now, if a philosophical idea can be shown to have a European pedigree, it does not get counted as a religion—no matter the content. The philosophy could be theistic or make a case for unobservable facts, perhaps even life after death (such as much of Plato), but it would not be religious if it was argued for by a European and has a European pedigree. But if the same philosophical outlook is found somewhere else in the world it is religion. Even when we focus solely on religions formed on the doorstep of Europe's imperialism—Judaism, Christianity, and Islam—we find that "religion" is a label given only to those traditions as they have an extra-European pedigree. The vast majority of European philosophers from Plato on were theists but their theism is counted as philosophical and not religious so long as there is no explicit effort made to ground these ideas in an extra-European tradition. But if theism comes by way of the Middle East from outside of Europe, it is thereby religious.

Part of this transformation has to do with divorcing the idea of religion from a 'duty to the divine' but also secularizing what divinity amounts to (an idea of *SECULARISM* that I will call "Secularism$_2$"). We find this transition already afoot in Plato's *Euthyphro*, where Socrates criticizes the idea that the holy can be learned by tradition, and rather the holy has to be determined by some independent criterion that would legitimate some traditions as authoritative and others as not. Here we find Plato putting a wedge between holiness as a sociological phenomenon and one that is philosophical. With this wedge we find that European ideas of the holy from European philosophers are routinely treated as secular and philosophical while non-European accounts are religious and sociological even from philosophical sources.

Consider the following philosophical position. You should not worry about your individuality (or questions like whether god exists) but rather pay careful attention to your choices, for they have consequences. Some lead to beneficial results for all concerned, and others to suffering. In so far as beings can suffer, we ought to choose carefully so as to minimize suffering. If you believe this because you read Bentham (1781), your views would be called ethical. But if you believe this because you read the writings of Buddhists (cf. Goodman 2009) your views would be religious. When the argument is made by a European, it is philosophers who study the arguments. If the argument is made by a South Asian, it is primarily social scientists (scholars of religious studies, philologists, historians, linguists) who would study the matter. What is the difference? Race and ethnicity.

Or, consider the following philosophical option. Reality begins with the evolution of matter from a primal indistinct state of nature: a root state of nature. Through this evolution of matter from primitive undifferentiated states toward increasing complexity, we find that people arise on the scene. That is, while originally we could not find people within the natural world, people all of a sudden coincide with a high degree of differentiation in nature. A person is a center of consciousness—a perspective—and is the kind of thing that apparently can make choices. Some choices can be ethical and can lead to better outcomes of life, while others are immoral and lead to bad outcomes. But freedom comes to the individual when she observes the truth: that the only thing that has ever suffered or enjoyed life, has ever made choices bad or good, or had any type of life arc is matter. Everything is causally determined by nature and hence personal experience is at most epiphenomenal. If you came to believe this for reasons of European pedigree, you would be called a rationalist-materialist. This is 'secular.' If you came to believe this because you read Īśvarakṛṣṇa's second-century *Sāṅkhya Kārikā*, you would be a Hindu. This is 'religious.' A Sanskritist with no formal training as a philosopher is more likely to opine about your view. What is the difference? The pedigree.

One might suppose that the difference is that in the case of religion, we find a belief in the afterlife. So while Marxism shows many traits of organized religion (such as group rituals, symbols, traditions, and figures who are venerated such as Lenin or Mao), Marxists do not have a religion because they reject the afterlife. But it is far from clear that you have to believe in an afterlife to be religious. There are several Indian theories that are identified as religious that deny the reality of an afterlife and depict life after death as a confusion. Early Buddhist texts for instance affirm rebirth, but no transmigration: this is a criticism of the idea that you as an individual will have a life after your death (*Milindapañha* II.2). More radically, the *Sāṅkhya Kārikā* that identifies the individual as epiphenomenal undermines the idea that there is anything like a life for you once you are free of the delusion of agency—even nature will no longer flatter your pretense of having a life at that point (SK 59, 62–63). In a position that combines elements of both, the Vedānta philosopher Śaṅkara, regarded by many contemporary Hindus as their philosophical inspiration, describes the idea of individuality that could persist in time as a superimposition of pure subjectivity on the objects of experience (Śaṅkara (Ādi) 1994: I.i. preamble). At best after death there are new bodies born: you as an individual do not continue as you the individual were never real (Śaṅkara 1991: commentary on II.12). The expectation of hope beyond the grave is mistaken on these accounts. They are, however, very orthodox, 'religious' options from India.

When we are aware of the diversity of religion on a global scale, the usual effort to distinguish religion from secular philosophy on the basis of some basic philosophical doctrine or commitment is obviously mistaken. The idea that there is some type of doctrinal or substantive difference between the religious and the secular resides in profound ignorance of many non-western religions: especially Hinduism. Yet, the underlying narrative is clear. Non-western ideas are to be studied by non-philosopher, social scientific, scholars of religious studies. European ideas are studied by philosophers (who are not social scientists). What conclusion follows from this? European foundations for philosophical ideas are rational, but extra-European foundations are mysterious, traditional, and non-rational and involve commitments to matters that go beyond what we can reasonably expect based on the evidence. What further policy can we derive from this? European resources are treated as the content of public reason, and anything alien as beyond the pale of reason to be described ethnographically. Indeed, as a reviewer of this work noted, following this trend: when talking about Hinduism even when we are engaging in a philosophical investigation of it, we should not forget what falls outside of philosophy—Hindu practices. This commenter's response is not unusual. It is a common view: when Hindus do things it apparently has nothing to do with reason and philosophy according to many scholars. This is because Indians have no notable tradition of moral philosophy (Matilal 1989). It is all religion and mysticism (Danto 1972).

Irrelevant standards in the study of Indian thought

The asymmetry of scholarly concerns that leads to philosophers studying European ideas and non-philosophers studying non-European ideas leads to an imbalance in the scholarship. It seems like non-Europeans are more traditional and less philosophical simply as a result of the asymmetry in scholarship. However, the asymmetry is glaring: we do not send ethnographers to study the transmission of ideas of European philosophers over generations, and we do not subject their writings to philological scrutiny as the primary means of studying intellectual history. Yet, in the case of anything South Asian, this is the primary avenue of research: philology, historical anthropology, or some other form of social science. Even when the topic is explicitly philosophical, in Indology, one will be hard-pressed to find a philosopher trained by other philosophers doing the research: it will more likely be a linguist. As a result, when the challenge is posed to account for what an Indian philosophical text has to say (such as the *Yoga Sūtra*—YS) we will find armies of philologists trying to account for its content by philological means. They will substitute reading the primary text with reading commentaries that are less challenging though derivative and perhaps inaccurate, and we will find some trying to defer to questions of authorship to determine the content of the text. We find in this literature the astounding definition of a "critical scholar" as someone who is primarily concerned with commentaries, not the original text (White 2014: 5; Maas 2013; for further investigation of this phenomenon, see Ranganathan 2017). In other words, the research interests and methods of philology substitute for reading philosophy. It hence seems like the Indian text is mysterious and difficult to read and not rational philosophy—it will get called "religious." But this is a function of the research interests and methods of scholarship.

The malpractice of research into philosophy where Indian thought is concerned runs deep. The first matter that we teach our students as philosophers is that answers to philosophical questions cannot be solved by bringing a good dictionary to class. Indeed, the very idea that there are definitions that will settle philosophical questions is a mistake. The reason? Any definition of, say, "good" or "ethics" that we care to proffer will be controversial too for definitions at most encode a perspective that is at issue in a philosophical debate. Utilitarians define "goodness" as happiness. Kantians define "the good" as the will determined by the Categorical Imperative. When Utilitarians and Kantians offer their definition of the good as a means of solving a philosophical debate, they are really trying to pass off their theory of the good as though it is the meaning of "good." So in light of the reality that a definition merely encodes a controversial theory and is by no means the uncontroversial condition of thinking philosophically about the topics they define, philosophers prevent students from trying to solve philosophical problems by thinking about them as a problem of linguistics. Yet, when we come to the study of Indian philosophy, the issue is routinely treated as a linguistic question about what our words like "ethics" or "moral" mean and what Indian terms like "dharma" mean. (We shall examine this widespread phenomenon in Indology in further chapters.) The study of Sanskrit and philology eclipses the study of philosophy. Indeed, even in the *Journal of Indian Philosophy*, the salient journal dedicated to the study of Indian thought and philosophy, one will routinely find articles that have nothing to do with philosophy but are on philological matters.[3] The study of Indian thought and philosophy has been overcome by research interests that are outside of philosophy. This is certainly an embarrassment for the study of Indian philosophy but it also speaks to the wider disvalue people attach to the study of philosophy. We shall see the usual myth that there is nothing like research in philosophy and nothing objective to study is false, but this idea makes room for substituting the study of philosophy with social scientific topics that are viewed as more objective. This is in part how the depiction of the mystical essence of Indian thought is sustained.

The categorical origins of 'religion'

So often we talk about religion in a bubble as though the criteria and conditions under which we come to identify something as a religion are divorced from politics or the history of imperialism. It is difficult to think of Judaism without understanding the history of political and imperial oppression that constituted its development and is immortalized in observances such as Passover. It is difficult to understand the historical event of the crucifixion of Jesus (central to Christianity) without acknowledging the Roman Empire as its instrument. In reality, no one in Asia ever thought of themselves as having a religion (or in need of religious rights or freedoms) before the *W*est showed up on its doorstep. As the religious studies scholar and Buddhologist, José Ignacio Cabezón (2006), notes, the idea of religion and religious studies originates out of the *W*est's exploration of *alterity* (the other).

I will invite my readers to draw a distinction between being ethnically or geographically western (small "w") and politically *W*estern (capital, italicized "*W*" that leans on the "est"). One can be western without being *W*estern. I am western by birth and upbringing and I *choose* not to be *W*estern: no one has to be *W*estern by virtue of birth or ethnicity. It is a bad philosophical choice but one made without much thought.

The *W*est as a cultural force is interpretation with a European origin. It is *W*estern imperialism—an imperialism that treats the European outlook as the basic framework that everything must conform to in order to be understood. What connects interpretation and Europe is the central doctrine of the *W*est's intellectual tradition: *the linguistic account of thought*.

This goes back to the Greek idea of *logos*—a single word for 'thought,' 'opinion,' and 'word,' but also 'reason.' Accordingly, thought and conceptual content is the meaning of what we say in our language. If thought (*logos*) is the meaning of what we say in our language (*logos*), then:

> our reasons (*logos*) that we can rely on are what are culturally encoded in our language as its semantics.

But:

> as these reasons are semantically encoded in our language, we cannot refuse to endorse them without saying something that is a contradiction in terms (analytically false).

Hence,

> to rely upon these linguistically encoded meanings as our reasons is to believe them (*logos*).

But then,

> as thought and belief are thereby conflated as our reasons, then all rational explanation becomes explanation by way of our beliefs: explanation by way of belief is *interpretation.*

However,

> as the model of interpretation derives from this characteristically *W*estern (European) account of thought, beliefs that derive from Europe's intellectual tradition are employed by the *W*est in its interpretation of everything else.

Yet,

> interpretation can only explain what is internal to the beliefs employed in interpretation: everything else it depicts as irrational—or at least, non-rational—and mysterious—or at least, traditional, a matter of habit, and not a consequence of theoretical or philosophical reflection.

So,

> given the last two observations, anything that is non-*W*estern is depicted by the *W*est as irrational and mysterious, or non-rational and a matter of tradition—to be studied social scientifically, and not philosophically.

*W*esterners are committed to a strong distinction between philosophy and religion: for them, religion is something objective to be studied—not a consequence of a bad account of explanation (interpretation). Religion is what falls outside of the interpretive resources of the *W*est, or rather, what we call "religion" is simply what the *W*est cannot interpret satisfactorily. The category *RELIGION* is how alien philosophy looks when it is interpreted, and in a *W*esternized world everything is interpreted from a Eurocentric perspective. If there were more than one intellectual tradition wedded to the linguistic account of thought, there would be more than one way to define the secular in contrast to the religious. Yet, the European intellectual tradition is unique in being founded on this basic doctrine, which constitutes a continuous thread from its ancient to its modern manifestations in Continental and Analytic philosophy.

Given the basis of the *W*est in the linguistic account of thought, authors who work in the paradigm of the *W*est (such as Orthodox Indologists) treat the challenge of understanding the thought of others not primarily as an exercise in philosophy but a social scientific inquiry: a matter of understanding the language and culture of aliens—this allows the substantive beliefs of the interpreter to never be the direct object of philosophical research and instead function as measures of alien thought. Studying Indian philosophy in this *W*estern paradigm is reduced to the exercise of discerning whether Indians say things believed by *W*esterners. For an Indian to have a view on moral or political theory, they would have to agree with *W*estern accounts of morals and politics, and if their outlook diverges, they would apparently have no views on the matter.

Indian thinkers often engaged in *mīmāṃsā*: reflection, examination, investigation. This is often incorrectly translated as "interpretation." Interpretation is not *mīmāṃsā* for it is not a form of investigation: it is the attempt to treat one's own beliefs as a standard that everything else must measure up to. It is in essence the opposite of investigation: it decides answers to substantive questions by relying upon one's beliefs, and all that is left is the task of filtering the world through these assumptions.

There are several logical and philosophical problems with the *W*est. First, the linguistic account of thought (as we shall see in subsequent chapters) is a disaster: it confuses the anthropological and the culturally contingent (what is linguistically encoded) with thought (what can be true or false) and hence creates philosophical problems that it cannot solve that have to do with reality and truth beyond our cultural vantages. However, as the linguistic account of thought that leads to interpretation has problems understanding anything that is not derivable from the culturally encoded beliefs it relies on, it creates a narrative of its cultural background as the default fountain of reason (philosophy) and everything else as mysticism (religion). As there are no alternative models of thought in the *W*est (indeed, the imperialist methodology of this tradition would not allow it), this narrative, based on the incapacity of interpretation to understand diversity, is taken as a vindication of the tradition: the *W*est is logical and everyone else traditional mystics. So, the methodology of the *W*est parlays the cultural contingency of the *W*est into a privileged background that is then used to judge and assess everything that diverges. But there is an important problem with it: interpretation runs afoul of the basic mode of explanation in philosophy—*explication*—which is founded on the essence of logic: validity. Whereas interpretation tries to explain by way of what the interpreter takes to be true, *validity* is concerned with what follows *if* premises of an argument are true. Explication based on validity hence does not flatter the starting points of the believer, and seems like a threat to interpretation—and the *W*estern tradition.

On a global scale, the *W*estern tradition stands out for its conflicted relationship to philosophy itself. It begins with the murder of a philosopher, Socrates, is defined for much of its history by centralized doctrinal authorities that decided what everyone could believe without persecution, is punctuated by the persecution of intellectuals, and is distinguished by an imperial and colonial expansion that killed dissenting perspectives as part of its globalizing hegemony. All of this vitiates against the openness and tolerance of philosophy to dissent and divergent perspectives. The pathological relationship of the *W*est to philosophy stands in sharp contrast to the role of philosophers in non-*W*estern philosophical traditions—especially South Asia where they were and are still venerated as *ācārya*-s (pedagogical authorities). Whereas martyrdom (dying for one's philosophical commitments) is a well documented phenomenon of the *W*est, it has no obvious corollary in other philosophical traditions. When it arises, there is an ancestral relationship to the *W*est.[4] One could be as philosophically quirky as one wanted to in ancient South Asia and with no centralized doctrinal authority to enforce an official position, no one seemed to care.[5] If your brand of philosophy was counterculture, you could try to gain followers as a philosophical outlier (*śramaṇa*). Most were unsuccessful, but some, such as the Buddha, had legions of followers. Hinduism, a collection of quirky, tenuously connected and often disagreeing and antagonistic traditions is also evidence of this openness. It has sometimes been observed that there was no central authority in Hinduism that settled doctrine for followers. This is not strange. What is strange is that there was such a thing in Europe. Too often the hegemony of the European tradition is taken to be an expression of a standard and general feature of human society and the diversity of Hinduism and India is treated as strange. To understand Hinduism we need to understand how the tradition of Eurocentric interpretation gets us to believe the paradox that diversity is strange and the uncritical hegemony of Europe is the content of reason.

In a *W*esternized world where *W*estern theory is considered to be the content of public philosophy (thanks to its tradition of interpretation), this marginalization serves to maintain the *W*est's imperialism. But the primary victim is the discipline of philosophy itself. In calling upon the idea of *RELIGION* to quarantine non-*W*estern philosophy, the *W*est puts a fence around philosophy, and leaves its own narrow tradition of thinking (what Alfred North Whitehead called a "series of footnotes to Plato"—1978: 39) as the content of public discourse. But as this tradition all goes back to a single source, its diversity is limited: variations on a theme. Diversity in options and theories is central to the health of philosophy for philosophy involves looking at our concepts, thoughts, and theories from differing critical perspectives. It thrives on disagreement and debate, and the segregation of non-western philosophy from *W*estern theory kills philosophy. Every religion is a philosophical option or set of options hived off by the *W*est to be quarantined from diversity. The result is that the *W*est is a maimed tradition of philosophy. Hinduism is that part of philosophy the *W*est thought it could bite off but could not chew: it is too big. It is philosophy itself. Ironically, the *W*est in its effort to interpret everything from a Eurocentric perspective alienates philosophy from itself. We have to study the religion Hinduism to recover what it lost.

One of the implications of these considerations is that religion as what cannot be interpreted by the *W*est in many ways functions as race: it is a device of marginalization with the European self occupying the primary role as the universal self—everyone else is derivative and primitive in contrast (cf. James Accessed 2016; Mills 1997). Just as the only people who have no color are Europeans and their descendants while everyone else is 'colored' so too does the European have no religion save for what comes from outside of Europe and everyone else is religious (unless they convert to something European as say when the Chinese adopted Marxism). While this is generally the case with religion, "Hindu" being a historically western term for people living in India (Hawley and Narayanan 2006: 3–10) is a most explicitly racialized account of a religion, in which comparisons to the European self as primary abound.

One of the challenges for those of us with an interest in non-*W*estern traditions is that the very narrative generated by the *W*est can and is often transplanted to non-western contexts as a function of its imperialism and the result is that non-westerners start to understand themselves by way of the framework of the *W*est—by way of religious identities that would never have otherwise taken foot. In a world that naively identifies the secular as the *W*estern and the religious as what deviates (call this idea of secularity "Secularism$_2$"), failing to appreciate that Hinduism is the microcosm of philosophy with a *masala* twist leads to marginalizing philosophy from public discourse in a 'secular' country like India. The only kind of Hinduism that can play into Secularism$_2$ assumptions about religion, the only one left over after philosophy has been banished as religion, are the *rākṣasa* (demonic) varieties—that are unphilosophical, intolerant of dissent and diversity (Sharma 2011). This variety of Hinduism, the 'secular' (Secularism$_2$) state understands: it plays into the idea that religion lies outside the bounds of reason. Getting to the objectivity of Hinduism involves not only chipping away at the philosophical tenets of the *W*est, but opening ourselves up to a more genuine secularism (Secularism$_1$): the freedom to philosophically disagree. This is Hinduism in its non-*W*esternized form.

Much of this will seem controversial. If we are to embrace a philosophical investigation into Hinduism, we should become comfortable with controversy as philosophy is nothing if not controversial. Hinduism is that religion that is the controversies of philosophy with a South Asian presentation. One obstacle to such an investigation is:

- a tenacious, subconscious endorsement of the *W*est in the form of the identification of philosophy with the European tradition, and everything else as religion.

This is a very entrenched intuition and is merely another version of the *W*est's own narrative of acclamation. One fatal error with this intuition is that the only way to generate it is by endorsing interpretation: as we shall see, when we endorse the contrary, explication, all we find in our investigations is philosophy and never religion. Another fatal problem with this intuition is that philosophy is not a tradition but a discipline, and disciplines are venues of disagreement. So in so far as religions contribute to philosophical disagreements on a variety of matters, including how to live, and what to aim for, we need philosophy to understand the options. But then an investigation into Hinduism has to be philosophical if we want to even make sense of the supposed difference of Hinduism to the *W*est's own acclaimed picture of itself. Hinduism is not outside philosophy but contributes to it, and the line between religion and philosophy melts. Moreover, Hinduism is a peculiar religion: the only way to understand it synoptically is as philosophy, the disagreement.

What is philosophy?

Our philosophical investigation into Hinduism will lean on a clear account of philosophy as distinct from other avenues of research—an account of philosophy that shows how philosophy is in many ways the most basic of yogas (disciplines). It is certainly not the only academic discipline but the failure to give philosophy a pride of place in our account of knowledge leads to confusion and the blurring of distinctions that should be kept clear. Our way to understanding philosophy begins with a general consideration: objects. The topic of objectivity will be explored in detail in this book, but for now, we start with the humble object.

Objects that we know are what we can observe from differing vantages and to the extent that we can disagree about what we are viewing we know what we are viewing is objective. In contrast, illusions and subjective opinions are only observable from a specific vantage. This distinction allows us to tell mirrors apart from their reflections. A mirror is objective as we can view it from differing perspectives, and in so far as it explains our disagreements about what we are observing in this case, we know we are viewing an object, the mirror. A reflection from a mirror in contrast is viewable from one perspective only: if we move relative to a mirror, we see different reflections or none at all. What we view in a mirror is hence subjective. If we believe that what we view in a mirror is objective, we are under an illusion. Truth is the property of thoughts and representations—it reveals (or corresponds to) the content of thought.[6] When a thought or representation reveals an object, it is objectively true. When our representation reveals what is subjective, it is not objectively true, but subjectively true. False representations and thoughts reveal nothing objective or subjective. (Theories of truth are examined in greater detail in Chapter 8.) For instance, a description of a mirror is objectively true if it reveals the objectivity of a mirror (what we can view from multiple perspectives) whereas our description of what we see when we look in the mirror is subjectively true—it reveals to us the content of a subject's experience. Truth and objectivity are not the same. Indian philosophers have celebrated objectivity as something distinct from truth. The Jain parable of the blind men feeling different parts of an elephant, with each providing perspective-relative descriptions (the one holding the leg says it is a tree, the one holding the ear says that it is a leaf) is one such illustration: each description is true from some perspective, but the objectivity of the elephant transcends such subjective truths. Famously, the Hindu deity Viṣṇu reclines on the cosmic snake of many perspectives, while holding a conch. The conch is especially symbolic of objectivity as it is a perfectly asymmetrical object, which appears different from every orientation. He objectifies himself as a disk of mutually imposed triangles. Given the elementary observations about what an object is, to know an object is to know it from differing perspectives, and hence to be objective as a knower is to triangulate. To know oneself as objective would be to triangulate oneself from a differing vantage. This is the dynamism of Viṣṇu himself as the disk—the triangulated self-triangulating. This allows Viṣṇu to be clearly distinct from the other objects of the world, and hence this disk is his 'good view' (*Sudarśana*) of them, but then his own practice reveals what is objective: he is in some sense objectively true of what he knows—his self-practice of objectification reveals the objectivity of other people. His concomitance with such objects of knowledge allows him to be not their creator, or destroyer, but their preserver.[7]

The famous Buddhist philosopher, Nāgārjuna, argues in his *Mūlamadhyamakakārikā* (XXIV.8–14) that ultimate truth is empty (like a conch) for there is no canonical description of it from all perspectives. Ultimately, truth lacks *svabhāva* (autonomy, or essence) on this account. The Emptiness of truth is its objectivity. Hence Nāgārjuna argues that Nihilism is a mistaken inference from the observation that everything is empty, and that the opposite is true: we should choose carefully for action has objective consequences (karma).

Philosophy is perhaps the oldest of disciplines, though it is certainly not the only discipline. Disciplines are not theories, or perspectives. Disciplines take controversies as their objects and aim at a thorough and comprehensive account of the object. If objects are what we can triangulate from differing perspectives, we need some common axis to coordinate differing perspectives on common objects: this is the job of the discipline as we can practice the same discipline from differing perspectives. In empirical science, the objects of disagreement are the characterization of what we can experience (observe) from all perspectives. These objects are the laws of nature, and the accurate scientific theory—the true theory—aims at revealing these objects. In mathematics, as in logic, the objects of inquiry are claims and their constituents (what we can disagree about), and the true claims (properly understood) reveal their derivability from more basic systems. Identifying what can be derived mathematically tells us what is true in mathematics. 2+2=4 can be derived from arithmetic and it also reveals what can be derived, but 2+2=5 is neither and thus false.[8]

Philosophy too has its objects: they are our perspectives, their constituent propositions (thoughts), and the constituents of propositions: concepts and other objects. These relate as reasons for conclusions, and the study of such relations is philosophy. We say that reasons entail a conclusion when the conclusion has to be true if the reasons are true. Arguments that have this property are called *valid*. You and I can converge on an argument's validity from differing theoretical perspectives, while disagreeing about whether the reasons and the conclusion are true. This shows that validity is objective. The process of studying a perspective's reasons so as to understand its conclusions is *explication* for it renders *explicit* what seems implicit. Explication allows us to identify the subset of reasons of a perspective that entail particular controversial claims about a topic *t*. When we compare competing theories on *t*, we find that what they converge on while they disagree is the concept *T*—call this comparison the *consilience of entailments*. Philosophers engage in explication without much fanfare. For instance, when a philosopher wants to understand what a Kantian perspective (*P*) has to say about ethics (*t*), she looks at the reasons that constitute the Kantian perspective that entail the Kantian uses of the term "ethics" (this would be the Kantian theory of ethics) and then she further compares competing theories of 'ethics' (she would have to explicate them too) to discern what the common substance of ethics is about: this is what theories of ethics disagree about, which is *THE RIGHT OR THE GOOD*. As John Rawls notes: "The two main concepts of ethics are those of *THE RIGHT* and *THE GOOD* . . . The structure of an ethical theory is . . . largely determined by how it defines and connects these two basic notions" (Rawls 1971: 24).

The first step in the process of explication relies on validity, and as noted it is objective. Moreover, as the resulting concept is identified as what we can converge on while we disagree, it too is objective for objectivity is merely this property of what we converge on while we disagree. In other words, explicating a philosophy and understanding its substance requires no agreement or assumptions about controversial matters: we rather discover this by studying a debate. While philosophy appears to start with the modest concern for tracking reasons for conclusions, it allows us to understand the objective concept at the heart of a debate, such as *THE RIGHT OR THE GOOD* in the case of moral philosophy, as something that is *abstract* (as it comes apart from the particular theories of ethics) but also *general*, as it is something relevant to the competing theories that allow us to isolate the concept. So from a seemingly modest concern for reasons and conclusions, we arrive at a defining trait of philosophy: that its substance is at once *abstract* and *general*. As truth is the property of thoughts that *reveals* what it is about (false propositions reveal nothing), explicating philosophy and isolating its basic concepts by the consilience of entailments allows us to identify revealing claims about the objects of philosophy and these revealing claims are thereby objectively true. Contrary to myth, philosophy is objective, as objective as any discipline of research, and philosophers too can work to uncover objective truths about philosophy by research. This is typically missed and underappreciated by scholars who are not philosophers and unarticulated by philosophers.

At this point it is worth reflecting upon the difference between psychology and philosophy, belief and thought. Common parlance confuses these two and even some famous philosophers—such as the British imperialist and colonial administrator of India, John Stuart Mill—confused psychology with philosophical truths of logic (Mill 1882). This view is called *psychologism* and we will see in our chapter on Logic that there is a non-accidental connection between *psychologism* and imperialism. (Mill has a false reputation for being a liberal—an impression we get by ignoring his voluminous output justifying colonialism and his explicitly racist claims in his political works.[9]) We shall see that *W*estern liberalism comes with constraints that undermine freedom. (Hinduism in contrast has a shot at being a genuinely liberal platform.) The father of phenomenology, Edmund Husserl (1970, also a *W*estern imperialist) was initially sympathetic to *psychologism*, but after being criticized by (the closet anti-Semite) Gottlob Frege (cf. 1980) he temporarily recanted though he reverted to it in rolling out his project of phenomenology (Husserl 2001, see the "Prolegomena" for the recantation and the subsequent investigations for the psychologism). We shall see (in Chapter 4) that the politics of these philosophers of logic are more than relevant to our investigation. Logic is concerned with how we should think. Human psychology or dog psychology might be empirically describable but yet fail to live up to the ideals of logic. The reason that the two issues get confused is that both can be described as tracking thought. Philosophers are concerned with thought—propositions—and their components (such as concepts), while psychologists are apparently also concerned with our thoughts. What is the difference?

For starters, it is important to distinguish between propositional attitudes, and propositions (thoughts). A propositional attitude, such as believing, is an attitude of assent with respect to a proposition *p*. I can *believe* that *p*, just as I can *fear* that *p*, or *question* that *p* or perhaps even *joy* that *p*. Philosophy as something that tracks the objectivity of propositions is concerned with *p* from multiple angles and perspectives. This is what allows us to appreciate the objectivity of *p*. Philosophers might know this as analysis. Hindus should know this as *yoga*: the control of thought (YS I.2). As Patañjali notes, yoga, the practice of controlling our thoughts (YS I.2), situates being critical about thoughts in a public realm where we can take diverse perspectives on a thought, concept, or object (YS II.33–IV). Being free from confusion depends upon distinguishing a thought from our propositional attitudes, but this requires that we transcend our selfishness (YS IV.29) that ties us to a thought via an attitude that we might call a prejudice (*saṃskāra*). This is what we aspire to in Analytic philosophy—or at least, that is why it is worth taking seriously. But that is yoga as Patañjali describes it. Psychology in contrast takes an interest in attitudes, but it takes an interest in attitudes for it is an empirical science, and empirical science is concerned with the objectivity of empirical laws of *x*—in the case of psychology the *x* includes our attitudes.

What is certainly interesting and important about psychology is that it allows us to treat something subjective—our attitudes—as the topic of objective laws of nature. Philosophy, however, is not concerned in the first instance with describing our attitudes, but with our thoughts and their components. That leads us to be objective about them in a manner that permits *criticism*. One might question this: couldn't we be critical about our beliefs?

We shall revisit this issue in Chapter 4, Chapter 5, and Chapter 6. But for now it is worth noting that belief, and any described propositional attitude (Rāhu, a demon we will investigate in Chapter 4), is a most curious creature. A belief builds into a claim an attitude of assent (as a fear builds into a claim an attitude of revulsion), while a thought does not. Hence, the belief 'I believe that it is raining outside' (or the fear, 'I fear it is raining outside') includes in it the proposition 'it is raining outside' and an attitude that ties some person to a thought. The trouble here is that my belief (or fear) about it raining outside is answerable to nothing outside of me and its truth depends upon my attitude. A belief is hence quite different than a mere description of a subjective experience, such as 'it seems rainy outside' or 'I observe rain phenomena.' The latter is assessable from one perspective (a putative inside looking out) but its truth depends on more than mere attitude. 'I believe it is raining outside' is true if I believe it. This has logical implications. I can for instance infer that 'if it is raining outside' that 'it is raining outside.' I can inductively infer from the subjective claim 'it seems rainy outside,' to the objective claim 'it is probably raining outside.' I cannot infer (deductively) from 'I believe it is raining outside' to 'it is raining outside.' Even inductively (probabilistically), it is quite implausible to infer from 'I believe that it is raining outside' to 'it is probably raining outside.' The former is true because of the attitude of belief, and the latter is true given the probabilities, matters quite disconnected. So whereas subjective claims may be false, though you believe them, a belief in contrast is true simply by virtue of one's attitude of belief. Hence while I might disagree with your assessment that 'it seems rainy outside' (I might look outside from your vantage and come to a differing assessment) I cannot disagree that you believe that it is raining outside, if, indeed, you believe it. So belief makes a claim on everyone's assent, even if the substance of a belief is controversial and false. So whereas thought is something we can be critical of, propositional attitudes, whether beliefs or fears, are not, for their truth depends upon the attitude contained in the claim.

The common careless practice of treating 'belief' and 'thought' as interchangeable (*psychologism*) causes many problems for clear thinking. This sheds light on why psychology and philosophy are sometimes confused. Psychology is concerned with our attitudes and thereby our beliefs, fears and other propositional attitudes, but propositions in their abstraction are the topic of philosophical investigation. Based on this confusion of conflating the psychological (attitudes) with thought (the truth assessable), it seems like the proper topic of philosophical investigation into the thoughts we think is a psychological or sociological enterprise. Given this confusion, it seems like we need social science to study philosophy. On the basis of this confusion, it would seem like a philosophical investigation into Indian philosophy and Hinduism consists in studying what Indian philosophers and Hindus believe. But once we dispel this confusion, the only objectivity that we can inquire into, where Hindu and Indian thoughts are concerned, is not the belief but the thoughts relevant to Indian and Hindu philosophy, which we study objectively via explication. These are likely what Indians and Hindus have positive attitudes toward, but we cannot determine what they are as inferential entailments from Indian and Hindu beliefs any more than we can derive 'it is raining outside' from 'I believe it is raining outside.'

If our only way to a thought is via our beliefs, we can never be critical of our thoughts: our thoughts will always be what we believe. But if we can practice some philosophy we put aside beliefs and interest ourselves with perspectives, which contain reasons for conclusions that are objective (remember, objective does not mean 'true' it only means that we can disagree about them). By swapping out belief and replacing it with a theoretical perspective, we exchange what is not objective, with something that is, for the theoretical perspective has logical implications—implications that are logically valid and hence objective. We can hence distinguish between a *valid argument*—an argument whose concluding thought follows from the premises (whose conclusion has to be true if the premises are true)—and a valid argument with premises that we want to believe, or is worth believing because the premises are true. We might even discover something strange: that the argument worth believing is not the one based on premises we believe. Stranger still: we come to appreciate that the arguments worth taking seriously in the first instance are not worth taking seriously because our only reason for believing the argument is that the premises are true. Invalid arguments can have true premises and conclusions. What renders the argument valid is not the truth of the premises or the conclusion but the relationship of entailment: if the premises are true the conclusion has to be true. Reasonable arguments can have false premises, and irrational arguments can have true premises. Truth is neither necessary nor sufficient for logic. This shows us that the validity of reasoning is *objective*: we can converge on it from differing disagreeing perspectives and whether we believe the premises or not has to do with our perspective and not the content of reason. Indeed, the entire controversy over the truth or falsity of an argument (of its premises and conclusion) is moot with respect to its validity for validity comes apart from the truth of premises and conclusions. But, importantly, we cannot determine whether an argument is *sound* (valid with true premises) if we do not first determine its validity, for unsound arguments can have true premises and conclusions. So contrary to popular opinion (encouraged by the *W*est we shall see), our first duty in critical reasoning is not to the truth but the objectivity of reason, which is to say, what we can disagree about from differing perspectives. In our chapter on Logic we shall see that this feature of objectivity (our ability to disagree about the topic) is characteristic of reason but absent in the case of *psychologism* and imperialism.

For now we might draw the further observation: failing to distinguish between your beliefs and thought leads you to be unable to distinguish what can be thought and what you think is true. The thinkable is conflated with your perspective if you do not draw a distinction between thought and belief. But then you render disagreement unintelligible for the thinkable is the same as what you believe. Anyone who renders disagreement unintelligible acts imperiously as though their perspective is the only possible and reasonable perspective, but they also undermine the objectivity of their thoughts, for one can only see a thought from their perspective. So the irrationality of *psychologism* and imperialism are deeply connected. *Psychologism* denies the logical possibility of disagreement by swapping thought for belief. Imperialism denies the political possibility of disagreement. Worse if you cannot distinguish between thoughts and beliefs, you cannot appreciate the objectivity of an argument as something independent of your perspective. (This is an outcome of the *W*est given its conflation of thought and belief.) In other words, you will have difficulty distinguishing between what you think is true and what is reasonable. This is the essence of irrationality. Philosophy is our way out of this quagmire. It involves seeing thoughts and arguments, as well as all mental content, from differing perspectives to discern their objectivity. This is accomplished by taking control of our relationship to what we contemplate so that we do not define it in terms of our perspective: yoga (YS I.2). Free of perspective—belief—we are free of *psychologism* and are thereby rational and qualified to think clearly. However, this involves understanding that all objects of contemplation exist in a public world where you can take differing perspectives on the same thing. Diversity of perspective is what we have to accept if we are reasonable. This is natural for philosophers and yogis: difficult for everyone else.

These considerations help us understand how a philosophical investigation into any topic is not the same as a psychological or social scientific investigation that tracks propositional attitudes. But, then, a philosophical investigation into

Hinduism will not have anything to say about what Hindus believe. The concern to track Hindu beliefs is motivated by the conflation of thought and belief, which is characteristic of the *W*est.

Looking ahead

In this chapter, I have engaged in a preliminary inquiry into philosophy in contrast to other salient forms of inquiry. The issues that arise in this introduction into Hinduism as a topic of philosophical investigation will continue in our investigation into Hinduism. Some might find the approach I am taking unsatisfying. They might believe that we should settle all methodological issues at the start, and allow this to frame the presentation of Hindu resources. One of the benefits of studying Hinduism philosophically is that these methodological issues of research are part of the philosophical sophistication of Hinduism and hence to study it is to study these methodological issues. Appreciating that Hinduism is a philosophical disagreement and not merely a comprehensive doctrine, leads us to appreciate that Hindus have methodological constraints of philosophy that they can fall back on that make sense of their diversity, and moreover what allows Hindus to make sense of their philosophical disagreements helps us say something synoptic about Hinduism—and philosophy. The entire project, however, will provide a prophylactic to interpretation. In general:

- For every substantive philosophical topic, the goal will be to identify an Indian resource that can be used to model what philosophers have to converge on while they disagree.
- In each such case we will have identified the relevant representative Hindu idea for the topic at hand.
- Representative Hindu ideas are not what Hindus agree on as Hindus, nor do they have to believe it to be a Hindu: rather they present what Hindus converge on when they philosophically disagree.

In Chapter 2, "Hinduism and the Limits of Interpretation," I revisit two models of understanding—interpretation and explication—that result in very differing outcomes given the same epistemic challenge. With this backdrop we are in a position to identify *Hinduism* as a category that defies the interpretive expectations of the *W*est: it is a religion merely because it could not be fully explained by the *W*est. While all religions are what cannot be reduced to Eurocentric explanations, Hinduism is the very limit of the *W*est: it is a religion because it is philosophy and for that reason it falls outside the hermeneutic resources of the *W*est, driven as it is by belief, not thought.

In Chapter 3, "Bhakti: The Fourth Moral Theory," we will look more closely at the question of Indian discussions of *dharma* and how, with a toggle of a switch, we can go from viewing them as expressions of religious mysticism via interpretation to moral philosophy via explication. Explicated, theories of dharma are theories of morality and via the consilience of entailments we discover it is the term that expresses the concept of *THE RIGHT OR THE GOOD*. It hence functions as the representative Hindu term for ethics. Indians in general, including Buddhists, Jains, and followers of other traditions with distinct religious identities, disagree about moral theory at a very basic level. In comparing the basic options of dharma theory in the Indian tradition, we identify a popular Hindu, fourth, theory, not obviously present in the *Western* tradition: *Bhakti*. It is often confused with theism but we shall see that in many ways the theories are mirror image opposites of each other. Bhakti is a radical procedural ethics that defines the right as an approximation to a regulative ideal—the Lord, unconservativism and self-governance. We see here too that many popular Hindu deities are procedural ideals, and account for values of Indian moral theory. While most religions are defined by a single moral theory, the basic options of moral philosophy are internal to Hinduism.

In Chapter 4, "Logic: The Nectar of Immortality," we will return to the questions of the foundations of logic and we will use the Hindu story of the Churning of the Milk Ocean as a model for logic. It is a great story, saturated with major and minor gods of Hinduism and is a symbol of the diversity of Hinduism itself. On a more explicitly philosophical level it tells us about what it is to be reasonable in a public world and it identifies a god as someone who knows how to disagree. Moreover, it elucidates reason as the nonempirical transitivity that we encounter when we acknowledge the force of a third-party perspective that we do not have to agree with. It also teaches us that the foundation of validity is not an *a priori* rule but what we converge on while we disagree about reasons. Reason is objective, for we converge on it from differing perspectives as we disagree.

In Chapter 5, "Subcontinent Dharma, the Global Alt-Right, and the Philosophy of Thought," I compare two models of thought: the standard model (thought is the meaning of what we say), and a yogic model (thought is the disciplinary use of meaning) with roots in Patañjali's *Yoga Sūtra*. The standard model is the definitive model of thought of the *West* going back to the Greeks: *logos*, which conflates thought, opinion, and language. I compare these two theories on Subcontinent Dharma: a place where a community's language is defined by its national theory of dharma. We can add to this folks who arrive late on the scene in Subcontinent Dharma and ask how and whether people across such communities can disagree about whether, for instance, it is dharma to persecute certain people, or whether meat eating is dharma. The standard account of thought generates imperialism, totalitarianism, nationalism, xenophobia, racism, and Orientalism. Turned in on itself, it creates skepticism and the peculiar phenomenon of easily hurt cultural or religious sentiments but also an increasingly familiar discourse of *anti-research, reactionary conservativism*, which paints educated critics as biased elites. Here we examine how the standard model of thought entails and generates the conflation of belief and thought, and as a result those who operate with it are powerless to respond to the discourse of anti-research, reactionary conservativism. A Yogic account of thought in contrast can respond to such criticism, for thought on its account is not in any way shape or form a belief: it is what we have to converge on while we disagree about thoughts. An upshot of this account of thought is that it is nothing peculiar to humans. If we think, we think by virtue of our semiotic activity having significance for a discipline or research.

In Chapter 6, "*Jñāna: Pramāṇa, Satya* and *Citta* (Not: Justified, True, Belief)" I tackle the question: what is the representative Hindu account of knowledge? Any such account of knowledge would reveal to us the objectivity of knowledge as what we converge on while we disagree theoretically about knowledge. Put this way, the concept of knowledge is the disjunction of *THE TRUE OR THE JUSTIFIED* for theories of knowledge disagree about truth and justification. Like the four moral theories that account for the basic ethical concept of *THE RIGHT OR THE GOOD* (reviewed in Chapter 2), four basic theories of knowledge are possible, and Yoga is an option unheard of in the *W*estern context because Yoga takes aim at the belief-thought conflation. The Indian and Hindu resource that models the objectivity of knowledge is a list of five ostensibly moral values: the *Mahāvrata*-s, or Great Vows. The objectivity of knowledge so understood is not the same as belief or language use. It is what thinking beings converge on when they disagree about knowledge.

In Chapter 7, "Moral Standing: Who Counts, Gods, and the Afterlife" I consider the openness of popular and traditional forms of Hinduism to moral standing. According to the Hindu landscape, people come in all sorts of biological forms—humans by no means are the paradigm case of moral agents. The gods too take on various animal forms, and the Earth herself is a Goddess. I review the disagreements of moral standing in the *W*estern and Indian traditions and note that it is reducible to a disagreement between two kinds of basic options: one claims that standing is determined intrinsically by the thing with standing or that is determined by extrinsic considerations. This is the disjunction of *SELF-GOVERNANCE* or *UNCONSERVATIVISM* (*SVĀDHYĀYA* or *TAPAS*): this is the objectivity of the debate of moral standing. Objects of intrinsic value have an interest in the former, moral patients have an interest in the latter, and people (*puruṣa*-s) have an interest in both. The Lord, as a procedural abstraction of bhakti, entails moral standing as such. Not only do Hindus have resources to represent and model the objectivity of standing, standing objectively understood entails many common Hindu conclusions about what types of beings have moral standing.

In Chapter 8, "Metaphysics: Two Truths," I move to the question of reality. Chapter 4 and other preceding chapters help make the case that the gods are objective—we can converge on them while we disagree. But what is real? The real pertains to the *factual* and the facts are true thoughts. As we will see in Chapter 5, the essence of a thought (the kind of thing we can disagree about) is disciplinarity, but then the facts of the world are all of them explained by disciplines, such as empirical science, mathematics, or philosophy. These comprise a first level of truth—the truths of the world. As they are each creatures of disciplinarity they instantiate the essence of disciplinarity: the Lord, or unconservativism and self-governance. But we can entertain competing theories about these first-order truths and the accurate theory about the first-order truths would be a second order truth. It is at this level that philosophers disagree about metaphysics. When we disagree about the second-order truths, we converge on our common Lordliness—to contest the facts. Reality so understood is distinct from our beliefs, and we may have grounds to revise our beliefs about reality in light of disciplinary findings. Reality—the facts—so understood is objective: it is what we converge on as we disagree about reality. Rāmānuja's Viśiṣṭādvaita is the Hindu philosophy that models the objectivity of the facts and its connection to disciplinarity and the Lord at both levels.

In Chapter 9, "The Politics of the Milk Ocean: *Mokṣa*," I consider what a representative Hindu politics and society would look like. To this end, I differentiate between two models of secularism. Secularism$_1$ is characterized by the philosophical freedom to disagree. Secularism$_2$ treats the *W*est as the secular and everything that deviates as the religious. A representative Hinduism is Secularism$_1$. Given the preceding findings, a representative Hindu Secularism$_1$ would also be non-speciesist: it would not be restricted to humans but would understand public participation more broadly to include non-human animals and the Earth herself. The Hindu resource that models Secularism$_1$ is the term "*mokṣa*." *Mokṣa*, freedom, is the objectivity of political disagreement, and what we actualize by endorsing the various representative Hindu accounts of philosophical disagreement.

In Chapter 10, "Conclusion," I will summarize the findings of each chapter, summarize the findings of the book on the whole, and respond to some objections.

Notes

1 For instance, the idea that there is some package in the Indian tradition developed by thinkers such as Vijñānabhikṣu, Mādhava, and Madhusūdana Sarasvatī that forms the foundation for later views about what Hinduism is, is a version of Comprehensive Hinduism (Nicholson 2010). Or, one might identify modern Hinduism with a pro-Vedic, Brahmanical Vaiṣṇava Pañcarātra or Śaiva traditions that was formed by the end of the first millennia CE (Sanderson 2015). Similarly, the thought of Neo-Vedāntins, who depict Advaita Vedānta (a specific school of Indian philosophy) as the basis of Hinduism seem to engage in making a case for Comprehensive Hinduism. According to advocates of these positions, there is something like a Hindu attitude of openness and tolerance that instantiates the openness of Hinduism (Radhakrishnan 1961: 37). Some might even hold that this attitude defines Hinduism as a world religion, and should be contrasted with Hindu nationalism (Long 2007). There is also the defense of Hinduism as a unity in diversity, where each option reflects the diversity of the totality (Malhotra 2014).

2 Thanks to my York colleague the historian Benjamin Kelly for clarifying these issues for me. For further sources, see Beard, North, and Price (1998), and Gordon (2008).

3 Examples of recent such papers include: "How Many Sounds Are in Pāli?" (Gornall 2014), and "Defining the Other: An Intellectual History of Sanskrit Lexicons and Grammars of Persian" (Truschke 2012). Whether this is good or bad scholarship is beside the point: it is not philosophy, yet it takes up place in the salient journal devoted to Indian philosophy.

4 In South Asia, there is the latter case of Sikh martyrs but this is something that occurs at the hand of Muslim rulers. While popular discourse does not associate Islam and the *W*est, Islamic philosophy is highly influenced by ancient Greek philosophy (Leaman 2009) and was part of the conversation of *W*estern Medieval philosophy. Martyrdom here does not arise out of a clash of indigenously Indian philosophical traditions.

5 It is difficult to think of examples of the persecution of intellectuals in the early South Asian tradition. There is the ninth-century case of Jayanta Bhaṭṭa who was imprisoned (Potter 2015: 342). I am grateful to Purushottama Bilimoria for reminding me of this. Then there is the case of the eleventh-century persecution of Śrī Vaiṣṇavas by a Chola King (Narasimhacharya and Sahitya Akademi 2004: 25). In the stories of the *Mahāvastu*

we find passing accounts of kings killing off ascetics for having the wrong views (*Mahāvastu* 354–372). Thanks to Justin Fifield for bringing this to my attention. Of course, if we count literature there are many cases of evil kings whose sin is intolerance of Brahmins and sages. These discussions serve to reinforce the dominant line of the just king as one who is open to intellectuals. This is a dominant theme in India's popular literature across traditions: good kings revere intellectuals while the evil kings do not. A fabled example of a lost philosophical school in India is the Cārvāka—who were known for materialism or naturalism. Our knowledge of this school was for a long time entirely from secondary sources (Chattopadhyaya and Gangopadhyaya 1990). Yet, at the time of the Buddha, there were many popular philosophical teachers who espoused such a view. Glimpses into the philosophical diversity of the ancient world are found in early Indian philosophical texts (cf. "Samaññaphala Sutta: The Fruits of the Contemplative Life" 1997). Moreover, materialism or naturalism itself was not an oppressed option but widely endorsed by divergent and even orthodox schools such as Sāṅkhya, not to mention early Buddhism. The one extant philosophical text attributed to the Cārvāka appears to hold a radical nihilism (Jayarāśi Bhaṭṭa 1967). As the school traces its roots back to the sage Bṛhaspati, it is within the options of Hinduism.

6 There are competing accounts of truth. In this investigation, I identify truth as the property of thoughts or more generally representations (or even presentations) that reveal what they are about: the false lacks this revelatory character. This is such a basic feature of the concept of truth that it is consistent with, and often entailed by the major options. For more see Chapter 8, *Metaphysics: Two Truths*.

7 This conch is sometimes called "Pāñcajanya" and one way to translate this is as "born of the five senses." This entails the idea that objectivity is what we discover when we observe from multiple perspectives. For an overview of the conch and its relationship to Viṣṇu, see Varadpande (2009: 19). For a discussion of how Viṣṇu appropriates this protective shell of a demon (who hides innocent victims from view), see *Bhāgavata Purāṇa* (10.45). Objectivity is rendered benign by Viṣṇu.

8 It is a worthy question whether there can be mathematical claims that are both derivable, but representatively inaccurate and thereby failures at revealing what can be derived. In logic there are many such examples. Sentences such as "this sentence is underivable" derived from a conjunction of this sentence and a second would be an example of a claim that is derivable but fails to represent what can be derived. On some telling of Gödel's incompleteness theorem, it appears that the problem with Gödel sentences is that they are derivable from a suitably complex mathematical system but contradict their derivability (Tieszen 2011). Yet on other accounts, they show that "there are statements of the language of *F* which can neither be proved nor disproved in *F*" and "a formal system cannot prove that the system itself is consistent" (Raatikainen 2015). Given the distinction between the truth and objectivity, Gödel seems to show that much math is objective, though not true, which is what we should expect if it is a discipline.

9 Mill was an officer of the British India company, in charge of writing 'dispatches' (propaganda) (Zastoupil 1994; Lal Accessed October 2014). Mill was not embarrassed about his job as an imperialist but thought of it as an important function for liberals such as himself (Mill 1861 [Accessed Fall 2014]: 573–579). His many writings on politics and economics touch upon imperialism, and he defends it explicitly in his supposedly liberal tract: *On Liberty* (I.10).

References

Bartley, C.J. 2011. *An Introduction to Indian Philosophy*. London; New York: Continuum.

Beard, Mary, John A. North, and S.R.F. Price. 1998. *Religions of Rome*. 2 vols. Cambridge; New York: Cambridge University Press.

Bentham, Jeremy. 1781. *The Principles of Morals and Legislation*. www.econlib.org/library/Bentham/bnthPMLCover.html.
Bilimoria, Purusottama. 1989. "Hindu-Mimamsa against Scriptural Evidence on God." [In English]. *Sophia: International Journal for Philosophy of Religion, Metaphysical Theology and Ethics* 28: 20–31.
Bilimoria, Purusottama. 1990. "Hindu Doubts about God: Towards a Mimamsa Deconstruction." [In English]. *International Philosophical Quarterly* 30, no. 4: 481–499.
Cabezón, José Ignacio. 2006. "The Discipline and Its Other: The Dialectic of Alterity in the Study of Religion." *Journal of the American Academy of Religion* 74, no. 1: 21–38.
Chattopadhyaya, Debiprasad, and Mrinalkanti Gangopadhyaya. 1990. *Carvaka/Lokayata: An Anthology of Source Materials and Some Recent Studies*. Translated by Debiprasad Chattopadhyaya and Mrinalkanti Gangopadhyaya. New Delhi: Indian Council of Philosophical Research in association with Rddhi-India Calcutta.
Danto, Arthur Coleman. 1972. *Mysticism and Morality: Oriental Thought and Moral Philosophy*. New York: Basic Books.
Dasgupta, Surendranath. 1975. *A History of Indian Philosophy*. 5 vols. Delhi: Motilal Banarsidas.
Doniger, Wendy. 2010. *The Hindus: An Alternative History*. Oxford: Oxford University Press.
Doniger, Wendy. 2014. *On Hinduism*. Oxford: Oxford University Press.
Frege, Gottlob. 1980. *The Foundations of Arithmetic: A Logico-Mathematical Enquiry into the Concept of Number*. Translated by J.L. Austin. 2nd rev. edn. Oxford: Basil Blackwell.
Ganeri, Jonardon. 2001. *Philosophy in Classical India: The Proper Work of Reason*. London; New York: Routledge.
Ganeri, Jonardon. 2007. *The Concealed Art of the Soul: Theories of Self and Practices of Truth in Indian Ethics and Epistemology*. Oxford; New York: Oxford University Press. www.loc.gov/catdir/toc/ecip0712/2007008548.html.
Goodman, Charles. 2009. *Consequences of Compassion: An Interpretation and Defense of Buddhist Ethics*. Oxford: Oxford University Press.
Gordon, R. 2008. "Superstitio, Superstition and Religious Repression in the Late Roman Republic and Principate (100 BCE–300 CE)." In *The Religion of Fools?: Superstition Past and Present*, edited by S.A. Smith and A. Knight. Oxford: Oxford University Press.
Gornall, Alastair. 2014. "How Many Sounds Are in Pāli?" *Journal of Indian Philosophy* 42, no. 5: 511–550. http://resolver.scholarsportal.info/resolve/00221791/v42i0005/511_hmsaip.
Harrison, Victoria S. 2006. "The Pragmatics of Defining Religion in a Multi-Cultural World." *International Journal for Philosophy of Religion* 59, no. 3: 133–152.
Hawley, John Stratton, and Vasudha Narayanan. 2006. *The Life of Hinduism*. Berkeley, CA: University of California Press.
Hiriyanna, Mysore. 1995. *The Essentials of Indian Philosophy*. 1st Indian edn. Delhi: Motilal Banarsidass.
Husserl, Edmund. 1970. *The Crisis of European Sciences and Transcendental Phenomenology: An Introduction to Phenomenological Philosophy*. Northwestern University Studies in phenomenology and existential philosophy. Evanston, IL: Northwestern University Press.
Husserl, Edmund. 2001. *Logical Investigations*. Translated by J.N. Findlay. International Library of Philosophy. 2nd edn. 2 vols. London; New York: Routledge.

Inden, Ronald B. 1990. *Imagining India*. Cambridge, MA: Blackwell.
Īśvarakṛṣṇa. 1948. *Sāṅkhya Kārikā*. Translated by S.S. Suryanarayana-Sastri. Madras University Philosophical Series, no. 3. Edited by S.S. Suryanarayana-Sastri. 2nd rev. edn. Madras: University of Madras.
James, Michael. Accessed 2016. "Race." In *Stanford Encyclopedia of Philosophy*, edited by Edward N. Zalta. http://plato.stanford.edu/archives/spr2016/entries/race/.
Jayrasi-Bhatta. 1967. "Tattvopaplavasimha." In *A Source Book in Indian Philosophy*, edited by Sarvepalli Radhakrishnan and Charles A. Moore. Princeton, NJ: Princeton University Press. Original edition, Sukhlalji Sanghavi and Rasiklal C. Parikh, *Gaekwad's Oriental Series*, vol. lxxxvii. Baroda: Oriental Institute, 1940.
Knott, Kim. 1998. *Hinduism: A Very Short Introduction*. Oxford: Oxford University Press.
Lal, Vinay. Accessed October 2014. *Organic Conservatism, Administrative Realism, and the Imperialist Ethos in the "Indian Career" of John Stuart Mill*. Originally published as: "John Stuart Mill and India", a review article. *New Quest*, no. 54 (January–February 1998): 54–64. www.sscnet.ucla.edu/southasia/History/British/jsmill.html.
Leaman, Oliver. 2009. *Islamic Philosophy: An Introduction*. Cambridge: Polity Press.
Long, Jeffery D. 2007. *A Vision for Hinduism: Beyond Hindu Nationalism*. London: IB Tauris.
Maas, Philipp A. 2013. "A Concise Historiography of Classical Yoga Philosophy." In *Historiography and Periodization of Indian Philosophy*, edited by Eli Franco. Vienna: De Nobili Research Library.
Mahāvastu. 1956. Translated by J.J. Jones. vol. 3. Luzac.
Malhotra, R. 2014. *Indra's Net: Defending Hinduism's Philosophical Unity*. Delhi: HarperCollins Publishers India.
Matilal, Bimal Krishna. 1989. "Moral Dilemmas: Insights from the Indian Epics." In *Moral Dilemmas in the Mahābhārata*, edited by Bimal Krishna Matilal, 1–19. Shimla; Delhi: Indian Institute of Advanced Study in association with Motilal Banarsidass.
Matilal, Bimal Krishna, and Jonardon Ganeri. 2002. *Mind, Language, and World: The Collected Essays of Bimal Krishna Matilal*. New Delhi; New York: Oxford University Press.
Milindapañha. Accessed September 25, 2013. Translated by T.W. Rhys Davids. (The Questions of King Milinda). *Sacred Text Internet Archive*. www.sacred-texts.com/bud/milinda.htm.
Mill, John Stuart. 1861. "Considerations on Representative Government." In *The Collected Works of John Stuart Mill, Volume XIX: Essays on Politics and Society Part 2*, edited by John M. Robson. http://oll.libertyfund.org/titles/234, Accessed Fall 2014.
Mill, John Stuart. 1882. *A System of Logic, Ratiocinative and Inductive, Being a Connected View of the Principles of Evidence, and the Methods of Scientific Investigation*. 8th edn. New York: Harper & Brothers.
Mills, Charles W. 1997. *The Racial Contract*. Ithaca, NY: Cornell University Press.
Mohanty, J.N. 1992. *Reason and Tradition in Indian Thought: An Essay on the Nature of Indian Philosophical Thinking*. Oxford; New York: Clarendon Press; Oxford University Press.
Mohanty, J.N. 2000. *Classical Indian Philosophy*. Lanham, MD: Rowman & Littlefield.
Narasimhacharya, M., and Sahitya Akademi. 2004. *Sri Ramanuja*. New Delhi: Sahitya Akademi.
Narayanan, Vasudha. 2004. *Understanding Hinduism: Origins, Beliefs, Practices, Holy Texts, Sacred Places*. London: Duncan Baird.
Narayanan, Vasudha. 2010. *Hinduism*. New York: Rosen Publishing.

Nicholson, Andrew J. 2010. *Unifying Hinduism: Philosophy and Identity in Indian Intellectual History*. New York: Columbia University Press.

Potter, K.H. 2015. *The Encyclopedia of Indian Philosophies, Volume 2: Indian Metaphysics and Epistemology: The Tradition of Nyaya-Vaisesika up to Gangesa*. Princeton, NJ: Princeton University Press. https://books.google.ca/books?id=aZJ9BgAAQBAJ.

Raatikainen, Panu. 2015. "Gödel's Incompleteness Theorems." In *Stanford Encyclopedia of Philosophy*, Spring 2015 edn, edited by Edward N. Zalta. http://plato.stanford.edu/entries/goedel-incompleteness/.

Radhakrishnan, S. 1961. *The Hindu View of Life. Upton lectures, 1926*. London: G. Allen & Unwin.

Ram-Prasad, Chakravarthi. 2001. *Knowledge and Liberation in Classical Indian Thought*. Houndmills: Palgrave.

Ram-Prasad, Chakravarthi. 2007. *Indian Philosophy and the Consequences of Knowledge: Themes in Ethics, Metaphysics and Soteriology*. Farnham: Ashgate. www.loc.gov/catdir/toc/ecip0616/2006021582.html.

Ranganathan, Shyam. 2016. "Hindu Philosophy." In *Oxford Bibliographies Online*, edited by Alf Hiltebeitel. www.oxfordbibliographies.com/.

Ranganathan, Shyam. 2017. "Philosophy, Religion and Scholarship." In *The Bloomsbury Research Handbook of Indian Ethics*, edited by Shyam Ranganathan, 35–58. London: Bloomsbury Academic.

Rawls, John. 1971. *A Theory of Justice*. Cambridge, MA: Harvard University Press.

Said, Edward W. 1978. *Orientalism*. 1st Vintage Books edn. New York: Vintage Books.

"Samaññaphala Sutta: The Fruits of the Contemplative Life." In *Digha Nikaya*. 1997. www.accesstoinsight.org/tipitaka/dn/dn.02.0.than.html.

Sanderson, Alexis. 2015. "Tolerance, Exclusivity, Inclusivity, and Persecution in Indian Religion during the Early Mediaeval Period." In *In Honoris Causa: Essays in Honour of Aveek Sarkar*, edited by John Makinson, 155–224. London: Allen Lane.

Śaṅkara. 1991. *Bhagavadgītā with the Commentary of Śaṅkarācārya*. Translated by Gambhirananda. Edited by Gambhirananda. Calcutta: Advaita Ashrama.

Śaṅkara (Ādi). 1994. *The Vedānta Sūtras with the Commentary by Śaṅkara (Brahma Sūtra Bhāṣya)*. Translated by George Thibaut. Sacred Books of the East, no. 34. www.sacred-texts.com/hin/sbe34/sbe34007.htm.

Sharma, Jyotirmaya. 2011. *Hindutva: Exploring the Idea of Hindu Nationalism*. Delhi: Penguin.

Tieszen, Richard L. 2011. *After Gödel: Platonism and Rationalism in Mathematics and Logic*. Oxford: Oxford University Press.

Truschke, Audrey. 2012. "Defining the Other: An Intellectual History of Sanskrit Lexicons and Grammars of Persian." *Journal of Indian Philosophy* 40, no. 6: 635–668.

Varadpande, M.L. 2009. *Mythology of Vishnu and His Incarnations*. New Delhi: Gyan Publishing House.

White, David Gordon. 2014. *The Yoga Sutra of Patanjali: A Biography*. Lives of Great Religious Books. Princeton, NJ: Princeton University Press.

Whitehead, Alfred North. 1978. *Process and Reality: An Essay in Cosmology. Gifford Lectures*, 1927–28. Edited by David Ray Griffin and Donald W. Sherburne. Corrected edn. New York: Free Press. Originally published New York: Macmillan.

Wittgenstein, Ludwig. 1958. *Philosophical Investigations*. Translated by G.E.M. Anscombe. 2nd edn. New York: Macmillan.

Zastoupil, Lynn. 1994. *John Stuart Mill and India*. Stanford, CA: Stanford University Press.

2 Hinduism and the limits of interpretation

Introduction

The *West*—a theory of thought, namely, that it is linguistic, with a European origin—comes apart from the west. Indeed, most theories that are western do not obviously or explicitly defend the *West*. Yet, the development of western philosophy in light of the dominant tradition of the *West* has certain implications. For instance, thinking about thought in terms of language, an essentially human artifact, which is characteristic of the *West*, leads to anthropocentrism, which characterizes most philosophy that is historically western (Steiner 2010: 2). Similarly, thinking about thought by way of language, and language as encoding the semantics of thought, and this further being nothing one can deny without saying something absurd, leads to conceiving the goal of philosophy as what we know from the *right* perspective—the perspective encoded in and revealed by *logos*. We find this most explicitly at first with Plato in the *Republic* and *Phaedrus* but in Aristotle too. The difference is a matter of emphasis. Plato emphasizes the objects that we are aware of from the right perspective (the elevated perspective) and while these objects include the essence of ordinary experience (forms of ordinary objects like chairs and tables), we also get a glimpse into the Good—the form of forms. This apparently makes Plato a non-naturalist. Aristotle in contrast in his *Nicomachean Ethics* stresses the role of social epistemology—the right upbringing that allows us to reflect on the good. Not everyone has this kind of good upbringing and unfortunately, it is not clear what this amounts to without having the right upbringing in the first place. This apparently makes Aristotle a naturalist. However, both agree: there is a unique or special place from which we see everything—for Plato it is high up, for Aristotle is it your society that affords you the right kind of upbringing. Moreover, occupying this special seat is essential for knowledge. Medieval philosophy was dominated by Aristotle and Plato. The modern period of philosophy in the *West* coincides with the imperial and colonial expansion of Europe on a new scale. Philosophical traditions that reach back to the Greeks (including religious traditions of the west) were already spreading past their homelands. But with the modern period, this shift is often regarded as a secular expansion. One might think that this intensified contact with non-*Western* peoples would temper the idea that there is one right perspective and that reality is the kind of thing we see from many perspectives. Yet there is a continued interest in the idea of the right perspective from which we understand the world in modern philosophy. The epistemological projects of the rationalists and the empiricists are best described as efforts to describe the right epistemic conditions (the right epistemic perspective) from which we have knowledge. This comes to a head in the writings of Kant:

> If intuitions must conform to the constitution of the objects, I do not see how we could know anything of the latter *a priori*; but if the objects (as objects of the senses) must conform to the constitution of our faculty of intuition, I have no difficulty in conceiving such a possibility.
>
> (*Critique of Pure Reason*, B xvii)

Kant likens his move to understand objects in terms of our perspective as following "the lines of Copernicus' primary hypothesis." This move is comical in many respects. First, it is an admission of incompetence, but one Kant treats as a conceptual constraint on knowledge. Moreover, on the basis of this move he constructs a theory about the *a priori* structures of the human mind that constrain the possibility of anyone having knowledge in his *First Critique*. The most ironic aspect of this passage is that Kant gets the revolutionary ideas of his time wrong. What he describes is not at all a Copernican revolution. The Copernican revolution involves decentralizing our frame and criticizing the notion that our perspective is privileged in the world. The old geocentric view (from Aristotle) that the Earth is the center of the universe and that we see the world from this privileged perspective is false. If we buy it, we have an inexplicably complicated heavens, replete with stars that move in epicycles with apparent retrograde motions—as though for our amusement. The simpler explanation is the decentralized account of reality, where what we see is a function of our contingent and dynamic vantage relative to other contingent and dynamic vantages. The model of how things are really like if we keep up to date with astronomy is more like that of the solar deity Viṣṇu, reclining on the cosmic snake of many perspectives, with the Goddess Earth, Lakṣmī. As Viṣṇu understands himself as the autonomous triangulating self-triangulation, he can distinguish himself as this autonomous disk from others and maintain the self-governance of his lover, Lakṣmī. Leaving things preserved involves treating the decentralized vantage as privileged. A decentralized vantage is one that accommodates other objects (like the conch) and persons (like the Goddess Lakṣmī Herself). This is the vantage from which disagreement is intelligible.

Hindus contemplate the idea of a centralized or privileged vantage in the God Śiva (the benign), symbolized by the phallus or *liṅga*—which also means 'spot.'

Like Plato's gods of the *Phaedrus* who climb beyond the Earth, Śiva resides on high (Hindus regard him on the peak of Mount Kailash) looking down on us small critters below. But his role is that of destruction. The prioritization of a central or elevated vantage forces everything else to accommodate its centrality and this means that other things have to change to accommodate Śiva. This forced change is destruction. Śiva can be terrible (then he is Rudra, the terrible) and is complemented by his consort and Viṣṇu's sister, often simply known as *Śakti* (power). In benign form, she seems like Lakṣmī (the Goddess of wealth and prosperity) and she is known as Pārvatī. In a more ambiguous role, she is Durgā, the warrior Goddess, who resembles Viṣṇu in presenting the disk, mace, conch, and Lakṣmī (as Padma, Lotus), and as the angry and horrid form, she is Kālī, who resembles the undead (cf. Kinsley 1989: 3–5). It is a curious matter as to how one complement to Śiva could have so many presentations, but the association of Śiva's power with *māyā* or illusion (cf. *Devī Māhātmyam*) is useful. As Śiva's power, Śakti is the full range of his illusory experiences. This is a theme latent and picked up by philosophers in the Kaśmīrī Śaiva tradition, who identify Śiva as the only reality, and Śakti as Śiva's path of self-recognition (*ahampratyavamarśa, pratyabhijñā*) via his expansion and control of the universe (Somānanda and Utpaladeva 1934). If Śakti is illusion—the confusing of the subjective with the objective—then Śiva comes to recognize himself as all via the illusion that is his power.

The philosophical influence of Kant on the subsequent tradition is immense. For those who take the split between Continental and Analytic philosophy seriously (we shall see it is quite superficial) Kant is the last major philosopher that both traditions draw upon and his influence resides in the implicit assumption in subsequent philosophy that what is knowable has to be explainable by our vantage as humans. This is a naturalized version of Plato's theory that biologizes the position. Whereas the forms that we observe from an elevated position on Plato's account arise from philosophy, Kant puts these into the *a priori* structures of the human mind as a natural endowment. Later philosophers in the Continental and Analytic traditions tend to move to the more classically Greek position, which maintains this move to locating thought with humans: it is about language. What I find humorous about Kant's 'Copernican' revolution is his effort to take over the world (like other Europeans of his day), but whereas everyone else would do it by military and economic means, Kant would do it through theorizing: everything objective—the entire universe of experience—has to conform to Kant's perspective and constitution to be understood. And far from a triumphant takeover, it is an admission of incompetence: he can only understand something from his perspective. As we explore Hinduism, we shall see this is mistaken.

The philosophical world of Europe after Kant shows many Kantian elements, but they are Platonic or more basically *W*estern. Essential to this tradition is the idea that knowledge is what we know from a special perspective. The difference between the subsequent tradition and Plato is that as the history of the *W*est progresses, there is a tendency to Aristotelian and naturalized versions of the doctrine. The special perspective becomes increasingly our empirical perspective and hence knowledge becomes apparently relativized. Especially in contemporary philosophy we find this tendency: in the idea of Wittgenstein that we know from specific forms of life (*Philosophical Investigations* I.241); in the Quinian and Davidsonian idea that knowledge depends upon interpreting the world and other people in terms of what we think is true (Quine 1960: 58–59; Davidson 1996a: 463; 2001b: 137), in Heidegger's (1962) failed attempt at rewriting the conceptual scheme that we should share with others to avoid Platonic excesses, and finally in Hans Georg Gadamer's idea that everyone's tradition provides the backdrop of justificatory resources for understanding (Gadamer 1996: 292). Indeed, so apparently inescapable is the relativization of knowledge to one's perspective that Gadamer claims that being critical of prejudice is merely prejudice about prejudice (Gadamer 1996: 270).

There are some notable resistors to this tendency toward relativization, but they are Kant's children. We find in Peirce the idea that what is true is what we could converge on at the end of inquiry. Similarly we find earlier in Hegel that thought strives toward a balance of opposing tensions. Hegel is in some sense extremely prescient in appreciating that this balance is tenuous and unstable (like the waves of the Milk Ocean) but his approach like the standard *W*estern options idealizes the resolution of discord in the synthesis of contrary perspectives.

There are a host of problems that are generated from this approach to philosophy—the approach that strives to identify knowledge relative to the *right* perspective. The idea that knowledge is defined by the right perspective problematizes objectivity for objects are what we understand from multiple perspectives. To assess a topic objectively is to disown the idea of there being a right perspective on the topic. Rather, objective truth comes about by revealing or representing what we can see from multiple perspectives. The problems of philosophy, such as the problem of other minds, the reality of the external world, and the value of philosophical inquiry and discovery, themselves hinge on the identification of knowledge with the right perspective, for from this perspective, we lack any *independent* evidence for taking what we believe seriously. Incidentally, Kaśmīrī Śaivas appreciated that these were concerns for their view as they too identified knowledge with Śiva or the right perspective but in their philosophical account there is the Goddess too (they further theorizer her as the voice of Śiva), which is to say an acknowledgment of the reality of illusion. With this, we can temper some of the skeptical outcomes of taking one's perspective too seriously. We can know for instance that what is observed from the 'right' perspective is illusion, which means that what is real (what makes the illusion possible) lies somewhere beyond our vantage (cf. Lawrence 1998; Rastogi 1986). But lacking this appreciation of *māyā* of the privilege perspective we revert to the standard problems of philosophy.

In this chapter I will contrast two models of understanding, one that is *W*estern—interpretation—and one that is central to the discipline of philosophy—explication. The two are at odds with each other and this accounts for the *W*est's troubled history with philosophy and its creation of religion out of diversity. Interpretation derives from the standard *W*estern account of thought as *logos*, or the meaning of what we say. Interpretation is the model of taking your perspective too seriously as though it exhausts the knowable and everything else is mysterious. Given the western origins of this model of understanding and thought that conflates the contingency of how things seem to you from your perspective with the content of thought, everything non-western is problematized and then normalized as religion for the *W*estern is treated as the default model of thought. This is easily misunderstood as a prejudicial view of the intellectual history of the west as though merely being western, or of European heritage is sufficient to generate prejudice and imperialism: it is not. The origins of the problem of prejudice (*saṃskāra*) is the conflation of one's perspective with thought, which has dominated the tradition coming out of Europe via the more illusive and basic theory that thought is linguistic (more on this in Chapter 5). With this background, and by progressively elucidating the distinction between interpretation and explication, I shall clarify the idea of *HINDUISM*. Hinduism, the philosophical disagreement, lies outside of the *W*est's misgivings with philosophy. Properly understood it is a prophylactic to the spread of interpretation. This implies that the proper means of studying Hinduism is not the social sciences, but philosophy.

*W*estern imperialism and non-western philosophy

When we explicate a perspective, we look to the reasons that constitute the perspective to explain its controversial conclusions about a topic *t* (any topic), and the explanation here is logical: when the reasons entail the conclusion (that is, if the reasons are true the conclusion has to be true) we have identified the perspective's theory about *t*. When we compare competing such theories about *t*, what they disagree about is the concept *T*.

As an example, let us look at the term "thought" and the concept *THOUGHT*. For instance, when we explicate Descartes' position about thought in his *Meditations*, we look to the reasons that he provides that constitute his perspective that entails his conclusions. In this famous dialog, Descartes entertains successive hypotheses of doubt and uses it to generate skeptical conclusions. But he moves past each of these perspectives and their theories to a final perspective of what he depicts as ultimate doubt, and from here he identifies his famous *cogito* as his conclusion: I think therefore I am. He claims that this cannot be doubted, but it is not as though the conclusion is without reason. Accordingly, no matter what we are doing when we are doubting, we are thinking, but then, he reasons, he has to be there to reason otherwise there would be no reasoning. Hence, he cannot doubt himself as he thinks: the fact of thinking entails his reality. This is Descartes' theory of thought. We can imagine and identify a contrary theory of thinking, where thinking begets more thinking, and there is no evidence of a thinker aside from thought. This is the early Buddhist account as we find in dialogs such as *Questions of King Milinda*. When we compare these competing accounts of thought, we are in a position to discern what the concept *THOUGHT* is about. From this cursory comparison, it seems like the concept *THOUGHT* tracks what we can draw inferences from, for this is something in common with both theories as they disagree. The entire process of identifying the substance of the philosophical debate requires *valid reasoning* in the technical sense, but it does not require that we have any beliefs about what thought is, or what the right position on the topic is. Rather, we discover the concept by following the disagreement.

Philosophers study philosophy via the objectivity of explication. This means that they explicate a variety of philosophical perspectives about *t*, whether 'reality,' or 'knowledge' or 'reason' and they understand the concept of REALITY, KNOWLEDGE, or REASON as what competing theories of 'reality,' 'knowledge,' or 'reason' converge on while they disagree. The entire process is one of discovery, and hence in order to understand the basic substance or concept at play in a debate, we have to explicate a large number of philosophical theories before we are in a position to appreciate what the issues are.

If we were to line up competing theories of morality and identify what they converge on while they disagree, we would find the concept MORALITY. This explains our moral disagreements. What we observe when we inspect this concept is that it further decomposes into two related concepts: the RIGHT (procedure) or the GOOD (outcome). What is important here is that for the enumerable uses of "morality" that are often at odds with each other, there is only one concept of MORALITY and this explains the theoretical disagreement about morality. "Ethics" and "morality" are functional synonyms in philosophy for when we line up theories articulated with either of these terms, we find that the common concept is that of THE RIGHT OR THE GOOD. This is what the disagreement about ethics or morality is about.

Indian philosophers and Indian culture stretching back to very ancient times also had and has a term that can be explicated: "dharma." "Dharma" is a term that almost everyone used to explicate and articulate their own philosophy from a third-party perspective. For instance, Buddhists called their entire platform "dharma" as did Jains. Philosophers and texts that we identify with Hinduism also had extensive things to say about 'dharma.' Aside from the Brahmanical tradition of *Dharmaśāstra*-s that has much to say about ritual purity, virtually every major school of Indian philosophy had something to say about 'dharma.' Indeed, foundational texts of the Pūrva Mīmāṃsā and Vaiśeṣika schools (schools within the Hindu tradition) explicitly start out with the aim of explicating their own view on dharma. (The *Vaiśeṣika Sūtra* I.i.1, commonly known for its tradition of ontological realism, begins: "Now, therefore, we shall explain dharma.") Even the schools that have a reputation for focusing on freedom (*mokṣa*) have much to say about dharma, and most frequently (except in very rare cases) theories of dharma will be explicated in relationship to theories about freedom. On top of this the term figures prominently in the philosophically imbued popular literature of India, such as the epics (the *Mahābhārata* and *Rāmāyaṇa*—in all their versions) and the mythologies. It is hard to find an Indian school of thought without a view on dharma, and harder still to find a school that regards it nihilistically as a realm of philosophical concern that is false. The latter is the minority view in Indian philosophy (Ranganathan 2007a).

To explicate dharma would be to look to a perspective (*darśana* in Sanskrit) to logically explain its use of "dharma" in the way that we look to a perspective to logically explain its use of "morality": the reasons of a perspective that entail its use of "dharma" is just its theory of dharma. Studying such a philosophical theory is careful *philosophical* work that is not at all like philological research for the following reason: any theory of dharma that we arrive at by studying a perspective *P* will be something we arrive at by employing our own logical skills in drawing inferences from the propositions that comprise the perspective *P*.

The theory of dharma or morality that we arrive at will be a deductive entailment of the perspective *P* but it will often be simpler and more economical than the entire perspective and this may take us far beyond the philological facts of a text. The actual theory we discover that explains the controversial claims of a text may not be explicitly stated in a canonical or standard form (with premises clearly set out from conclusions) and quite implicit in the mass of what is written. Anecdotally, I have come to observe that Indologists often call this activity "reconstruction." Philosophers call this *reading philosophy*, or explication. The main difference is that philosophers do not believe that they are re-presenting or reconstructing a text when they explicate: they are rather distilling the philosophy, in the way that a scientist would distill the scientific theory of a scientific text, or a mathematician would distill the mathematics of a mathematical text. (So while I am flattered that some might regard me as doing something creative and new, as a philosopher I regard myself as rendering explicit what is already implicit in philosophy and the traditions we are investigating.) Moreover, there is further gold ahead: once we have distilled many philosophies we are in a position to compare them and what they converge on while they disagree is the common concept of their disagreement. The entire process is one of discovery and research: philosophical research.

What we find when we explicate is that if we line up theories of dharma, they converge while disagreeing on the concept *DHARMA*, and this decomposes into the *RIGHT*, or the *GOOD* (Ranganathan 2017)—a matter that we will further explore in Chapter 3. *DHARMA* is the same concept as the one instantiated by our "ethics" and "morality." To clarify: for the explicator, the conceptual identity of "dharma" and "morality" does not rest upon these terms being defined by the same theoretical outlook—just the opposite. These terms express the same concept as they concern the same kind of disagreement.

Explication allows us to be critical of people's claims about their own philosophy. If my job as an explicator is to explain your uses of "morality" by your theory of morality, then I have a means of criticizing your mentions (second-order claims) about your own theory of morality or about your usage of moral terms. It might be that your mentions are out of step with your uses as explained by your theory of morality. Explication is the basic and first step of philosophical research. In order to arrive at some representation of the options in philosophy that could be philosophically true, we need to survey the options and that is what explication allows us. We find it being employed with some skill by Socrates in Plato's dialogs when he questions his interlocutors about their use of philosophical terms. We also find it in the Indian convention of identifying the *pūrvapakṣa* (opponent's position) at the start of philosophical treaties. This is standard practice in advanced philosophical research and any philosopher who knows what they are doing will spend some time explicating alternatives as part of their argument.

Explication is a methodology of *research* for two reasons. First, it involves a scrupulous distinction between the beliefs and reasons of the explicator (the explicator's first-party reasons) and the third-party reasons of what is studied. These may coincide, but that is an accident. Explication allows for this distinction as it involves discerning entailed theories of *t* (whatever the *t*) implicit in a perspective *P* that entail the perspective's employment of *t* with no reliance on interpreter prejudices about *t*. Hence, when I discover a theory of morality implicit in the Kantian perspective, I discern the implicit theory of morality in this perspective that logically explains its use of the word "moral" and other synonyms. And I do this without relying upon my own prejudices about morality. My philosophical beliefs are not employed in explication—even my belief that I should be explicating plays no inferential role in the conclusions I derive via explication. When I read philosophy as an explicator, my first job is to discern the reasons implicit in a perspective that logically explain its *t*-claims. I succeed when the theory that I discern from the perspective entails the perspective's *t*-claims. I might find a theory I agree with or disagree with, and it might be that in some respects I agree and in other respects I disagree. (I could explicate the philosophy of interpreters, for instance.) Whatever I discover, it is objective, for I can arrive at the same conclusion regardless of my own substantive convictions, which play no inferential role in the explication. (Interpreters will find this difficult as they tend to confuse explanation in terms of what they believe with being reasonable.) Second, the concept of *T* that we arrive at by comparing theories of *t* is a matter of discovery. (Hence, the concept of *MORALITY* that we arrive at by comparing theories of morality is a matter of discovery. It is the disagreement.) There is no way to discern the concept at play in a philosophical debate on a whim. You have to do the research and what you arrive at is a contingency (the objectivity of the concept) but via the *a priori*, non-empirical means of philosophy. This is nothing that we frequently speak about in academic philosophy for curious historical reasons (we shall investigate these in Chapter 5). But for now it suffices to note that philosophy is not without its objects of research and what we discover is a contingency at the heart of a disagreement.[1]

Interpretation has been the standard approach to Indian thought, and interpretation is something that, though frequently defended by philosophers in print, is nothing that we actually employ in research. One cannot employ interpretation in research as it is completely subjective.

INTERPRETATION is often confused with *TRANSLATION*. The two concepts are often treated interchangeably—particularly in the Hermeneutic ('interpretive') tradition (Heidegger, for instance, was reputed to have held that every translation is itself an interpretation, cf. Lilly 1991: vii; Gadamer 1996: 384, 387)—but there are important differences between the two. Translations and interpretations both function as proxies for original texts. However, an interpretation is an explanation: it seeks to explicitly shed light on a distinct corpus. It is an intermediary. A translation, in contrast, takes on the literary identity of the original (Ranganathan 2007b, 2011). To interpret some package *P* is for the interpreting subject S to use their own beliefs (or if you prefer, 'premises,' 'assumptions,' 'truths,' and even '*tradition*') *in* the explanation of *P* (cf. Gadamer 1996; Davidson 2001b, 2001a). Interpretation is regarded by many as the basic fact of understanding. Central to interpretation is the idea that whatever we explain, even someone else's philosophy, cannot transcend the explanatory resources of the interpreter.

What you explain has to follow from what you believe as your beliefs here act as premises that entail what is explained. But then, surprisingly, whatever you explain becomes part of your stock of beliefs as it is entailed by what you believe.

The reason that anyone would take interpretation seriously is a respect for truth. If you think that truth is the end of inquiry, you might also believe that our *means* of arriving at answers to questions should be guided by truth. Interpretation treats what the interpreter believes to be true (whether it is true or not) to be the means of inquiry. The result of the interpretation—the explanation of some perspective—by the interpreter's beliefs follows from what the interpreter takes to be true. In this respect, it seems like a certain conclusion. Moreover, if interpreters can produce interpretations on the basis of beliefs that *are* true, then it seems like the outcome of interpretation is something we should take seriously. As all beliefs are true by virtue of attitude, there are no false interpretations. But they are yet problematic.

Troubles for interpretation

When interpreters are faced with a philosophy *P* that diverges from their background beliefs, they have two strategies open to them. They can *domesticate* the alien philosophy by revising their own background beliefs. In this case, they have conversion so to speak, but once converted they have no way to identify the alien *P* as anything but the contents of what they take to be true. Interpreters can opt to *religify* what is alien to their reasons: in this case they define what is alien as *underivable* from their reasons, yet traditional.

For instance, if I were to interpret your philosophy of morality, I would rely upon my beliefs about morality to make sense of your theory. Instead of laying off my beliefs (as explicators do), I put them to work. I can *domesticate* your theory: this would be for me to revise my beliefs so that I adopt your theory as my beliefs. Then your theory would be a deductive consequence of my beliefs as they amount to the same thing. If I choose not to change my beliefs, I can *define your theory* of morality as *underivable* from mine at those points where your views diverge from mine. This is to *religify* the alien theory—it is to acknowledge it as alien, but also underivable from the contents of reason to the extent that it departs from the interpreter's perspective. What is remarkable in the strategy of religification is that the sheer *underivability* of an alien perspective from the interpreter's reasons has the effect of depicting the alien perspective as mysterious, a matter of faith and beyond the presumed scope of reason. And yet the alien moral perspective, in so far as it is a theory of *The Right or the Good*, will specify practices and objectives. Even if it is not explicitly on *The Right or the Good*, the fact that it is endorsed by the alien, without any obvious reason depicts it as a matter of tradition and habit, and not as a matter of philosophy. But then, this alien moral theory deemed inexplicable by the interpreter's resources appears mystical, faith bound, and nevertheless a traditional goal-oriented practice. In a word, it seems like religion. What happens when we line up the religions that we so identify? If they were merely religified alien moral theories we find some overlap on questions of the right or the good and we might claim as Kant attempted to that this is pure morality at the heart of religion (Kant 1998). To get to this conclusion you have to fail to be objective about the alien theories, try to understand them from your perspective, and then opine on what you find.

But the problem with religification is that it seems to auger the failure of interpretation itself. One way around this is for the interpreter to try to reclaim the mystified alien claims by treating them as malapropisms. We diagnose others as malaproping when they say something that we would rather replace with what we would say in that context. And this is appropriate in the case of speakers of our own language, who ostensibly do not understand our shared language. Archie Bunker, America's loveable bigot, said "we need a few laughs to break up the monogamy." Donald Davidson points out in a classic paper, that what we do in this context is not correct Bunker but replace what he says with what we would say: "we need a few laughs to break up the monotony" (Davidson 1996b: 465). This is to acknowledge that Bunker misspoke. But note, if Bunker sometimes uses "monogamy" as we would use it and sometimes when we would say "monotony," we now correlate Bunker's use of "monogamy" with at least two concepts: *MONOGAMY* and *MONOTONY*. And imagine if Bunker were to use "monogamy" in yet a third unrelated way, we would correlate this third usage with a third concept, which we would deploy in the same context. In other words, to treat others as misspeaking is to multiply the concepts associated with their use of a single word, relative to our outlook. If we did not think that Bunker was an idiot, we would explicate his speech and we might come to appreciate that he was not misspeaking but he has a different theory of monogamy that leads him to say "we need a few laughs to break up the monogamy." But it seems inappropriate in the case of Bunker to give him so much credit as he is not a critical thinker endorsing an alien theory, but an uncouth bigot who is ignorant about his own language, so it is best to treat him as malaproping.

Ironically, what we find in Orthodox Indology is that Indian thinkers and philosophers are not explicated. If Indian thinkers were explicated, each would be treated as articulating or exploring theories of *DHARMA*, and the common concept would be understood not in terms of our preferred language use but the disagreement across theories of dharma. Explicated, there is only one concept *DHARMA*. But instead, Indian thinkers are treated like Archie Bunker: as people who do not know how to speak their own language. In this case, the Indologist correlates uses of "dharma" with what they would be inclined to say in the same context, and this multiplies concepts associated with "dharma." But this is the only way open to interpreters who maintain that alien utterances have to be explained in terms of the interpreter's own perspective. Here is a small and by no means exhaustive list of examples of this treatment of Indian sources:

- We cannot reduce the meanings of *DHARMA* to one general principle; nor is there one single translation which would cover all its usages (Halbfass 1988: 333).
- "Dharma" is one of those Sanskrit words that defy all attempts at an exact rendering in English or any other tongue (Kane 1990: I: 1).

- DHARMA is a concept difficult to define because it disowns or transcends distinctions that seem essential to us, and because it is based upon beliefs that are . . . strange to us (Lingat 1973: 3).
- It is difficult to define DHARMA in terms of Western thought (Van Buitenen 1957: 36).
- "Dharma" is used in so many senses that it eludes definition. It stands for nature, intrinsic quality, civil and moral law, justice, virtue, merit, duty and morality (Rangaswami Aiyangar 1952: 63).
- The word "dharma" . . . is used in very different senses in the different schools and religious traditions of Indian thought (Dasgupta 1975: IV: 2).
- The term "dharma" seems to be one impossible to reduce even to a few basic definitions. It is ubiquitous throughout the texts of the Indian tradition, ancient and modern, and has been used in a bewildering variety of ways (Larson 1972: 146).
- One must avoid identification of 'dharma' as directly equivalent to any of the various components of its meaning, such as law, duty, morality, justice, virtue, or religion. All of these are involved, but we should cease looking for an equivalent for translation, inasmuch as premature identification with Western concepts tends to blind one to the particular multifaceted structure of meanings in the Hindu dharma (Creel 1977: 2).
- Because the term ["dharma"] has been used in a bewildering variety of ways, it has no single semantic equivalent in English. In various contexts the word may mean law, justice, custom, morality, ethics, religion, duty, nature, or virtue (Hudson 2013: 36).

To be clear: one cannot arrive at these conclusions by explicating 'dharma.' To get these conclusions you have to interpret 'dharma' from a non-Indian perspective, *religify* uses of "dharma" as they depart from your perspective, and then correlate distinctions between the *religified* theory and the domestic theory. As noted, Donald Davidson describes this process in detail as what we have to do when we come across a malaproper like Archie Bunker. Just as Archie Bunker is a funny bigot, stuck in his ways and immune to evidence and reasoning, so too do Indians appear via interpretation. Moreover, it is our choice to toggle: if we explicate Indian thought, we will find dharma philosophy everywhere, which is the same as moral philosophy. If we interpret, we see only noise that speaks of parochialisms of Indian, tradition-bound mystics and their mysterious views on dharma.

It is hence unsurprising that if we want to talk about Indian religion, we talk about dharma. This tradition of interpretation has been so influential that even modern India understands itself this way. In the constitution 'dharma' is conscripted to stand for the idea of RELIGION, in India's articulation of its own secularity: it describes itself as (*dharmanirapekṣa rājya*) "a country not wedded to any dharma" (Government of India 1950)—though the error appears to be noticed now (Mantri 2015). If Indologists and the Republic of India had explicated Indian philosophy a very different view would be established: Indians disagreed about the concept DHARMA, which is the concept of THE RIGHT OR THE GOOD.

To the extent that such disagreements were freely tolerated in South Asia, it was secular—free thinking.

Why interpretation is a disaster

Certain general observations of interpretation are in order. First, no matter what strategy I adopt as an interpreter (domestication or religification), the result of an interpretation (its conclusion) entails the premises that get me there. Interpretations are thereby question-begging as the essence of a question-begging argument is that the conclusion entails the premises, such as *P* therefore *P*. The problem with question-begging arguments is not that they are invalid: they are *all* valid. The problem is that in begging the question, I explain nothing, for the premises of a question-begging argument are no different *logically* from the conclusion: *P* therefore *P* is question-begging and for this reason valid—if the premise is true, the conclusion has to be true. It also fails to explain why we should take *P* seriously as it is circular (this is what it is for the conclusion to entail the premises). So Indian thought interpreted explains nothing.

Second whereas explication draws a distinction between first-person and third-person reasons, interpretation collapses the distinction. For me to make sense of your ideas as an interpreter I have to somehow show that they are derivable from my reasons—even if this means that I have to define them as underivable from my reasons. This is the trick of religification, for what it does is it serves to embed your views within mine as something acknowledged by my reasons to be quite distinct. But your reasons are thereby acquired by my stock of reasons as colonists acquire alien land. Yet it protects the expectation that my conclusion about your perspective follows from my reasons. Like imperialism, in general, interpretation brooks no disagreement. If anything intelligible has to be derivable from my reasons, then I thereby render myself incapable of acknowledging a disagreement, which rejects my reasons. Religifying alien views is the limiting case that acknowledges the difference of alien views by denying a disagreement. It treats the alien view as 'underivable from my reasons' but this is not the same as 'disagrees with my reasons.' It is the normalization of the violence done by interpretation to alien views.

Third, the results of interpretation are completely subjective. Whether an alien use of "morality" means what you mean by "morality" has to do with your perspective: change your perspective and you would change the outcome of an interpretation. The only reason that the foundational subjectivism of interpretation is not apparent is privilege: a shared perspective in 'research' that constitutes the backdrop for interpretation. For then interpreters will tend to agree. But the numerosity of persons occupying the same perspective is not at all the same as the numerosity of perspectives that converge on what is objective. Intersubjective agreement gets confused with objectivity for interpreters.

The fourth problem with interpretation is that it is enthymematic and yet it employs assumptions to frame data. These assumptions are first-person beliefs. As the first-person reasons frame data, it seems like interpreters can do research—without critically exposing their assumptions as controversial. For instance, as an interpreter, as I assume a definition of "ethics" to study Indian uses of "dharma," I do not acknowledge that my perspective on ethics is controversial the way that explicators do. Rather, what I want to show is that the text I am interpreting corresponds or agrees with my beliefs, for this is what it is to explain the text or perspective I am studying in light of my perspective, which is interpretation. So it seems that I have to copiously pore over the minutia of language use in a text or perspective to establish this concordance. Here I have to be a good philologist who apparently grounds my account of a text on the text. Interpreters will hence be motivated to swap research into philosophy with an exercise in philology. It will all seem very scholarly, and often held up as paradigm work in Indology (cf. Halbfass 1988). But the catch is that all the evidence of a text (uses of "dharma" for instance) are weighed and assessed in accordance with my beliefs and the beliefs of those with whom I agree. The interpretive writings can be vetted by peer review, and so long as everyone interprets and shares the same privileged perspective, this peer review process will be of no help in weeding out the arbitrariness of the project. The supposed rigor of this kind of research is an illusion. I will call this the *rigor of solipsism*. It consists in a very careful fact-checking exercise where the 'facts' are defined by one's uncontested perspective. In actual cases, this often plays out in interpreters insisting that any account of the wide moral significance of "dharma" is forced, and consists in the imposition of a contrary perspective on the text (cf. White 2011; Burley July 2012; 2014: 226; Taylor-Rugman 2012).

Fifth, as we shall see in Chapter 4, interpretation is irrational. But for now, we can note that those who interpret employ a subjective methodology of research. Hence, they have no grounds for criticizing contrary interpretations. But as interpretation treats the interpreter's perspective as factual and the basis of explanation, interpreters will confuse peer review, their capacity to interpret alien traditions and their widespread intersubjective agreement with other similarly placed interpreters with objectivity, and they will ironically claim that contrary accounts of the same matter are speculative and not supported by the evidence. The decisive trick that interpreters employ to give their narratives a veneer of scholarly credibility is that they will be compulsive about *referencing* works, and quoting words from the original text in isolation. This is a trick for it gives the interpreter an opportunity to avoid explicating (which involves understanding how words and sentences are used to generate certain conclusions—something that runs through a text) and instead explain the words and references in isolation by way of their beliefs. This is the method of Orthodox Indology, where "dharma" is said to have many meanings.

Those who complain that there is a bias in Indology are not wrong, but the challenge is to explain how we overcome this. The knee-jerk reaction to replace one interpretation (that is perhaps Eurocentric) with another (Adluri and Bagchee 2014) is no solution as interpretation is the problem. Explicators in contrast have an alternative: treat the data as controversial, and the study of philosophy as the study of reasons that entail controversial claims. The researcher's biases are simply unemployed in this exercise, and the objective data is what determines the explication, with the use of the explicator's reasoning skills. Explication is logically rigorous and relies upon textual data, but the explicator has no motive for showing that a text *agrees* with them. They are rather concerned with rendering explicit what is implicit. So explicators will explicitly disown a fetish for close philological referencing for this does not reveal the theory of a text: it is our logical skills as philosophers working with texts that does the work. Ironically, the explicator's approach is unbiased and objective, but will be treated by interpreters as speculative for they do not agree with its outcomes.

The West *and interpretation: the vector*

Interpretation is threatening to diversity because it does not acknowledge disagreement. If you do not share the interpretation of your interlocutors, your perspective is unacknowledged by them. However, as we inhabit perspectives, this failure to appreciate the room to disagree is a threat to one's own place in the world. The rational response to this aggression is explication, for explication undermines interpretation that makes this aggression possible. But most people when threatened respond in kind: aggression with aggression, interpretation with interpretation. Interpretation hence spreads like a disease, but it can also spread ideas as it disenfranchises contrary perspectives. Essential to this transmission of interpretation is a failure to explicate. Explication acknowledges disagreement and contrary perspectives and hence makes room for those who can disagree in a public world.

The means by which interpretation spreads ideas is political. When dominant powers interpret people inhabiting contrary perspectives, they can not only pass along the strategy of interpretation, but also beliefs of the colonizing culture—including interpretive beliefs of how the colonized culture seems from the colonizer's perspectives. Once in charge, the dominant power presents itself as the *de facto* perspective, and colonized individuals *internalize* the colonizer's perspective. This results in a *colonized consciousness* (more on this in Chapter 5). But if the initial batch of beliefs that characterizes the initial interpretive outlook is Eurocentric, this Eurocentric frame will be transmitted the world over as interpretation, the vector, spreads. Along the way, interpretation can even domesticate completely alien views that it initially religified by reclassifying it as the 'official religion' and these too can spread with the colonizing culture. What is doing the spreading is not the 'official religion' but interpretation. All religions in our world gain their status as religions via interpretation that starts with Europe as constituting the framework. From a Hindu perspective it can seem that the aggression of the *W*est is Christianity or Islam forcing its way into India. This is an illusion (what we see when we take our vantage too seriously). Really, it is interpretation that is spreading, and Hindus catch it all the time too.

The *W*est, which starts with the ancient Greeks and connects up to contemporary traditions of Analytic and Continental philosophy via Medieval philosophy, is constituted by a basic commitment to interpretation. The origin of interpretation is the Greek idea of *logos* that unites separate ideas in one concept: belief, thought, reason, and language. It is a model of thought that has been profoundly important for cultures and traditions that draw upon Greek philosophy[2]—but one that we do not find uncontested elsewhere. The idea of *logos* conflates your opinion—belief—with thought and identifies this with the meaning of what you say. To think about someone else, on this model, is to subsume them under the meanings encoded in your language that you believe to be the content of your thought. This is to explain aliens in terms of what you take to be true, your tradition and its beliefs. This is interpretation.

In recent *W*estern theorizing much has been made of the linguistic turn, famously associated with Frege (Dummett 1973: 667–669) but also the Continental tradition and its early Hermeneutic philosophers (Lafont 1999). But as the Continental philosopher Jacques Derrida notes, this has been a mainstay of the European tradition (1974: 3). What characterizes this tradition on his account is the idea that the content of thought is a sort of *presence* when in reality the linguistic foundations are hidden (1974: 12). This is an astute observation: if thought is the linguistic meaning *x* of what we say, then we will appreciate thought in terms of *x*—the content we are present to as speakers of a language. What is not apparent to us is that we have endorsed a theory that says that thought is the content of what you say. Moreover, the very content is often not linguistic—that is, the linguistic approach to thought characteristic of the *W*est is not the view that language is the content of thought. It is the view that the meaning of language is the content of thought.

Given the historical origins of this account of thought, the historical beliefs that are encoded in this tradition's language will be treated as the frame to subsume all else. As this tradition begins in Greece, it grows as the dominant tradition of the *W*est, creating and keeping European culture as the interpretive frame for all else: everything that deviates from this is religion. The *West* is that peculiar cultural force, part theory of thought, part history, which together have been influential but not for good, for the theory of thought is interpretation, and interpretation is a failure as it is deeply subjective.

The contemporary view that the move to language is a recent turn in western philosophy shows an ignorance about the history of western philosophy. This is not uncommon in the *W*est and this lack of insight into the history of one's own perspective is an artifact of interpretation. As interpretation leads us to identify the thinkable with our perspective, it undermines our ability to be critical of the history of our perspective, as the thinkable is conflated with whatever we believe from our contemporary vantage. (This is a topic that we shall further explore in Chapter 5.)

A tradition that embraces the complex significances of *logos* as identical—the idea that thought is perspective, but also the content of language—will likely display certain features.

1. It will identify communication and who you can get along with as those within your community: ethical questions will be primarily about community membership.
2. Aliens in other communities who are humans will be viewed with suspicion as people who are presumptively not reasonable (after all, they lack your language) and one's obligations to them will be unclear if not apparently non-existent as obligations (as per 1) exist for people within the same community only.

3 Extending the model of duty and obligation (as per 1) to people outside your community involves bringing them into your community. You will see this as an act of kindness—an extension of your sense of fellow-feeling and consideration. Everyone else will see this as imperialism, colonialism, and an act of aggression.
4 Non-humans who ostensibly do not speak language will be branded non-persons who cannot reason because they lack language.

The *W*est's tradition of moral philosophy from the very start to the present is characterized by communitarian anthropocentrism. Plato, Aristotle, the Medievals (Platonists and Aristotelians), Kant, all the social contract theorists (Hobbes, Locke, Rousseau), and Mill, and important recent exponents such as Rawls, understand moral questions primarily in terms of community membership. Even Kant, who introduces an emphasis on self-governance as central to all ethics understands this in terms of what we would agree to in an ideal community (the Kingdom of Ends). In rare exceptions do we find philosophers in this tradition think about the rights of non-human animals. Here too, as in the case of Bentham, there will be an effort to account for our duties to animals in terms of their inclusion in a *community* that we are all part of (*Introduction to the Principles of Morals and Legislation*, ch. 1: IX). Moral theories that are fundamentally individualistic—like most of the theories that I can think of in the Indian tradition—will come across as beyond the pale of moral theory to someone who takes communitarian anthropocentrism as the basic framework of all ethics. Indian moral theories will often adopt a strong line about the transcendence and cosmological significance of dharma, transcending community bonds (cf. Halbfass 1988: 311–312) but also transgressing and criticizing understanding people in terms of biological species. To be a person for a *W*esterner in contrast is the same as (minimally) being human: animal rights do not apply to humans (as though humans are not animals). It is a rarity to find a defense of the rights of those beyond our species and community in the *W*estern tradition (for a rare exception, see Singer 1972, 1989).

These implications of the logocentric account of thought create the impression that there is a 'secular worldview'—the worldview of human life from within a community. Religion will seem doubly beyond the pale, but this is not because religious views have nothing to say about community life, but because they are religified by interpretation and thereby depicted as mysterious, while the implications of the European origins of the linguistic account of thought are treated as uncontroversially secular. Meanwhile these same implications consist of an insular communitarian anthropocentrism, rendering 'secular' people quite uninterested in the welfare of those who are in other communities and species.

Hinduism: a class of its own

That *W*estern theory is dominated by the concern for the *right perspective* is an expression of the interpretive model of the *W*est. The concern for the 'right' perspective is the effort to retain the interpretive model while acknowledging that there could be more than one perspective that we can adopt. Putting together the observations from the previous section, it entails that *W*estern imperialism is nothing but the vector-function of interpretation with a Eurocentric starting point. Generalizations and simplifications of the *entire tradition* are made easy because interpretation ensures that basic ideas that frame the initial interpreter's worldview get retained like *saṃskāra*-s (tendency impressions) that get passed on historically via the vector of interpretation. What is retained is not only interpretation, but also Europe as the archetypal homeland of understanding, relative to which everything alien and foreign is religion.

Interpretation religifies what it cannot derive from its reasons. Explication (the basic model of understanding for philosophers) is a model of understanding that is underivable from interpretation. It would hence be a religion if interpretation ever ran into it. I think something like this happened and now what we have is Hinduism. Philosophy (explication) is depicted as a religion by the *W*est for the same reasons anything counts as a religion. But what is alienated is philosophy. But as it is religified, it appears from afar as a kind of unified perspective, endorsed by all Hindus. But this myth is a function of interpretation that tries to understand everything in terms of the perspective of the interpreter: as interpreters have a perspective, it seems to them that Hindus have to have one too.

As a preliminary clarification of Hinduism, it is worth visiting the distinction between a class and a kind. A category with an essence—a *kind*—is a category defined by necessary and sufficient conditions of identity. For an object to be a member of such a category is for it to instantiate the defining traits of the category. The category and the object in this case share an identity. We can call such a category a *kind* or *type*. It has been observed (I hear anecdotally by the philosopher Donald Davidson) that Socrates was never happy with proposed definitions of this kind except for one: *MUD*, which can be defined as a combination of Earth and water. Indeed, though we expect essences in our categories, we often have to settle for something else. This is the less famous but equally important variety of category that we could call a *class*. Classes have no essence. They are kept together by naming conventions. This means that objects that are members of a class do not display the criterion of class membership that defines the class. Rather, it is the diversity of members in a class that contribute to the character of the class. The logical properties of these varieties of categories differ.

Consider the case of *FRUIT SALAD*. Fruits, and their varieties, are kinds. We need this kind—*FRUIT*—to make sense of *FRUIT SALAD*, which is a class. An orange of variety *x* has an essence that is downward transitive to all its components. A piece of an orange of variety *x* will share the essence of the whole orange and we know that by virtue of being a piece of orange of variety *x*, the piece will share this identity. We could attempt to treat *FRUIT SALAD* as a kind, but then every component of a fruit salad would itself have to be fruit salad. But really, this is not the case. Some parts of fruit salad are pieces of fruit with essences, such as oranges of variety *x*. We might even pull this piece of fruit aside and note that it is a piece of orange of variety *x*, and we would have no reason to call this lonely piece "fruit salad." When we combine differing fruits with differing essences together, we get fruit salad. So the characteristic of being fruit salad is not downward transitive.

In point of fact, most religions are kinds: they are definable by a founding figure or text. This provides necessary and sufficient conditions to identify what falls within the category—the members of the category will instantiate or bear witness to the category criteria. Buddhism has the Buddha, Jainism has the Ford Makers, Islam has Mohammad and the *Quran*, Judaism has the *Torah*, Sikhism has Guru Nanak, Christianity has Jesus. The defining trait of the category entails that any member of the category in the case of kinds has to instantiate or display the criterion of class membership. Hence, if *Christianity* is a kind, then all things Christian will bear witness to the central importance of Jesus. I think the same would follow for the other religions that are also kinds. What this entails is that we can as a matter of conceptual clarity criticize claims of class membership in the case of religions that are kinds if they fail to exemplify the category trait.

Some have attempted to argue that there are essential elements to Hinduism, but the moment we find such arguments we find that the list of things that make up Hinduism are disjunctive.

For instance, Klaus Klostermaier (2007) accounts for Hinduism in terms of four disjuncts:

> (1) the traditions of the original inhabitants of India, perhaps preserved by *ādivāsis*, or "first-dweller" groups; (2) influences from the Indus civilization in northwestern and northern India; (3) the ancient Dravidian culture, represented by Tamils in contemporary south India and possibly preserving features of the Indus civilization; and (4) Vedic religions codified by Aryan groups and spread through settlement, conquest, and persuasion.

Very few versions of Hinduism exemplify more than one of these options, but this means that the Hindu religion can be identified by just one of these disjuncts. But some of these strands are so open (such as the idea of the 'original inhabitants of India') that any philosophical movement in India, that is not itself reducible to the others, could be Hindu.

It is worth noting that there is a vast literature on the definition of Hinduism (Llewellyn 2005; Patton Accessed 2016). If Hinduism were a kind, with an essence, it would be a largely open and shut case as to the essence of Hinduism: any Hindu thing or artifact would bear the group essence of Hinduism and then a very cursory survey of Hindu artifacts and persons would tell one everything about the essence of Hinduism. Moreover, we would expect there to be wide consensus on this as everyone involved would need the same essential definition to talk about Hinduism. But as Hinduism is a class that is wide open, we can operate with many different essential definitions of Hinduism, and any proposed definition will have some evidence in its favor.

Hinduism is not a religion that can be easily overlooked. There are one billion Hindus the world over today. The word "Hindu" designates a South Asian tradition that its adherents often regard as ancient, stretching back to the time of the Vedas (1500 BCE – 500 BCE). Historically, Hinduism appears to have spread out over parts of South East Asia, and today Hindus can be found the world over.

Yet, the term "Hindu" does not appear in the ancient literary materials that Hindus often call their own. To investigate Hinduism is to investigate a relatively modern grouping of often ancient ideas and traditions. To investigate Hinduism philosophically is to employ philosophy and its resources to inspect, analyze, and understand Hinduism as such. Framed this way, the philosophical investigation into Hinduism is a philosophical investigation into the category *HINDUISM*.

The term "Hindu" had no significant life in India prior to British colonial rule. According to the *Monier Monier-Williams Sanskrit* Dictionary, the term "Hindu" (originally "Hindū") appears to be medieval Persian and was used to talk about South Asian phenomena (1995: 1298). As T.N. Madan notes, the geographic region of the "Sindu" becomes "Hindu" for the Persians, and "Indos" for the Greek (Madan 2003: xii). Our word "India" comes from the Greek. At some point under British colonial rule (Lorenzen 1999), "Hindu" became used to classify Indians. If any stock can be placed in this etymology, then Hinduism is Indianism. It is a racial categorization like all racial categorizations: it does not arise via affiliation (like ethnic identity) but from the outside. Originally, the term was employed by the British to distinguish an indigenous Indian religion from Islam (Gottschalk 2012). Of course, things became more complex. Traditions that could be traced to a unique founder in India were eventually granted their own identity: some were designated as Buddhist, some as Jain, others as Sikh, and virtually *everything else* retained the designation "Hindu." Now most of Indian thought is understood as Hindu (cf. Flood 1996). In this act of naming we find that the door is wide open to what counts as Hinduism. "Hinduism" becomes the designation of what is *South Asian but with no common founder*.

This concept *HINDUISM* is a class concept: one can be a member of the category Hinduism and not display the criterion of class membership.

These observations about what it is to be Hindu suggest the following: that while being a Christian or a Muslim is to not be a Hindu, it is not at all obvious that a Hindu cannot be a Christian or a Muslim in some way. This is made possible by the logic of classes: the members of a class can be kinds, because the class itself entails no essential constraint on its members. Hindus can and do worship Jesus as the Lord, and they can and do pray to Allah. Further back in history, we find the Buddha, commonly known as the founder of Buddhism, being identified as an incarnation of the Hindu God Viṣṇu. There is nothing contradictory about this *if* 'Hinduism' is a class without an essential definition.[3]

The non-prohibitive definition of Hinduism is empirically adequate as it will be consistent with anything that we care to identify as Hindu. This has been known for some time, and is especially relevant to the legal and practical understanding of Hinduism in contemporary India. Accordingly,

> the test of whether a person is a Hindu . . . starts with ethnic and geographical tests, which raise a presumption that can be rebutted not by proof of absence of belief or presence of disbelief but only by proof of exclusive adherence (or conversion) to a foreign (i.e. a non-Hindu) faith.
>
> (Derrett 1968: 52)

J.A.B. Van Buitenen's entry on "Hinduism" in the *Encyclopedia Britannica* states:

> As a religion, Hinduism is an utterly diverse conglomerate of doctrines, cults, and ways of life . . . In principle, Hinduism incorporates all forms of belief and worship without necessitating the selection or elimination of any . . . A Hindu may embrace a non-Hindu religion without ceasing to be a Hindu.
>
> (Van Buitenen 1974: 519)

Similarly the legal historian of India, Marc Galanter, writes:

> Heterodox practice, lack of belief, active support of non-Hindu religious groups, expulsion from a group within Hinduism—none of these removes one from the Hindu category. The individual could venture as far as he wished over any doctrinal or behavioral borders; the gates would not shut behind him so long as he did not explicitly adhere to another religion.
>
> (Galanter 1971: 471n)

Hinduism is not a comprehensive doctrine—much like religion itself has no essential doctrine. It is an inclusive category open to all philosophy. This shows that comprehensive definitions of Hinduism cannot be right. But it also shows how some of the seemingly plausible comprehensive versions of Hinduism get so much attention. These are the versions of comprehensive Hinduism that claim that Hinduism is an open and tolerant religion and that this attitude of openness characterizes all things Hindu. Call these *Inclusivist accounts of Hinduism*. There are Indian antecedents to Inclusivist Hinduism. We find for instance Hindu sources claiming that all gods are reducible to the one Brahman (*Bṛhadāraṇyaka Upaniṣad* IX.9), or Kṛṣṇa's claim in the *Bhagavad Gītā* that no matter what god one is worshiping, one is worshiping Kṛṣṇa (*Bhagavad Gītā* 9:23). Inclusivist accounts of Hinduism take such sources in the Indian tradition as paradigmatic of Hinduism. These accounts of Hinduism attempt to treat the openness of the class of Hinduism as though it is a kind. This is a logical mistake but understandable. What is worth noting though is that the effort to depict Hinduism as a kind, like most other religions, is itself an outcome of Eurocentric interpretation. As the familiar varieties of religion from the Eurocentric perspective (the orientations that received the status of 'religion' earliest) are kinds, it seems true that religions are kinds, and then a great amount of effort is devoted to depicting Hinduism in this light. This is a mistake. Hinduism is special and unusual as religions go but that is because it is not a kind but a class that is wide open in the way of philosophical diversity.

William Cantwell Smith observes that there are Hindus but no Hinduism (1963: 65). The opposite is true if we are to be responsible and open about what counts as Hinduism. There is such a thing as the category of HINDUISM, but in understanding this we do not define or essentialize Hindus. Hinduism is not like most other religions that are kinds: understanding what Hinduism is entails nothing substantial about what Hindus believe or practice.

As *Hinduism* the class places no essential constraints on what a Hindu can advocate or endorse, there are no interpretive constraints on being a Hindu. Hindus do not have to share beliefs to be a Hindu nor do they have to share practices that are entailed by their perspectives—it is not as though Hindus all have to go to temple or engage in the same rituals or holidays to be Hindu. The upshot is that Hinduism does not require interpretation to sustain itself. Hindus are free to explicate as a way to understand their own religion. Moreover, to appreciate what they have in common, Hindus have to explicate each other's philosophies—for what they have in common is a philosophical disagreement on everything. It seems to me that this is how traditional and *very* orthodox Hindus relate to each other—Hindus that are so orthodox the term "Hindu" never comes into their descriptions of their traditions. They are able to discern the reasons of third parties without endorsing them and in understanding third parties as having different reasons, Hindus lean on their first-party reasons to understand the world as they see it. Orthodox Hindus, unlike *W*esterners, can keep clear the distinction between what they believe and what others believe, and this is because interpretation plays no major role in the philosophical landscape of orthodox Hinduism. Indeed, if it did, India would not have had such a robust and diverse tradition of philosophy. Everyone would have got behind a unified, centralized doctrinal authority.

But then the means of Hindus relating to each other is a philosophical disagreement that is rendered transparent by explication. Recent and contemporary Hinduism is another matter. Hindus can and do catch the interpretation bug. Symptoms of this include the tendency of Hindus or folks of South Asian descent to re-describe Hindu and Indian commitments (such as a commitment to action or karma) as concerned primarily with humans, and to fret about the doctrinal unity of Hindus as though to be Hindu one must share a belief system (De Smet 1968). (Another symptom is the tendency of Hindu groups to identify their tradition and commitments as Hinduism as such.) This can lead to two further conclusions: (a) either "Hinduism" is not a religion but a misdescription of several religions, or (b) that Hindus really do share an outlook. Neither is true as a representation of the objectivity of Hinduism. If Hinduism is objective, we can disagree about it and in it.

Ironically, the peculiarity of Hinduism as a class and not a kind sets it apart as an objective religion. But that is because it arises out of the effort of the *W*est to identify the religion of India, when all it was and is is philosophy. Just as philosophy is objective—what we can disagree about—so too Hinduism.

Objections

I want to consider nine objections to my argument.

Your argument is an interpretation

Interpreters tend to identify anyone's explanation as an interpretation: this is a psychological, self-fulfilling prophecy of endorsing interpretation as the only method of explanation. It arises from confusing the psychological question of whether someone believes something, with the fact of that belief playing a role in explanation. This conflation is itself interpretation. If we explicate, our own beliefs are not the data of explanation and hence, explication is not interpretation. Another source of this objection is that interpretation makes disagreement unintelligible so interpreters, committed to interpretation, will thereby conclude that explicators are not doing something different for they cannot make sense of the alternative—it is forbidden by their method of understanding. Explication gets around this problem by simply not employing one's own beliefs in explanation. That I believe that explication is the better of the two methods of explanation is not a premise in my explication of an interpreter, such as Gadamer, for instance: Gadamer's various claims about the necessity of tradition and the unavoidability of prejudice are the data for my explication of his theory of understanding.

If religion is a designation that arises from interpretation, it follows that there is no such thing as religion or Hinduism

Hinduism as the microcosm of philosophy has a special claim to objectivity, as it is itself a disagreement. The objectivity of Hinduism hence is what Hindus perceive from their various disagreeing perspectives, but this objectivity also explains their disagreements. That the word "Hindu" comes from outside appears at first blush to undermine the objectivity of Hinduism. If it is an outsider who comes up with the name, then it seems like the outsider made Hinduism up. Much ink has been spilled in the effort to show that what we think of as Hinduism (some unified perspective) corresponds to traditional options in the Indian tradition, as though the accuracy of the definition of Hinduism depends upon it representing Hinduism.

But this inference that the external origins of the name "Hinduism" entails an external construction is not supported by thinking clearly about the philosophy of language.

Frege (1980), the famous and influential philosopher of mathematics and language, noted that we identify objects in the world via modes of presentation and our modes of presentation may not at all be accurate of the objects—and yet, the modes of presentation can mediate our beliefs about the objects they depict. For instance, humans in some cultures identified a bright object in the morning sky as the 'morning star' and a bright object in the evening sky as the 'evening star.' It turns out that neither are stars, and both are the same object: Venus. In naming Venus 'the morning star' humans created nothing but they did identify the object Venus with their geocentric perspective on Venus. The identification of Hinduism similarly has more than one component. There is the reality that it names, and then there are the expectations that we have about Hinduism that speak to our (*W*estern) perspective on Hinduism that lead us to give it a name. Comprehensive definitions of Hinduism are our modes of presentation of Hinduism—how Hinduism seems from specific perspectives.

Saul Kripke (1980) similarly argues that the meanings of our words are their referents and in so far as we have impressions about these objects we talk about they are causally explained by the referent. Gems cast illusions and shadows and our first impressions of an object are usually not our last impressions. Our task as scholars and philosophers is to look more carefully at Hinduism. What we find is the objectivity of philosophy: it explains the varied impressions that we arrive at about Hinduism when we are open to its objectivity.

Similarly Keith Donnellan (1966) argued that we can often *use* words with a certain descriptive content (like "religion") to refer to objects (Hinduism), and what we refer to may not actually conform to the descriptive content of the words we use. So while "Hinduism" may be defined by outsiders with a certain descriptive content, what it refers to may not at all conform to the description: it is still objective. The objectivity of Hinduism may indeed be unique amongst religions for objectivity is what we can disagree about, and there is no basic thesis that Hindus have to agree to in order to be Hindus. So Hindus can disagree about everything. This entails that Hindus do not need an external origin for the idea of *Hinduism* to take Hinduism seriously: its objectivity transcends its history.

It might be the case that some religions endorse the idea that their perspective is mystical, and hence the diagnosis that this depiction of the origins of religion as something external undermines the authentic experience of religious people

The argument from explication shows us that whether we are inclined to describe a perspective as mystical has to do with imposing an external standard of reason on the 'mystical' perspective. Certainly religious people can endorse this external characterization of their view but it is unclear how they can account for the mystery of their perspective without this external standard. For any perspective can be explicated, and what we find is that the perspective provides reasons that explain its descriptions of the world. They are mystical only in so far as they fail to meet up with external standards.

There are essential ethical practices that define Hinduism

The practice that is often claimed to be essential to Hinduism is caste. Hindus often want to drop mention of the practices of caste, but yet it is often important to non-Hindus to attribute a commitment to caste to Hinduism so as to make sense of the decision not to be Hindu (Monier-Williams 2003; Ambedkar Accessed 2016a, Accessed 2016b, Accessed 2016c; Nath 1993). The problem is that in India, most everyone endorses cast—even the Buddha, who, depicted as opting out of caste hierarchy, is also depicted as making use of caste concepts in his canonical articulation of Buddhism (*Dhammapadha* Ch.26). Indian Christians and Muslims also have castes, and it is a political institution that is quite separate from Hinduism as a religion (Guha 2013; Roberts 2015).

The deeper problem with the identification of caste with Hinduism is that it takes something controversial and identifies it as essential. But if it is controversial, then Hindus do not have to endorse caste (many do not). One might claim that this is generally true of religions: that if something is controversial, it is wrong to define a practitioner of a religion in terms of that controversial commitment. But most religions are ostensibly kinds, and if a practice is definitive of the kind, the practitioner of the religion is by definition committed to the practice. *HINDUISM* is a class not a kind. So in the case of Hinduism it is quite implausible to define it in terms of any commitment or belief. Anything that all Hindus believe or do is likely not unique to them, and anything that seems unique to them will not comprehend all versions of Hinduism.

The claim has been made that religion is a kind of racial categorization: one that comes from outside and moreover Hinduism with its strong association with "India" is racial. But race is something that one cannot opt out of, yet one can opt out of being Hindu

If Hinduism is a class, with no essential trait, it is not at all obvious how one opts out of being Hindu and in this respect it is very much like race: a categorization that one has little choice over. It is not as though claiming to be an atheist will do it, for one can be both Hindu and atheistic. One can decide to affirm a contrary religion, and this might entail the rejection of Hinduism. But how does one merely opt out of it without taking on a new religious identity? Even when a Hindu does take on a new religious identity, it is not obvious that they have endorsed anything that they could not have endorsed as a Hindu. In actual cases, it seems that people who opt out of Hinduism have to essentialize Hinduism, by defining it by some practice or belief, and then reject the practice. So for instance, the materialist philosopher Ramendra Nath (1993) in his "Why I Am Not a Hindu" defines Hinduism by a commitment to caste, and then rejects caste with the expectation that this is a rejection of Hinduism. But this is to treat Hinduism as a kind. We find this type of criticism from those on the left, going back to Marx and Engels. On their account, religion is a kind of mentalization of the problems of the world that diverts us from practical challenges characterizable by some essential concern. "Religion is the sigh of the oppressed creature, the heart of a heartless world, and the soul of soulless conditions. It is the opium of the people" (Marx and Engels 1957). Religion is itself a kind, on this account, which distracts us from the actual challenges of practical questions (caste as a normativization of social inequality is an example of this kind of distraction). But this is a classic move of *W*esternization (and interpretation)—it's incapacity to understand disagreement is then projected on to aliens as though a failure to be practical or critical is theirs. And this projection is part of the *W*est's colonization of everything outside of the *W*est. This ignores the imperial and colonial origins of religion as such. This kind of criticism is analogous to blaming racialized minorities for the ills that befall them. It shows a naïve view of the history of such troubles.

That Hinduism is controversial, or that Hindus disagree about everything does not entail that Hinduism is philosophy

There are at least two senses of the word 'philosophy.' We can talk about a philosophy—a perspective (what Indians would call a *darśana*) or explication—the process of distinguishing first-party and third-party reasons as a means of understanding—rendering what is alien explicit. Most all religions are philosophies in the first sense, if we include moral theory in the mix. The practices of religious folks are their moral theories lived. But Hinduism is philosophy in the second sense. There is no way for a Hindu to understand the diversity of options within Hinduism without explication and this is philosophy.

Hinduism is just mysticism: it is not about reason but about transcending reason

Whether a perspective appears like mysticism has to do with whether you insist upon judging it by third-party reasons. As interpreters draw no distinction between first-party and third-party reasons, they employ their own reasons to judge alien perspectives, which is to judge the alien perspective by reasons that are third party to it. All divergent alien perspectives seem like mysticism to the interpreter.

Hindu texts are not philosophical: they are either stories and literature, or they are dense aphorisms. Essays and monographs in philosophy come relatively late in the tradition

(Let us ignore for a moment the problem with this criticism: if the mythological nature of Indian texts renders them unphilosophical then we have to get rid of Plato, who constantly refers to myths.) Interpreters get everything backward. They expect philosophical texts to explain themselves. This feeds the naïve impression that anyone can read and understand philosophy and that the reader has to do no work to understand philosophy. But philosophy, explication, is a yoga (discipline) and philosophical texts are those that we have to engage philosophically, which means by explication—otherwise their content is locked. To the extent that we require explication to make sense of Hindu texts, the texts are philosophy. Explication, philosophy, is especially relevant to the study of texts that make little sense when we interpret them—exactly the texts interpreters call mystical. (More on this in Chapter 4.)

***It is difficult to find very many critical comments about religion in the intellectual tradition associated with the W*est**

According to my explication of the two competing options of understanding (interpretation and explication) but also the *W*est as a political force of interpretation tied to the European tradition, "religion" is a term for what the *W*est cannot rationally explain, and moreover, its mode of presentation (to use Frege's model) is something that exceeds the boundaries of reason and philosophy, defined by theories of a European provenance. Moreover, on this account, religion is a category of marginalization—much like race. It serves to quarantine Europe's intellectual tradition from having to deal with diversity. If this is true, we should expect the use of the term "religion" by major figures in the European tradition as a term of criticism and abuse, to marginalize and demean. Yet we do not see such critical use of the term until quite late in the tradition.[4]

Certainly recently, there has been an increasing move to disparage religion amongst those who identify with being 'secular.' But certainly, historically, this has not been the case. I think the reason we commonly do not see this type of disparaging usage of "religion" is that the very process by which we come to identify something as religion is the normalization of violence and exclusion to a non-*W*estern perspective. The point of identifying Hinduism as a religion (or anything as a religion), and not merely an open-ended contribution to philosophy, is to make it seem innocuous and nonthreatening to a tradition—the *W*est—which cannot tolerate disagreement. This allows the *W*est to treat European philosophy as the only default philosophy and everything else as religion. The reason that the *W*est cannot tolerate disagreement is that it is based on the linguistic account of thought, which leads to the conflation of thought and belief, which is made true by virtue of the attitude of the believer. This move from taking a proposition seriously to assimilating it to my belief (moving from *p* to *I believe that p*) changes the topic, from something we can disagree about (*p*) to something made true by virtue of my attitude (*I believe that p*), and moreover, something personal: if one were to disagree with *I believe that p* (said by me), they would be picking a fight with me—denying that *I believe that p*, when I do. This is the universe of the *W*est, which is a universe in which adherents are very sensitive to dissent: here, dissent is not possible, and if it happens, it's threatening. Within this universe, the way to keep the peace is to emphasize belief, piously, for the more we emphasize belief (secular belief and religious belief), the more we will find that we cannot really disagree with them (true by virtue of the believer's attitude), and in this observation we avoid a real and dangerous conflict which is entirely the creation of the conflation of belief and thought. So here, relative to the *W*est, religion will be taken most seriously, and piously, and talk of religion will be most respectful—all as a way to avoid dissent. This causes problems for understanding Hinduism, and anything non-*W*estern for that matter—including western philosophy. (More on this in Chapters 5 and 9.)

Conclusion

There is a toggle switch between interpretation and explication: if we kick the switch so as to appreciate the distinction between third-party and first-party reasons, then the theories of dharma become transparent, and the concept of *DHARMA*, or *ETHICS*, as what moral philosophy disagrees about is also transparent. In this case, we look to the objects of criticism to provide the reasons to account for their philosophical claims—the controversial ones—and we know we have discerned these reasons when the theory based on them entails the controversial claims of the third-party perspective. Further, when we line up explicated theories, we find that the common concept explains the disagreements across theories. It is disagreement that sheds light on the objectivity of the discourse. In this manner, the discourse of moral philosophy and dharma philosophy is simplified to a single concept of *THE RIGHT OR THE GOOD*. If we kick the switch in the other direction and deny the distinction between third-party and first-party reasons, then we use some assumed frame—the *W*est—to study Indian thought, then we multiply meanings of 'dharma' and conceptual distinctions beyond their means. From this interpretive vantage, what would be straightforward moral theory becomes religion if it is from the other side of the world. The strangest of all such religions is Hinduism, which seems to not even agree on moral theory.

The *W*est—interpretation with a Eurocentric frame—is the tradition of Rudra with no Pārvatī: it is an aggressive prioritization of a perspective, with no accommodation of others who might dissent. In scholarship this leads to the Orientalist depiction of alien perspectives (say on ethics or dharma) as inexplicable and confused, and it creates the idea of religion as what is underivable from the Eurocentric frame. Orthodox Indology as a project outside of philosophy buys into this methodology.

Hinduism is the wall that the *W*est hits. It undermines all the expectations we have about outsiders because the resources of the interpreter such as anthropocentric communitarianism makes no sense of Hinduism. Hindus do not form a community, do not agree on the rules for the communities they would endorse, they do not agree on basic philosophical explanations, they are not on the whole humanists, and they do not as a whole believe as a matter of being Hindu that others have to share their beliefs in order for them to have a conversation. What they have in common is that they disagree about their religion. Hinduism is hence objective, which means that it transcends perspectives. For Hindus to understand the objectivity of their religion requires that they distinguish between first-party and third-party reasons. In short, to make sense of their religion, they have to do what philosophers do: explicate. Why is Hinduism a religion? Ask the *W*est.

Notes

1 What we find in philosophy when we explicate it is much like what we often associate with religion: "a system of beliefs, the breaking in of a transcendent reality, and human attitudes of ultimate concern, meaning, and purpose" (Meister 2009: 6). The transcendence is the objectivity of what we talk about in philosophy and the meaning and purpose that we find in religion is the meaning and purpose of the various axiological matters we study philosophically.

2 We find for instance the connection between language and thought continuing on in Arabic. The Arabic verb "*nataqa*" means *to speak* or *utter*, "*mantiq*" is the word for logic, and "*natiq*" is often the word used for *RATIONAL*. (For instance, in Arabic discussions of Plato's tripartite division of the soul, the rational soul is often referred to as: *al-nafs al-natiqah*.) I have this on the good authority of Muhammad Ali Khalidi. He is the translator and editor of *Medieval Islamic Philosophical Writings* (2005).

3 For a scholarly Hindu's inclusion of Jesus in his comprehensive Hinduism, see Shaunaka Rishi Das's "Jesus in Hinduism" (2009). Das is the director of the Oxford Center for Hindu Studies, and Oxford University's Hindu Chaplain. For evidence of the inclusion of the Buddha in a Hindu pantheon, see the *Bhāgavata Purāṇa* (1.3.24), where the Buddha is described as an incarnation of Viṣṇu. For the use of "Allah" in a Hindu context, consider the popular Hindu devotional song, "Raghupati Raghava Raja Ram" (*īśvar allāh tero nām, sab ko sanmati de bhagavān*).

4 I would like to thank the series editors, Chad Meister and Charles Taliaferro for sharing this objection with me.

References

Adluri, Vishwa, and Joydeep Bagchee. 2014. *The Nay Science: A History of German Indology*. New York: Oxford University Press.

Ambedkar. Accessed 2016a. *Buddha and the Future of His Religion*. www.ambedkar.org/ambcd/.

Ambedkar. Accessed 2016b. *Philosophy of Hinduism*. www.ambedkar.org/ambcd/17.Philosophy%20of%20Hinduism.htm.

Ambedkar. Accessed 2016c. *Riddle in Hinduism*. www.ambedkar.org/ambcd/.

Burley, Mikel. July 2012. "Surprising." In *Customer Reviews, Amazon UK*. www.amazon.co.uk/PATANJALIS-YOGA-SUTRA-Penguin-Classics-ebook/dp/B008ET4FIC/ref=sr_1_1?ie=UTF8&qid=1426279077&sr=8-1&keywords=shyam+ranganathan.

Burley, Mikel. 2014. "A Petrification of One's Own Humanity? Nonattachment and Ethics in Yoga Traditions." *The Journal of Religion* 94, no. 2: 204–228.

Creel, Austin B. 1977. *Dharma in Hindu Ethics*. Calcutta: Firma KLM.

Das, Shaunaka Rishi. 2009. Jesus in Hinduism. *BBC (Religions)*, March 24. www.bbc.co.uk/religion/religions/hinduism/beliefs/jesus_1.shtml.

Dasgupta, Surendranath. 1975. *A History of Indian Philosophy*. 5 vols. Delhi: Motilal Banarsidas.

Davidson, Donald. 1996a. "Belief and the Basis of Meaning." In *The Philosophy of Language*, edited by Aloysius Martinich, 456–464. New York: Oxford University Press.

Davidson, Donald. 1996b. "A Nice Derangement of Epitaphs." In *The Philosophy of Language*, edited by Aloysius Martinich, 465–475. New York: Oxford University Press.

Davidson, Donald. 2001a. "On the Very Idea of a Conceptual Scheme." In *Inquiries into Truth and Interpretation*, 183–198. New York: Oxford University Press.

Davidson, Donald. 2001b. "Radical Interpretation." In *Inquiries into Truth and Interpretation*, 125–140. Oxford: Clarendon Press.

De Smet, Richard. V. 1968. "The Indian Renaissance: Hindu Philosophy in English." *International Philosophical Quarterly* 8, no. 1: 5–37.

Derrett, John Duncan Martin. 1968. *Religion, Law and the State in India*. London: Faber & Faber.

Derrida, Jacques. 1974. *Of Grammatology*. Translated by Gayatri Chakravorty Spivak. 1st American edn. Baltimore, MD: Johns Hopkins University Press.

Donnellan, Keith S. 1966. "Reference and Definite Descriptions." *Philosophical Review* 75: 281–304.

Dummett, Michael A.E. 1973. *Frege: Philosophy of Language*. 1st U.S. edn. New York: Harper & Row.

Flood, Gavin. 1996. "An Introduction to Hinduism." In *Points of Departure*, edited by Gavin Flood, 5–22. New York: Cambridge University Press.

Frege, Gottlob. 1980. "On Sense and Reference." In *Translations from the Philosophical Writings of Gottlob Frege*, edited by P. Geach and M. Black, translated by M. Black. Oxford: Blackwell.

Gadamer, Hans-Georg. 1996. *Truth and Method.* Translated by Joel Weinsheimer and Donald G. Marshall. 2nd Revised English Language edn. New York: Continuum. Originally published Tubingen: J.C.B. Mohr (Paul Seibeck).

Galanter, Marc. 1971. "Hinduism, Secularism, and the Indian Judiciary." *Philosophy East and West* 21, no. 4: 467–487.

Gottschalk, Peter. 2012. *Religion, Science, and Empire: Classifying Hinduism and Islam in British India.* Oxford: Oxford University Press.

Government of India. 1950. *Glossary of Technical Terms.* In *Constitution of India.* New Delhi.

Guha, Sumit. 2013. *Beyond Caste: Identity and Power in South Asia, Past and Present.* Brill's Indological Library, vol. 44. Leiden: Brill.

Halbfass, Wilhelm. 1988. *India and Europe: An Essay in Understanding.* Albany, NY: State University of New York Press. Originally published Basel; Stuttgart: Schwabe.

Heidegger, Martin. 1962. *Being and Time.* Translated by John Macquarrie and Edward Robinson. New York: Harper.

Hudson, Emily T. 2013. *Disorienting Dharma: Ethics and the Aesthetics of Suffering in the Mahābhārata.* New York: Oxford University Press.

Kane, Pandurang Vaman. 1990. *History of Dharmaśāstra: Ancient and Mediæval Religious and Civil Law in India.* Government Oriental Series, Class B, no. 6. 2nd rev. and enl. edn. 5 vols. Poona: Bhandarkar Oriental Research Institute.

Kant, Immanuel. 1998. *Religion within the Boundaries of Mere Reason and Other Writings.* Translated by Allen W. Wood and George Di Giovanni. Cambridge Texts in the History of Philosophy. New York: Cambridge University Press.

Kant, Immanuel. 2003. *Critique of Pure Reason.* Translated by Norman Kemp Smith. Rev. 2nd edn. Houndmills; New York: Palgrave Macmillan.

Khalidi, Muhammad Ali. 2005. *Medieval Islamic Philosophical Writings.* Cambridge: Cambridge University Press.

Kinsley, D.R. 1989. *The Goddesses' Mirror: Visions of the Divine from East and West.* Albany, NY: State University of New York Press.

Klostermaier, Klaus K. 2007. "A Survey of Hinduism." In *The Beginnings of Hinduism*, edited by Klaus K. Klostermaier, 17–29. Albany, NY: State University of New York Press.

Kripke, Saul A. 1980. *Naming and Necessity.* Cambridge, MA: Harvard University Press.

Lafont, Cristina. 1999. *The Linguistic Turn in Hermeneutic Philosophy.* Studies in Contemporary German Social Thought. Cambridge, MA: MIT Press.

Larson, Gerald James. 1972. "The Trimurti of Dharma in Indian Thought: Paradox or Contradiction?" *Philosophy East and West* 22: 145–153.

Lawrence, David Peter. 1998. "Śiva's Self-Recognition and the Problem of Interpretation." *Philosophy East and West* 48: 197–231.

Lilly, Reginald. 1991. "Translator's Introduction." In *(Heidegger's) The Principle of Reason, vii–xix. Studies in Continental Thought.* Bloomington, IN: Indiana University Press.

Lingat, Robert. 1973. *The Classical Law of India.* Translated by J. Duncan M. Derrett. Berkeley, CA: University of California Press.

Llewellyn, J.E. (ed.). 2005. *Defining Hinduism: A Reader*. London: Equinox.

Lorenzen, David N. 1999. "Who Invented Hinduism?" *Comparative Studies in Society and History* 41: 630–659.

Madan, T.N. 2003. "Introduction." In *The Hinduism Omnibus*, edited by T.N. Madan, xi–xxxvi. Oxford: Oxford University Press.

Mantri, Geetika. 2015. "The Secularism Debate: Dharma Nirpekshta vs Panth Nirpekshta Explained." *Catch News*. www.catchnews.com/national-news/the-secularism-debate-dharma-nirpekshta-vs-panth-nirpekshta-explained-1448539543.html.

Marx, Karl, and Friedrich Engels (eds.). 1957. *Marx and Engels on Religion*. Moscow: Progress Publishing. www.marxists.org/archive/marx/works/subject/religion/.

Meister, Chad V. 2009. *Introducing Philosophy of Religion*. London; New York: Routledge.

Monier-Williams, Monier. 1995. *A Sanskrit–English Dictionary: Etymologically and Philologically Arranged, with Special Reference to Cognate Indo-European Languages*, greatly enlarged and improved edn. Delhi: Motilal Banarsidass Publishers. Originally published Oxford University Press 1872, enlarged 1899.

Monier-Williams, Monier. 2003. *Hinduism and Its Sources*. New Delhi: Munshiram Manoharlal.

Nath, Ramendra. 1993. *Why I Am Not a Hindu*. Bihar Rationalist Society (Bihar Buddhiwadi Samaj). http://infidels.org/library/modern/ramendra_nath/hindu.html.

Patton, Laurie. Accessed 2016. "Defining Hinduism." In *Oxford Bibliographies Online*, edited by Alf Hiltebeitel. Oxford: Oxford University Press. www.oxfordbibliographies.com/.

Quine, Willard Van Orman. 1960. *Word and Object*. Cambridge, MA: MIT Press.

Ranganathan, Shyam. 2007a. *Ethics and the History of Indian Philosophy*. Delhi: Motilal Banarsidass Publishers.

Ranganathan, Shyam. 2007b. *Translating Evaluative Discourse: The Semantics of Thick and Thin Concepts*. Ph.D. Dissertation, York University. www.collectionscanada.gc.ca/obj/thesescanada/vol2/002/NR68573.PDF.

Ranganathan, Shyam. 2011. "An Archimedean Point for Philosophy." *Metaphilosophy* 42, no. 4 (July): 479–519.

Ranganathan, Shyam. 2017. "Moral Philosophy: The Right and the Good." In *The Bloomsbury Research Handbook of Indian Ethics*, edited by Shyam Ranganathan, 5–34. London: Bloomsbury Academic.

Rangaswami Aiyangar, Kumbakonam Viraraghava. 1952. *Some Aspects of the Hindu View of Life According to Dharmaśāstra. Sayaji Row Memorial Lectures*, 1947–48. Baroda: Director Oriental Institute.

Rastogi, Navjivan. 1986. "Theory of Error According to Abhinavagupta." *Journal of Indian Philosophy* 14: 1–33.

Roberts, Nathaniel. 2015. "Setting Caste Back on Its Feet." *Anthropology of This Century*, no. 13 (May) http://aotcpress.com/articles/setting-caste-feet/.

Singer, Peter. 1972. "Famine, Affluence and Morality." *Philosophy and Public Affairs* 1, no. 3: 229–243.

Singer, Peter. 1989. "All Animals Are Equal." In *Animal Rights and Human Obligations*, edited by Tom Regan and Peter Singer, 148–162. Englewood Cliffs, NJ: Pearson.

Smith, Wilfred Cantwell. 1963. *The Meaning and End of Religion*. New York: Macmillan.

Somānanda, and Utpaladeva. 1934. *The Śivadṛṣṭi of Srisomānandanātha, with the Vritti by Utpaladeva*. Pune: Aryabhushan.

Steiner, G. 2010. *Anthropocentrism and Its Discontents: The Moral Status of Animals in the History of Western Philosophy*. Pittsburgh, PA: University of Pittsburgh Press.

Taylor-Rugman, D.C.H. 2012. *Dharmamegha Samadhi in the Yoga Sutra of Patanjali*. MA Thesis, University of Wales Trinity Saint David. http://dspace.trinity-cm.ac.uk/dspace/bitstream/10412/282/1/CHARLIE%20TAYLOR-RUGMAN.pdf.

Van Buitenen, J.A.B. 1957. "Dharma and Mokṣa." *Philosophy East and West* 7: 33–40.

Van Buitenen, J.A.B. 1974. "Hinduism." In *The New Encyclopaedia Britannica, Macropaedia*.

White, David Gordon. 2011. "Yoga." In *Oxford Bibliographies Online*. Oxford: Oxford University Press.

Wittgenstein, Ludwig. 1958. *Philosophical Investigations*. Translated by G.E.M. Anscombe. 2nd edn. New York: Macmillan.

3 Bhakti

The fourth moral theory

Introduction

When I was 19, I took my first undergraduate class, and effectively my introduction to the philosophy of religion. I thought I grew up in a religious household. My parents and their family are devout Śrī Vaiṣṇavas. Home *pūja*, temple worship, the recitation of Sanskrit Vedas, the Tamil Divya Prabandham along with the veneration of the Āḻvārs (the twelve devotional, Tamil Vaiṣṇava saints) was a basic part of my family life in Toronto. Indeed, a commitment to these practices and outlooks were so important that my parents and their friends saw to it that all the Āḻvārs were installed in the local temple, replete with many other standard Śrī Vaiṣṇava fixtures (Veṇkaṭeśvara, Sudarśana/Nārasiṃha, Padma and Āndal, as well as a Rāma sanctum with Lakṣmaṇa, Sītā and Hanuman). But what I experienced in my philosophy of religion class was foreign to me. It was as though I had never been raised in a religious household if the problems that were being discussed in this class are the philosophical problems of religious people.

In retrospect, I came to appreciate that the topics we covered are often standard problems in the philosophy of religion: the problem of evil, the possibility of divine foreknowledge, the question of the relationship of scripture and science, miracles. The discussions assumed for instance that all religious folks believe in god—I knew then that they do not and it struck me even then that this theoretical commitment was at the center of the philosophy of religion—but moreover if they do believe in god, the god is a creator. Hindus overall acknowledge a creator (Brahma) but do not worship him but rather deities who regulate other concerns. It is as though (most) all Hindus side with the atheist: yes, if your god created you, he is to blame. At any rate, my god did not create me, I was taught. All people are eternal realities and my god adopts us even though we come with a ton of our own baggage. And, moreover, it is not one person, but a couple: Viṣṇu and Lakṣmī. And they live with this cosmic baby: Ādi Śeṣa—the serpent of many perspectives. Divine foreknowledge seemed to be the least of the problems of a god tasked with fixing what goes wrong—choice and action change everything and hence there is nothing to know independently of what one chooses, but then, knowledge is not foreknown so much as determined by our choices. It still strikes me as very odd to worry about the relationship between religion and science—and the tension never arose in my background. What we called religion in my household was about practice and objectives (dharma), science is about natural explanation (*prakṛti*). They occupy different roles in our lives and the extremely orthodox people I knew never saw a conflict between higher learning in science or mathematics and their very orthodox observances and veneration of Śrī Vaiṣṇava icons and ideals. Indeed, the story has it that the famous Śrī Vaiṣṇava mathematician (Ramanujan) thought that his mathematical insights came from Lakṣmī herself in the form of the local temple deity Namagiri Thayar. So the question of miracles—the apparent suspension of laws of nature for divine purposes—never really arose. If something 'miraculous' happened it would be about timing and coordination of practice and natural regularities, and this is as miraculous as going to the gym and exercising.

I thought like many folks that I would not like moral philosophy or ethics: my associations with these topics were not very complimentary. What I found was just the opposite. Not only did I love my moral philosophy classes, the South Asian background that informed my family life came alive in these contexts. The idea that there can be competing theoretical explanations for choice and competing explanations for what we should be aiming for in relationship to our practice structured the South Asian backdrop that I had only a cursory knowledge of then. My family's "religion" made sense here, and not in the philosophy of religion class. Our God, Viṣṇu, was prone to giving lectures in moral philosophy, whether on the battlefield of the *Mahābhārata*, or as Rāma, trying to find his way out of one moral dilemma or the other.

I now think that not only does the study of Indian 'religion' really belong in moral philosophy, so does the study of all religions. What we call religion is moral theory that is alien to the *W*est. Part of why this is not apparent is that the *W*est replaces explication with interpretation, and renders alien moral theory mystical, because it tries to understand non-western moral theory by standards alien to it. Any theory will seem mysterious judged by external standards. Explication, the far more rigorous approach to understanding, shows us the basic logic of moral theory. It brings to the fore Bhakti as the fourth moral theory, in addition to Virtue Ethics, Consequentialism, and Deontology. While Bhakti explains a lot about popular Hinduism, what represents Hinduism as a philosophical disagreement is moral philosophy as such. The disagreements of moral philosophy are the disagreements of Hinduism. Hinduism is not the *sanātana* (ancient) *dharma* if by that we mean a specific moral outlook. However, it is the *sanātana dharma* if by that we mean moral philosophy—the disagreement. I suspect, however, that people who love thinking of Hinduism as the *sanātana dharma* are not too fond of disagreements.

Moral theory

Explication simplifies the matter by leading us to an appreciation of the common concept of *ETHICS/DHARMA* philosophy: this is the concept of *THE RIGHT OR THE GOOD*.

Philosophers need not agree about what this concept amounts to and they do not as far as it is objective. Indeed, there are at least four ways to resolve the apparent ambiguity of the concept. One might hold that: (1) the good is the condition of (causes) the right, (2) the good justifies the right, (3) the right justifies the good, and (4) the right is the condition of (causes) the good. Call the first two options *teleological* as they prioritize the good over the right. Call the second two options *procedural* as they prioritize the right over the good. Here I quickly and generally explain these four moral theories as we find them in Indian—and Hindu—ethics.

Virtue Ethics

The first theory is *Virtue Ethics*. Virtue Ethics takes a good state—usually the character of the good agent—as primary in moral explanation, and accounts for right action as derivative of the goodness of the agent (Hursthouse 1996; Annas 2004). In Sanskrit, this is the view that *vīrya* precedes karma in moral explanation. According to Virtue Ethics, to account for ethical choice primarily as a question of right action is a confusion that overlooks the essential condition of right action: virtue. In the western tradition, Plato and Aristotle exemplify this approach to ethics, though their views—especially that of Aristotle's—is a bit more complex as his view is more properly *teleological*. From India we find one prominent philosophical tradition taking up the cause of virtue: Jainism. Jain philosophers regard *vīrya* (the Sanskrit cognate of 'virtue') to be an essential trait of the living agent (*jīva*) and action (karma) to be a contingent feature that clouds our self-understanding by removing us from our strengths (Jaini 1998: 104; see also 102–106 for the other innate qualities). What we need to do according to the Jains is prioritize virtue, but this means that any laudable action has to be derivable in some way from our virtue. As virtue is not action, laudable actions will in some way leave no mark on the external world, and hinder no other being's freedom to choose. *Ahiṃsā*, or non-harm, becomes the primary ideal of action, and Dharma—ethics itself—is the motion or disposition of the self. The guides in moral practice are a group of pioneering virtuous individuals (*Tīrthaṅkara*-s) who show the way of a virtuous life. Like all individuals, they are immortal: the difference is that as people who live from virtue, they are free. One of the ideals of this practice is abandonment of the body (*kāyotsarga*)—that is, of doing anything at all—and the ritual fast unto death: *sallekhanā*. These are procedural outcomes of the Jain commitment to virtue as a thoroughly distinct moral property from action (Soni 2017).

Virtue Ethics is popular the world over. We find in China Confucius teaching us that *li* (*propriety*) is what follows from the superior man of virtue who is a man of humanity (*jen*) (Confucius 2010). This contributes to the Confucian doctrine of being morally moved (Wang 2010). Taoism too emphasizes the importance of virtue (*te*) but on its account it is not what we cultivate but what is spontaneous and natural: this spontaneity is strength in light of the overpowering force of the Tao ((Laozi) 2010). In this category we find too a group of thinkers who are usually excluded from philosophy, narrowly conceived: Theists. A theist is someone who believes minimally in an all good, all powerful and all knowledgeable being—God. God so understood is the paradigm virtuous agent in both the moral and effective sense. Theists hence regard God as central to determining questions of how we should live, and seek God's guidance on these matters. Right action on this account cannot be fully grasped without taking God seriously for the virtues of God show the way to right living.

Theists are often depicted as having mysterious views. God, we hear from some Theists, is a mysterious agent who acts according to "ways known unto Himself" (cf. Vatican Council II 1965: 7). But virtue theorists are famous for criticizing the idea that right action is algorithmic: the virtuous agent can consider principles, universal reasons, in making a decision. Yet the virtue of the virtuous agent is the ultimate condition of right action and hence there might be no other reason to justify an action but that it flows from the character of the virtuous agent (Hursthouse 1996). In short, the mysterious activity of God is just the activity of virtue that is not algorithmic. As for divine command ethics, which is often associated with Theism, this might seem inconsistent with Virtue Ethics as divine command theory is a theory of action based on rules from God. Yet, the source of these rules and procedures is the goodness of God, and hence the presence of divine command theory in Theism is not evidence against it being a version of Virtue Ethics, but rather consistent with this theory (Austin 2006).

If Theists are virtue ethicists who treat God as the paradigm virtuous agent, then disagreements between Theists on the character of God, or God's actions in relationship to other agents—theology—becomes of first importance and to this extent the history of God's actions will become important too. The reality of God will also be an important question for Theists as far as God, the *actual* virtuous agent, plays a role in their account of the right life.

A central account of dharma in the Hindu tradition is to be found in the *Vaiśeṣika Sūtra*, the foundational text of ontological realism of the Vaiśeṣika School. The text begins by claiming to be an elaboration of dharma and continues that from dharma is the accomplishment of the ultimate procedure (*niḥśreyasa*) (VS I.i.1–2). This results from the knowledge, produced by a particular dharma, of the Predicables, (which are) Substance, Attribute, Action, Genus, Species, and Combination by means of their resemblances and differences. (VS I.i.4). The dharma here is particular, which already indicates that it is the character of an individual. Much of the confusion over this section comes from a poor translation of '*śreyasa*' as "good" inspired by Platonic interpretations of Indian thought when it means "right" or the deontological idea of 'control'—we find this use of '*śreya*' for 'control' in the *Upaniṣads* (Ranganathan 2016). In this passage of the *Vaiśeṣika Sūtra*, we can discern perhaps indirectly that *śreya* is a procedural notion, as dharma that leads to *śreya* is defined by the knowledge of these epistemic categories (Chandrakānta 1923: 15) and is thus depicted as the character of the agent who knows. If the state of goodness is defined as the character of the virtuous agent, then the character gives rise to something distinct: choice. Indeed, this is the view of the commentator Śaṅkara Miśra (1923: 12), who identifies dharma as a sagely forbearance that results in this ultimate procedure. What follows is choice in accordance with this forbearance.

Later, the thirteenth century Hindu philosopher Madhva argues that our character is set and the difference between elevated and damned individuals are their character (Madhva/Ānandatīrtha 1993). Brahman (development, growth), which he identifies with Viṣṇu, has no character and is hence in this respect the ultimately free agent, but whether an individual will be able to participate in Brahman depends upon their character. He combines this account of virtue in conjunction with a deontological account of moral behavior: the virtuous individual is able to conform to the expectations of good behavior, while the unvirtuous individuals are forever damned (Ranganathan 2017). (Madhva is distinguished in the Indian tradition for his theory of eternal damnation—an entailment from his Virtue Ethics.)

Here is the tally: Jains, Confucians, Taoists, Plato, Aristotle, Vaiśeṣika-s, Madhva and Theists are all virtue ethicists. Of this list, only Plato and Aristotle are the 'non-religious' contributions. What is the difference? Ask the *W*est.

Consequentialism

The second option is what we might call Consequentialism. According to Consequentialism, the ends justify the means. There are two important versions of this theory—only one gets top billing. If the ends in question are agent neutral, then we call this theory Utilitarianism. If the ends are agent relative (defined perhaps by preferences) we often do not have a word for this theory, though it can be found in the writings of Hobbes and Hume. What is notable is that both philosophers conceive of reasoning in this manner, where goodness is merely what one wants or desires, and the right thing to do brings this about. But they both criticize this. Hobbes points out that there can be no justice under these circumstances (*Leviathan*, Part I, Chap 13). Hume thinks that morality is better explained by our fellow-feeling (*Enquiry*, Section IX, Part I, para 221). Consequentialism is often mistakenly—and popularly—depicted as the view that we should do what produces the most of a good outcome. The problem with this gloss is that Consequentialism entails what we might call the *moral symmetry principle*: accordingly, if an action A and an omission O have the same consequence, they are morally equal in value. So for instance, if telling your friend a joke (A) and thereby making her laugh, or leaving her to watch Seinfeld (O) have the same outcome (her laughter, assuming that she would be just as happy and tickled either way) and further either way she would be as happy as possible on this occasion, then telling her a joke (A) and leaving her alone (O) have the same moral status. But in the case of the omission (not telling a joke) one has not done anything to bring about a good outcome: one has merely not interfered with a good outcome. Yet Consequentialism that treated happiness as the good outcome would equally endorse both strategies. So Consequentialism is not the idea that we ought to do what produces the best outcome. The famous Utilitarians in the western tradition include Jeremy Bentham and John Stuart Mill. Their views span two options; either the right thing to do is justified by the best outcome on occasion, or the right thing to do is what is justified by the best outcome over time. As Charles Goodman has argued in his influential *Consequences of Compassion*, the prominent examples of Utilitarians in the

Indian tradition are Buddhists: the difference between early and later Buddhism being a difference between act Consequentialism and rule Consequentialism. The good that Buddhist Utilitarianism aims at is the minimization of *duḥkha*—suffering. The reason and solution to suffering has to do with the diagnosis that all things are ultimately familial and dependently originating. Hence, our expectation that there are objects with essences (*svabhāva*) has to do with our desires: as the Buddhist monk in the famous dialog *Questions of King Milinda* argues, our words are but convenient designations that fit our expectations. But as reality is dependently originating, things change, and our expectations can become frustrated. Solving the problem of suffering involves giving up desires, and this leads to a compassionate approach. This argument is summarized as the Four Noble Truths, and the solution is the Eight-Fold Path that leads us away from harmful ways of life. Later Buddhists, following Nāgārjuna, who apply this argument deconstructively to everything—including Buddhism and Buddhist teachings—also point out that our understanding of the lack of essences—that everything is empty—requires that we take responsibility for cognition so that we act prudently, but this requires the Dharma.

One misunderstanding about Buddhist accounts of dharma arises in part out of a misunderstanding about Consequentialism. Buddhists note that most everything is a dharma—the very constituents of your psychology or of reality are dharmas on their account (Conze 1967). Yet we can have attitudes of greed, envy, or anger, which are not right. Similarly, there can be realities of the world that are not right. But this seems to imply that some Buddhist discussions about dharma are not moral. This is a mistake that fails to take into account a distinction between the good and the right. If the right thing to do is justified by a good outcome, then the right thing to do might on occasions be to treat what seem like bad things, such as feelings of greed or anger, as good outcomes that *justify* an omission. For instance, if I have a feeling of anger or belligerence the responsible thing to do would be not to act on it: but my action here is justified by the outcome on Consequentialist grounds. Given the outcome of anger, my omission is the right thing to do. This is the Buddhist practice of Mindfulness—this is the final step of the Eight-Fold Path (*Maha-Satipatthana Sutta*). It treats all outcomes as justifications for appropriate choices, and puts us in the driver's seat of responsible action. We must come to this realization when we want to undermine suffering. Negative outcomes need some role to play in the moral life, otherwise we are irresponsible. When we practice Mindfulness we observe the contents of our mind without grasping them, and the contents of our mind that we have left over, once we have rooted out other vices in our life, are these negative outcomes. Nirvana, liberation, from trouble comes when we can treat everything as justifying appropriate and responsible choice. Certainly, some outcomes are the kind that we can emulate. Our feelings of friendship and sympathy, for instance, are described by the Buddha as what we should emulate. But other dharmas are not what we should emulate and being responsible is about choosing not to emulate them. This treats them as goods that justify moral choice: as responsible individuals, we see how all outcomes are good and aim at the minimization of suffering. Here we have a criterion for distinguishing dharmas. While all of them are good, some are models for behavior, while others are not. All of this makes sense of a Consequentialist ethics.

A Consequentialist approach to ethical reasoning is not unique to Buddhism in the Indian tradition. Philosophers in the Hindu logistics school of Nyāya argue that dharma (ethics) is to be justified by its end, and argue that the proper goal to justify moral action is ultimate freedom from trouble. Nyāya philosophers are also the notable Theists of the Indian tradition, who are famous for cosmological arguments for the existence of God (Chakrabarti 2017). Like many teleologists from the *W*estern tradition, their position combines elements of Consequentialism and Virtue Ethics.

Nyāya philosophers are not the only teleologists among Hindus. Kaśmīrī Śaivas, like Buddhists, stress compassion in their Consequentialism. But in the case of Kaśmīrī Śaivism, the emphasis is not on the reduction of suffering, but the maximization of bliss. There are interesting philosophical differences between the two schools that account for such differences. Buddhists stress the agent neutrality of good decisions. Kaśmīrī Śaivas in contrast stress that any criterion we have for selfhood is not numerically distinct, and hence all ethical decisions are relative to a common agency. From this common ethical point of view (which Kaśmīrī Śaivas identify with Śiva, the Hindu God of a centralized, and destructive perspective) the right thing to do is maximize happiness (Ratie 2009).

Here is the tally: Bentham, Mill, Buddhists, Nyāyikas, Kaśmīrī Śaivas are all Consequentialist. However, only Bentham and Mill are not religious, but everyone else is. What is the difference? Ask the *W*est.

Deontology

The third option in our list of ethical theories can be called Deontology. This position is misrepresented as the moral theory that is averse to good outcomes, or does not believe that good outcomes are relevant to assessing duty. The reason that Deontologists gain this reputation is that they are often vocal critics of Consequentialists. Consequentialists claim that the good *justifies* the right. The deontological view is the opposite. Right procedure justifies the *good* but the good outcome in question is a choice that we can repeat (duty) or a freedom that others are obliged to respect (a right).

The famous deontologist in the western tradition is Kant who makes no secret of his Christianity (*Groundwork of the Metaphysics of Morals* 4:409). Kant defines duties in accordance with a procedure—the Categorical Imperative. There are several versions of this imperative. What the versions have in common is that they identify duty with some good outcome (whether it be what we would choose to mediate our relationship in a Kingdom of Ends, what causal rule we would elect to govern nature, or how we should treat other humans, as not merely means but also ends in themselves). The duties so defined are justified on procedural grounds (*Groundwork* 4:421, 4:429, 4:431, cf. 4:432, cf. 4:436, 4:439). On Kant's account, these procedural grounds have to do with a reverence for duty.

The Hindu tradition is filled with examples of Deontology. The argument for Deontology can be found in the *Kaṭha Upaniṣad* (a text part of the Vedic corpus), where the God Death, pleased with the wisdom of the boy Nachiketa, who has to face death ahead of his time, advises the boy that the foolish prefer pleasures (*preya*) but the wise prefer control (*śreya*). He further advises the boy on what control consists in: responsible governance of mind, intellect, and body. Those who are able to practice this control take successful control of their body and land in the realm of Viṣṇu, the God of protection (*Kaṭha Upaniṣad* I.3).

A further famous example of Deontology in the Hindu tradition is Krishna's account of karma yoga (the discipline of action) in the *Bhagavad Gītā*: this is good action that we choose for duty's sake (*Gītā* II.38, 47, XVIII.47). It is better to do what ethics (dharma) demands of you badly than what ethics demands of someone else well on this account (*Gītā* III.35 and XVIII.47).

A very important contribution to Deontology to philosophy is the Pūrva Mīmāṃsā tradition of philosophy. This is often interpreted as a school of Vedic apologetics, tasked with making sense of the requirements of a life informed by the Vedas. This gloss ignores the philosophical argument at the base of the contributions of Pūrva Mīmāṃsā authors. The most notable such argument is from Kumārila.

Kumārila in his *Ślokavārttika* begins an important argument for Deontology via a criticism of Utilitarianism. It begins first with the observation that the idea that dharma is a means to happiness would support sexual affairs as this would result in an increase of happiness, though clearly it is immoral. But worse, he says, if we identify the ethical action in terms of good outcomes and further justify such actions by virtue of its goodness, we are locked in a circularity. Or, put another way, if we identify moral properties with natural properties, we cannot provide any significant further justification for such properties (*Ślokavārttika* II.242–247). This criticism prefigures Moorean criticisms of naturalism (Moore 1903). But whereas Moore argued that there is no definition of goodness, Mīmāṃsā does not endorse this claim that is roundly criticized as folly. To avoid this circularity, we do not need to criticize definitions of moral concepts but we need procedural means of determining what we should do. This allows us to identify action with its goodness, without falling into circularity. The Pūrva Mīmāṃsā approach in general is to define (*lakṣaṇa)* ethical (dharma) command (*codana*) in terms of beneficence (*artha*) (*Mīmāṃsā Sūtra* I.i.2) but to identify and justify what counts as ethics in terms of intuition (*śruti*) and any tradition (*smṛti*) that does not conflict with intuition (MS I.iii.2), and in cases where the two conflict, *śruti* takes precedence (MS I.iii.2–3). The contents of intuition on the Pūrva Mīmāṃsā account are filled out by the Vedas—but we can follow the moral philosophical argument here without agreeing that the contents of moral intuition are the Vedas. What is important about this argument is that it makes a case for Deontology on the basis of identifying ethics with good action: if that is what ethics is, we cannot appeal to outcomes to justify actions without circularity. Hence, we require a procedural justification. Moreover, if for some reason we feel that intuition cannot be a valid means of deriving moral knowledge, for it is too mystical, much less traditions and customs, then much of recent analytic ethics should be rejected as appeals to intuitions and traditions, especially in the form of cases, is common place here (cf. Kagan 2007).

Here is the tally: Kant, the *Kaṭha Upaniṣad*, the *Bhagavad Gītā* and the Pūrva Mīmāṃsā tradition all make cases for Deontology. Only Kant is the non-religious option here taught openly in secular philosophy classes—even though he is overtly a Christian. Yet one will typically have to learn about the rest in a Hindu Studies class. What is the difference? Ask the *W*est.

Bhakti/Yoga

The basic concept of *MORALITY, ETHICS*, or *DHARMA* is *THE RIGHT OR THE GOOD*, and each theory is an attempt to resolve the tension between procedure and outcome. Virtue Ethics prioritizes the good over the right, Consequentialism justifies the right by the good, Deontology justifies the good by the right, and there should be space for a fourth option: the right is prior to the good. This fourth option mirrors Virtue Ethics. It claims that the right brings about or causes the good. Of the four options this is the most procedural for it explains morality in a manner that makes the right basic. In order to complete the prioritization of the right in moral explanation, we need a way to think about the right without recourse to the good, and what fulfills this requirement is a regulative ideal that defines the right. Approximating this ideal constitutes moral practice and the perfection of this practice is the instantiation of the ideal. This is the good outcome. This fourth option is Bhakti (Devotion). It is by the devotion to the regulative ideal of a practice—the Lord of the practice—that we produce a good outcome according to the *bhakta* (devotee), and the good outcome is the outcome of devotion to the ideal. I regard this as an important discovery for two reasons. First, Bhakti is not a salient option of moral theory in the *W*estern tradition, yet it has many theoretical advantages over its rivals. Second, the usual efforts to compare Bhakti traditions of India with theistic traditions from the west fall flat and are mistaken as these theories are opposites. For the theist, God is good. For the *bhakta*, the Lord is Right. For the theist, the goodness of God entails that God is an outcome of reality—something to be discovered, and moreover as moral guidance flows from the character of God, knowing who is God or believing in it is an important part of moral deliberation. But if the regulative ideal, the Lord, is right, it is a procedural ideal—an abstraction from good practice. Questions of the reality of the Lord will be unimportant for the *bhakta*, and moreover, the *bhakta* will tend to define the Lord as constitutive of practices that, when perfected, get rid of evil. Just as there is no logical problem of the consistency of a cleaner and dirt, so too is there no obvious problem of evil for the *bhakta*: the Lord is antagonistic to all evil who we approximate as devotees and in so far as we approximate the Lord we become clean as we instantiate the Lord. Devotion to the Lord brings about our own Lordliness. Finally, because the Lord is a procedural ideal, it can be explicitly instantiated in icons and objects of veneration that can be observed in so far as the ideal is literally displayed in such icons. *Bhaktas* can be comfortable with idolatry: an idol is someone admired and to be emulated, and the worship of idols is the worship of someone to emulate. *Bhaktas* will have no qualms affirming that the Lord in the form of an object of veneration is literally the Lord, and will feel no need to explain this veneration as a symbolic gesture. But as noted, because it is an abstraction the *bhakta* will tend not to feel compelled to worry about arguments about the existence of God or the cosmological role of God in creation. Their moral practice will tend to avoid physical and cosmological questions about the universe.

The history of Bhakti in the Indian tradition is ancient. My late professor of religious studies, Joseph O'Connell pointed out to us in class that this tradition of devotion to deities goes back to the Vedas themselves. But the most philosophically rigorous account of the theory is to be found in the second century *Yoga Sūtra* by Patañjali (2008). We can hence also call the theory of Bhakti, "Yoga." The influence of this text is underappreciated. It was an important source of inspiration for Nāthamuni (White 2014), the Śrī Vaiṣṇava *ācārya*, and spiritual teacher of Rāmānuja and widely influential philosopher of Bhakti from the eleventh century known for his position of Viśiṣṭādvaita. Karl Potter the prolific historian of Indian philosophy notes:

> Rāmānuja, we have seen, elevates God to the supreme position in his ontology and elevates bhakti to the supreme position among the paths. In the last analysis, it is God's grace alone that can obtain freedom for us. Then what is the function of philosophy? Apparently Rāmānuja takes philosophy to be not the resolver of doubts, but rather the path of knowledge itself. This implies that doubts are to be encouraged, as they lead one to embark upon the path of knowledge . . . With its emphasis on bhakti and *prapatti* [surrender], this development of Rāmānuja's tradition can be said to represent one of the main arteries through which philosophy reached down to the masses, and it may be that Viśiṣṭādvaita is today the most powerful philosophy in India in terms of numbers of adherents, whether they know themselves by that label or not. Viśiṣṭādvaita is not, however, the philosophy which the West associates with India, nor is it the avowed position of the large proportion of nineteenth- and twentieth-century professional philosophers in Indian universities.
>
> (Potter 1963: 252–253)

We shall return to the topic of Rāmānuja's philosophy as it is in some respects a derivation from Yoga.

The *Yoga Sūtra* is in the primary instance a philosophical text about critical thinking: yoga is the control of our mental representations, so that we can think clearly (YS I.2–3). We observed why this is important: it allows us to be critical of our thoughts by divorcing them from our attitudes, while failing to draw the appropriate distinction between our attitudes and thoughts leads to an uncritical acquiescence in them. But the means of this practice of critical thinking according to Patañjali is thoroughly procedural. It involves changing our life. The chief means of bringing about success in yoga is devotion to the Lord, a special person Patañjali defines as untouched by afflictions and consequences of past choices (karma) (YS I.24, cf. IV.34). The Lord is the regulative ideal of the practice of Yoga.

When Patañjali moves to define Yoga as a practice, he distinguishes it in terms of three component practical ideals (YS II.1). The first is *Īśvarapraṇidhāna*—approximating the Lord. A second practice is *tapas*, which means 'heat producing.' To practice *tapas* is to go against the grain, to do something different. The last practice is *svādhyāya*, which means 'self-study.' In the context of Yoga, to study or learn is to control what one knows and hence, to study oneself is to practice self-governance. One who engages in *tapas* goes against the grain, is unconservative, and is hence untouched by the consequence of past choices. As one practices self-governance one is free of external coercion and affliction. In short, *tapas* and *svādhyāya* are the essential attributes of the Lord, and hence the approximation of the Lord takes these two ideals as its object.

For Patañjali as a principle theorist of this ethical theory, we talk about ETHICS—'*dharma*' (III.13–14,46, IV.29), '*ṛta*' (I.48) '*vṛtti*' (I.2)—when practice instantiates ideals. As you approximate this ideal we find Patañjali describing proper procedure in Yoga in terms of self-control, self-governance, and self-mastery (metaphorically described as *svarūpe'vasthānam*/abiding in one's form (YS I.3), *svarūpa-pratiṣṭhā*/standing on one's form (YS IV.34), and more literally *sva-svāmī*/own master (YS II.22)—essential features of Lordliness). The Lord is the one who is master of their own destiny, and this links the Lord analytically to self-governance. The term that the *Yoga Sūtra* uses to talk about perfected practice as the outcome of practice is the term for *independence* or *autonomy: kaivalya* (YS II.25, IV.34). This transformation is not mysterious on the Yoga account: it comes about by our own diligent practice of yoga, which consists in our devotion to the Lord.

What is obvious when we compare these three ideals of yogic practice and subsequent Vaiṣṇava reflections on the essential traits of the ultimate paradise of Vaikuṇṭha—Ādi Śeṣa, Viṣṇu, and Lakṣmī—is that the three deities are the Lords (regulative ideals) of the three practices of *Īśvarapraṇidhāna, tapas*, and *svādhyāya*. The devotional aspects of Ādi Śeṣa are a regular part of Hindu lore: as Viṣṇu's sibling in various stories, he plays the role of a devotee and certainly, in Vaikuṇṭha he constitutes the caring bed on which Viṣṇu and Lakṣmī reside. Viṣṇu the God of decentralization that objectifies himself dynamically as the disk is *tapas*—doing something different, going against the grain, in an objective world. Viṣṇu as a dynamic self-objectification is always untouched by the consequences of past choices as he is always doing something not predetermined. Hindu lore also depicts Viṣṇu as the quirky God, who frequently goes against expectations. When he starts to flirt with patriarchy (as in the case of his incarnation of Rāma), things go wrong (he is exiled to the forest for 14 years, has his wife kidnapped, and later on banishes her to the forest). Lakṣmī, the Goddess who resides on her own form of the lotus, governs herself—that is, she is *svarūpe'vasthānam* and *svarūpa-pratiṣṭhā*. This accounts for Lakṣmī's association with wealth, but also identity and authenticity: all things that are authentic have their identity as an intrinsic feature, and this is what self-governance allows: our identity is an intrinsic matter. In her case, things go badly when she does not get to determine her fate (as in being kidnapped by the demon Rāvaṇa). That these deities are the regulative ideals of these basic practices of Yoga answers some important questions. This observation also sheds light on how the Lord for Śrī Vaiṣṇavas decomposes into two persons: Viṣṇu and Lakṣmī for each accounts for one of the two essential traits of the Lord: unconservative (Viṣṇu) self-governance (Lakṣmī); *tapas* and *svādhyāya*, that rest on the bed of *Īśvarapraṇidhāna* (Ādi Śeṣa). So understood, the paradise of Vaikuṇṭha is the procedural ideals of yoga—and all of this floats on the Milk Ocean, literally described by the dense and superlatively meaningful *Yoga Sūtra* I.2: *citta-vṛtti-nirodha* (the rolling down, respectful checking, of opaque mental content). This is not at all surprising: Viṣṇu is depicted as the Lord of Yoga.

One of the advantages of Bhakti as a moral theory is that it explains any practice where the goal is improvement. Consider learning music. This involves identifying the abstract ideal of music, meditating on it, and practicing so as to approximate the ideal. At first one's performance will be bad, though the ideal remains regulative. As one practices one comes to instantiate the ideal itself. The goodness of the practice is just the perfection of the practice, and the practice is made possible by the ideal that we approximate. In the case of the theory of Bhakti in the *Yoga Sūtra*, we find a theory of practicing what it is to be a person, as the Lord defined by unconservativism and self-governance is the category essence of personhood. What it is to be a person on this account is to have an interest in one's own unconservativism and self-governance, and devotion to the Lord is about perfecting this potential we have. The reason that this is a broadly social matter is that the Lord as the essence of persons is not proprietary and in appreciating what the Lord is, we understand that there are other people like ourselves with whom we share this common bond. So in being devoted to the Lord, we endeavor to make a world that is political safe for people to perfect their own personhood. This is the substance of most of the *Yoga Sūtra* (certainly from YS II.33 till the end). Essential to this political world are the anti-colonial and anti-imperialistic values of the Yama Rules: non-harm, truth (as something we discover after we respect a diversity of perspectives), the respect of personal property, the respect of sexual boundaries, and non-acquisitiveness (YS II.30).

The general theory also makes room for a diversity of ideals. Patañjali notes that in practicing self-governance, we discover our chosen ideal (*iṣṭa-devata*) (YS II.45). This is often read as the idea that in the course of the practice of yoga, we choose a god to worship. But what this also implies is that we are really our own god as children of the Goddess Lakṣmī: we are accountable for who we are, not others, for in understanding ourselves, we discover the ideals that we have set for ourselves. This is a matter of self-responsibility that cannot be foisted on society or tradition. But we are also thereby accountable for the deities that we choose to venerate. In this room of bhakti, is space for a diversity of philosophical ideals, including many deities of popular Hinduism. In other words, this theory from the *Yoga Sūtra* provides a philosophical justification for the widespread practice of

Hindus to choose their own ideals and venerate them—even when these ideals are not necessarily those of one's family. We are all choosers of our own ideals, and understanding what ideals these are is part of our own self-governance. India hence has many traditions of bhakti, venerating and focusing on different ideals.

Patañjali's Yoga has had a profound influence. As noted, it was revived by Rāmānuja's spiritual teacher Nāthamuni. It stands at the back of Rāmānuja's philosophy. In Rāmānuja's account, reality is characterized as Brahman: development, growth, and expansion. At the center of Brahman is the Lord, which turns out to be Viṣṇu and Lakṣmī. The relationship of the Lord to Brahman is the relationship of the person to their body, and we as individuals are modes or expressions of this body. The Lord is our 'inner controller' (*Śrī Bhāṣya*, p. 55 I.i.1). It is easy not to see the connection of Rāmānuja's philosophy to the *Yoga Sūtra* if we ignore the relationship of the Lord on Patañjali's account of the individual. On both accounts, the Lord is the *normative* essence of what it is to be a person, and hence all persons are subsumed by the Lord in so far as the Lord is our regulative ideal. But then, each one of us is an expression, no matter how imperfect, of Lordliness, just as each one of us is a mode of Brahman. We are expressions of the Lord and Brahman for we are works in progress. Rāmānuja's analogy of person to body that explains the relationship of the Lord to Brahman and ourselves is the relationship we have to the Lord as the regulative ideal of personhood. When life goes well, we approximate this regulative ideal and the result is our freedom: *mokṣa*. This approximation is bhakti, which Rāmānuja places at the center of his philosophy (*Vedārthasaṅgraha* §239–241). Subsequent Śrī Vaiṣṇava tradition (taking a cue from Rāmānuja's writings) elaborates on the central importance of divine grace in bringing about freedom, and *Śrī* (Lakṣmī) is depicted as having a central role in mediating our relationship with Viṣṇu: certainly, self-governance is our means of actualizing anti-conservativism (*tapas*) that frees us from the consequences of past choices (karma).

Similar ideas are expressed in the *Bhagavad Gītā* and especially in Krishna's articulation and defense of bhakti yoga—sources on which Rāmānuja comments. This document ends with Krishna recommending bhakti as a means of overcoming problems: do not worry about dharma, come to me and I will relieve you of all faults (*Bhagavad Gītā* XVIII:66).

Philosophically the theory has the following virtue: in times of oppression when goodness is not allowed, a bhakti account provides a way to act for it defines right action without recourse to the Good. The Lord does not assume or require a good world to be the Lord, and our devotion to the Lord does not require that we are good to be devotees. This is because the procedure becomes the end when it is perfect, but the procedure is logically prior to the end.

The influence of the *Yoga Sūtra* goes beyond traditional Hinduism. Gandhi's philosophy of direct action (*satyagraha*) is actually a line in the *Yoga Sūtra*. In response to the challenge and opposition posed by those who would advocate tyranny and violence (the opposite of *ahiṃsā*), Patañjali argues that the yogi should appreciate that the source of this antagonism is past suffering, and not a well reasoned argument. The way to get the tyrant to renounce their hostility is to live in a contrary manner via non-harmfulness or *ahiṃsā* (YS II.33–35)—this permits the mutual objectivity of the antagonist and the yogi, and hence the mutual self-determination of all parties. This was Gandhi's strategy to gain India's *kaivalya* (independence). It is based on the insight that what we as people have in common is our interest in unconservativism and self-governance (the Lord) and hence even our enemies can become our friends, if we emphasize the importance of unconservativism and self-governance in our own life.

I mentioned these observations to the Gandhi scholar Bindu Puri at a workshop on India and Human Rights in Ottawa (Drydyk and Peetush 2015). She followed this lead and wrote a book that focused on the influence of Patañjali on Gandhi. She notes that there are over 200 references to the *Yoga Sūtra* and "Bhagwan Patañjali" in the *Collected Works of Mahatma Gandhi* (2015: 36). M.K. Gandhi gives credit to Patañjali for coming up with the idea of *ahiṃsā* (Gandhi 1947: vol. 59, 494). If we want to count the influence of Gandhi on Martin Luther King's conceptualization of direct action—an influence that goes back to Patañjali—the importance of this philosophy goes far beyond Hinduism, though it is certainly important for Hindus.

The tally: Bhakti/Yoga. Bhakti/Yoga is not obviously a theory of the *W*estern tradition. Yet it is an account of the relationship of the *RIGHT* and the *GOOD*. In mirror opposite to Virtue Ethics, it claims that devotion to rightness produces the good. There are reasons in support of this view, and, moreover, it requires no faith in the reality of a god that is supposed to exist as an outcome of the world. Bhakti identifies ideals of practices as the objects of practical veneration. Our goal is to approximate them: that is the point of devotion. Yet, Bhakti is often depicted as the epitome of Hindu religion and is not discussed in moral philosophy classes. I find this most peculiar, for the Lords of Bhakti are nothing but what they superficially claim to be: regulative ideals. Far from being the epitome of religion, the Lords of Bhakti are the proper objects of philosophical inquiry. But this is not acknowledged in standard presentations of moral theory and philosophy. Why? Ask the *W*est.

Hinduism as moral philosophy with a South Asian twist

Not only are the standard options of religion simply options within moral theory, but we really only come to understand the objective differences between the options of Bhakti and Theism if we situate them within the options of moral theory. Theology, as a discourse characteristic of Judaism, Christianity, and Islam, is a discourse within the discourse of moral philosophy—it is not a separate discussion. As Theism is perhaps the most influential form of Virtue Ethics, theology is a discussion within Virtue Ethics about the characteristics of the primary virtuous agent: God. I think we lack a good word to describe what intellectuals of the Bhakti tradition were engaged in when they write about the Lord—perhaps Bhakti is what we should call it. But if bhakti prioritizes the right over the good, it cannot be a version of Virtue Ethics, and hence cannot be a version of Theism. Nevertheless, it is an interesting and important alternative that comes to life when contrasted with the other option of moral theory.

A review of the options shows us that Hinduism has no primary or fundamental moral theory. Other religions apparently are identified by specific moral theories. Jainism is a kind of Virtue Ethics. Buddhism is a version of Consequentialism. The various Theistic religions are versions of Virtue Ethics. However, the options of Hinduism traverse the options of moral theory. What is a Hindu's moral theory? This question is presumptuous. It assumes that Hindus have only one to choose from. The reality of Hinduism is that it is nothing short of the disagreements of moral theory, and hence we can summarize Hinduism as ethics, in the sense of moral philosophy. This corresponds to the disagreements of Hinduism, which are the disagreements of moral philosophy. Indeed, so extensive is the philosophical disagreement of Hinduism that we find all the logical options with respect to causal theories of ethics (Virtue Ethics and Bhakti) as well as justificatory theories (Deontology and Consequentialism) in Hinduism. This puts comments like the following in sharp contrast:

> Professional philosophers of India over the last two thousand years have been consistently concerned with the problems of logic and epistemology, metaphysics and soteriology, and sometimes they have made very important contributions to the global heritage of philosophy. But, except some cursory comments and some insightful observations, the professional philosophers of India have very seldom discussed what we call "moral philosophy" today. It is true that the *Dharmaśāstra* texts were there to supplement the Hindu discussion of ethics; classification of virtues and vices, and enumeration of duties related to the social status of the individual. But morality was never discussed as such in these texts.
>
> (Matilal 1989: 5)

This is a famous passage from the influential Indologist Bimal K. Matilal. He is noted for having prominent students in Indology today—some of whom do good work. But with this passage, Matilal shows himself to be an incompetent student of philosophy. The only way that one can generate the conclusion that moral philosophy was not an important part of the Indian tradition is if one assumes the framework of the Eurocentric "we" as the backdrop to the rigor of solipsism. Then the only contributions to moral theory that one will notice are those that seem most like Europe's philosophies of anthropocentric communitarianism. These are texts that place a great deal of emphasis on matters such as caste—the *Dharmaśāstra* being one prominent example. Indeed, the rigor of solipsism is likely to highlight features of European thought that we find obnoxious, such as caste—defended by Plato in the *Republic*. That is, in treating the ethical theory of the 'we' as the rigor then we can only ever notice aspects of Indian thought that resonate with 'our' perspective, but as Indian philosophers were radically different in some ways from the Eurocentric we, the only features of their thought that will stand out are the features of their thought that they did not seem to take very seriously but reminds us of 'our' sins. These will tend to be under-justified and this will only augment its apparent injustice. When we look to the arguments of

Hindus we find a diverse range of theories that allow us to take a critical approach to matters of social justice—in virtually every case, matters such as caste are not basic moral principles. Bhakti is often noted as providing a strong ground for criticizing discrimination of all sorts. We shall return to this matter in our discussion of moral standing (Chapter 7). None of this justifies the idea that Hinduism and India was forever a perfect place free of injustice, but we do not need that myth to recognize that unjust practices are controversial given the full range of theoretical options within Hinduism.

These considerations show that one version of Comprehensive Hinduism that defines Hinduism as the *sanātana dharma*—the eternal ethics—is implausible, unless by this we mean that it was always moral philosophy, which means a disagreement about moral theory.

Objections

By now, we have seen that there is a kind of objection to taking Hinduism seriously that we can dismiss. The objection starts with the observation that Hindus are not committed to anything as a matter of being Hindu, and tries to conclude that hence, there is nothing like Hinduism. As objects are what we can disagree about, the disagreements of Hindus about moral theory are evidence of the objectivity of Hinduism. The objectivity of Hinduism is in large measure the objectivity of moral philosophy.

Here is a different kind of antirealist objection.

The idea that there is no ethics in Indian thought and Hinduism is just a perspective, like the view that Hinduism and Indian thought are filled with ethics

It all depends upon the perspective you adopt. Therefore, there is no truth to the matter. In other words, what is objective about Hinduism is that it is controversial whether Hindus disagree about moral issues. Cute. The problem with this objection is that it mischaracterizes how we come to the respective antirealist conclusion that Indians were not concerned with moral philosophy and the realist conclusion that they were concerned with moral philosophy. These observations are not a matter of perspective. They are a matter of what model of understanding we adopt. If we adopt interpretation with a Eurocentric twist, we will agree with Matilal. If we explicate philosophy, we will find moral theory everywhere in India and Hinduism. As interpretation is irrational (it confuses belief with thought) but explication is objective, my bet is with explication.

Speculation

Yet another objection can be derived from the predilection of interpreters. Interpreters treat their objects of criticism as something to be justified or derived from their batch of beliefs. Unlike explicators they do not treat these objects as third-party perspectives that have to account for themselves. Hence, the only connections interpreters see are those that are part of their batch of beliefs. So if they cannot derive a connection between Yoga and Vaikuṇṭha on the basis of what they take to be true, it is not there and the suggestion is speculation. Usually what they would want (in Hindu Studies, or Indology) is some type of philological or social scientific evidence of connections. There are two problems with this expectation. First when connections are basic and obvious for members of an intellectual tradition, no one talks about them (just as virtually no one talks about the *W*est's foundation on the linguistic account of thought except perhaps at crisis points and boundaries of the tradition): they merely engage with their ideas by way of such governing assumptions. So obvious connections for Hindus will appear baffling to the interpreter trying to understand the tradition from the outside by their beliefs. Second, the real cause of the error lies in what the Indian philosopher Ādi Śaṅkara notes is the error of superimposition (*Brahma Sūtra Bhāṣya* I.i. preamble). This is the error of imposing the subjectivity of the knower onto the object of what is known. The result is an ersatz reality, which, but for the choice of the knower, would not exist. Indology is largely this superimposition in so far as it is constituted by the imposition of the Indologist's substantive assumptions on to the objects of study. This ersatz reality then constitutes a bath of 'facts' that are used to filter out research. We avoid all of this by explication, which does not involve confusing the subjectivity of the explicator with what they explicate.

What about **mokṣa***?*

Hinduism is a disagreement not about dharma but about *mokṣa*—freedom. This objection does not have much teeth. For if we appreciate that Hinduism is just philosophy with a South Asian twist, we do not have to reduce Hinduism to any one debate of philosophy. The debates of ethics are central to philosophy and hence they are central to Hinduism, but Hindus are also free to disagree about what freedom amounts to. But the critic might have a more pointed concern: that *mokṣa* is a non-moral goal, and the central importance of *mokṣa* to Hindus means that their religion is not really about moral theory.

This objection confuses the concept of morality with the goals of morality. So indeed, while the concept of *FREEDOM* is not that of *THE RIGHT OR THE GOOD*, questions of the right or the good frequently bring up questions of freedom. This is the standard phenomenon of India. Indian philosophers will frequently contrast and connect their account of "dharma" with "*mokṣa*," and in each case, they will employ these controversial terms to articulate their own theories of ethics and freedom. There is no standard story for all concerned here just as there is no standard story about the connection between morality and freedom in philosophy as such. Indeed, there cannot be, for the relationship between dharma and *mokṣa* is controversial. Change your theory of dharma, and you will have to adjust your theory of *mokṣa*. All of this should tell us that the importance of *mokṣa* to Indian thought is not evidence against the importance of dharma to Indian thought. Indeed, if anything, the more basic concept is dharma, as one's theory of THE RIGHT OR THE GOOD will entail either a procedural account of freedom, or a teleological account of freedom. If your theory of ethics is teleological, you will likely have a procedural account of freedom. If your ethics is procedural, you will likely have a teleological account of *mokṣa*. Both accounts are moral in the sense that they follow from your theory of THE RIGHT OR THE GOOD. In so far as Indian moral theory has a balance of procedural emphasis—in comparison to the *W*estern spread—as it also has Bhakti, we will find more instances of teleological accounts of freedom in Indian philosophy than from the *W*est.

Bhakti is not about idols

Some Hindus, who endorse something like bhakti, object to calling consecrated icons "idols" and they may want to refer to their deity as a creator god, who explains the origins of the universe. (I have been surprised to find strong opinions on this matter.) This runs contrary to Bhakti as described here: accordingly, bhakti is the veneration of someone who is idolized (an idol) and the point of the practice is to transform oneself into an instantiation of the ideal—such an ideal plays little role in cosmological explanation as it is a procedural ideal. It cannot be a form of Theism for Bhakti is the opposite of Virtue Ethics, and Theism is a form of Virtue Ethics. Add to this that many Hindus, especially those who endorse some form of bhakti, seem to want to characterize their religious convictions in terms of a commitment to monotheism, and yet, Bhakti is not Theism as Theism is a version of Virtue Ethics, which is its opposite. *And*, importantly, bhakti traditions often acknowledge multiple deities, and rarely just one, and are hence not versions of mono-deitism, much less monotheism. There are two important responses to this concern. First, I think it is not possible to generate these kinds of strong views without assuming the *W*est, and religions imagined as associated with the *W*est (such as Christianity), as an interpretive frame to subsume Hinduism. For against the backdrop of such a framework, idolatry and the rejection of monotheism seem *bad* and irrational—not just wrong—as idolatry and the rejection of monotheism are not derivable from religions imagined as associated with the *W*est. Second, Hindus could adopt an anti-idolatry, Theistic position as votaries of Nyāya, perhaps, as the Nyāya philosophers were Theists who defended a cosmological argument for the existence of God (Dasti Accessed 2017). They could also invent new versions of Theism—no need for it to be derived from Nyāya. It could be derived from Christianity, and continue to be Hindu if there is some South Asian connection (and many South Asians are Christians). But this native Hindu Theism would be a contribution to the philosophical disagreements among Hindus: it would not be the default comprehensive view of Hindus—the position Hindus have to adopt to avoid a crass and inaccurate representation of Hinduism. And then, lo and behold, the position that was rejected (idolatry and the rejection of monotheism) would be revealed as a live option for Hindus to adopt—and a traditional option at that! Moreover, it is not an irrational option: it is one of the logically basic explanations of the relationship between THE RIGHT OR THE GOOD, which was influential the world over.

Conclusion

Indians were too busy being religious to worry about moral theory—that is the orthodox view in Indology. But when we look to the ubiquity of moral theory and moral philosophy in the Indian tradition, we have no occasion to identify any extra-religiosity left over and above Indian moral theories. Indeed, this generalizes. When we examine the breadth and possibilities of moral theory drawn along the line of possible resolutions of the relationship of the right or the good, the religions of the world fall into discrete options within moral theory, and we only really appreciate the distinctions between the options when we situate them within the debates of moral philosophy. Whether you believe in a theistic god, or the Lord of your bhakti-oriented practice, depends upon your moral theory. Moreover, the apparently atheistic options of moral theory, also identified as religious options, are to be found among Deontological and Consequentialist options in addition to Virtue Ethics. So, what conclusion should we draw about religion? One option is to claim that there is indeed something left over: the practice of religious people. But this is implausible for the practices are in any case a function of the moral theory that people adopt. Some varieties of ritual and social observances are justified by the Pūrva Mīmāṃsā Deontology. But the vast practices of Hindus of *pūja* and other worship of regulative ideas of Bhakti, in addition to social observances, are a function of a commitment to devotion as a moral theory, just as the rituals and prayers of Theists are a function of their version of Virtue Ethics that identifies God as the primary virtuous agent. The meditational practices of Buddhists are a straightforward application of their version of Consequentialism, and the Jain practices of *ahiṃsā* and finally *sallekhanā* are outcomes of their Virtue Ethics. Does it follow that there is no such thing as religion? Religion is a real outcome of interpretation from a Eurocentric perspective. Hinduism like all other religions gains its identity via this process of seeing everything in the world from a Eurocentric perspective. However, the catch is that the objectivity of Hinduism is just the disagreements of moral philosophy as religion is moral theory viewed through the lens of Eurocentric interpretation. There are no moral theoretical options outside of Hinduism as Hinduism is a disagreement about the *RIGHT* and the *GOOD:* it contains the four basic options of moral theory reviewed in this chapter. Bhakti is a notable fourth moral theory that adds to the familiar three options from the *W*estern tradition (Virtue Ethics, Consequentialism, and Deontology) and Hinduism might be unique in being home to this option, but then that is what we would expect if the objectivity of Hinduism is the objectivity of moral theory. Being serious about Hinduism is hence in large measure being serious about moral theory as something we can disagree about, and this disagreement is moral philosophy.

References

Annas, Julia. 2004. "Being Virtuous and Doing the Right Thing." *Proceedings and Addresses of the American Philosophical Association* 78, no. 2: 61–75.

Austin, Michael W. 2006. "Divine Command Theory." In *Internet Encyclopedia of Philosophy*. www.iep.utm.edu/divine-c/.

Chakrabarti, Kisor K. 2017. "Nyāya Consequentialism." In *The Bloomsbury Research Handbook of Indian Ethics*, edited by Shyam Ranganathan, 203–224. London: Bloomsbury Academic.

Chandrakānta. 1923. *Vaiśeṣika Sūtra (Gloss)*. Translated by Nandalal Sinha. In *Sacred Books of the Hindus*, edited by Nandalal Sinha. 2nd rev. and enl. edn. Vol. 6. Allahabad: Sudhindra Nath Basu, Panini Office.

Confucius. 2010. *The Analects of Confucius: A Philosophical Translation*. Translated by Roger T. Ames and Henry Rosemont Jr. New York: Random House.

Conze, Edward. 1967. *Buddhist Thought in India: Three Phases of Buddhist Philosophy*. Ann Arbor, MI: University of Michigan.

Dasti, Matthew R. Accessed 2017. "Nyāya." In *Internet Encyclopedia of Philosophy*, edited by James Feiser. www.iep.utm.edu/nyaya/.

Drydyk, Jay, and Ashwini Peetush. 2015. *Human Rights: India and the West*. New Delhi: Oxford University Press.

Gandhi, M.K. 1947. *Collected Works of Mahatma Gandhi (Electronic Edition)*. 95 Vols. Mahatma Gandhi Research and Media Service. http://gandhiserve.org/cwmg/cwmg.html.

Hursthouse, Rosalind. 1996. "Normative Virtue Ethics." In *How Should One Live?*, edited by Roger Crisp, 19–36. Oxford: Oxford University Press.

Jaini, Padmanabh S. 1998. *The Jaina Path of Purification*. New Delhi: Motilal Banarsidass.

Kagan, Shelly. 2007. "Thinking about Cases." In *Ethical Theory: An Anthology*, edited by Russ Shafer-Landau, 82–93. Blackwell Philosophy Anthologies. Malden, MA: Blackwell.

Kumārila. 1983. *Ślokavārttika*. Translated by Ganganatha Jha. Sri Garib Das Oriental Series, vol. 8. Delhi: Sri Satguru. Originally published 1909 Bibliotheca Indica. Calcutta: Asiatic Society.

(Laozi), Lao Tzu. 2010. *Dao De Jing: A Philosophical Translation*. Translated by Roger Ames and David Hall. New York: Random House.

Madhva/Ānandatīrtha. 1993. *Mahābhāratatātparyanirṇaya*. Translated by K.T. Pandurang. Edited by K.T. Pandurang. Vol. 1. Chirtanur: Srīman Madhva Siddhantonnanhini Sabha.

Maha-Satipatthana Sutta. 2000. Translated by Thanissaro Bhikkhu. *Access to Insight*. www.accesstoinsight.org/tipitaka/dn/dn.22.0.than.html, Accessed September 23 2013.

Matilal, Bimal Krishna. 1989. "Moral Dilemmas: Insights from the Indian Epics." In *Moral Dilemmas in the Mahābhārata*, edited by Bimal Krishna Matilal, 1–19. Shimla; Delhi: Indian Institute of Advanced Study in association with Motilal Banarsidass.

Moore, George Edward. 1903. *Principia Ethica*. Cambridge: Cambridge University Press.

Patañjali. 2008. *Patañjali's Yoga Sūtra: Translation, Commentary and Introduction by Shyam Ranganathan*. Delhi: Penguin Black Classics.

Potter, Karl H. 1963. *Presuppositions of India's Philosophies*. Prentice-Hall Philosophy Series. Englewood Cliffs, NJ: Prentice-Hall.

Puri, Bindu. 2015. *Tagore-Gandhi Debate on Matters of Truth and Untruth*. New Delhi: Springer.

Rāmānuja. 1968. *Vedārthasaṅgraha (Edition and Translation)*. Translated by S.S. Ragavachar. Mysore: Sri Ramakrishna Ashrama.

Ramanuja. 1996. *Vedanta Sutras with the Commentary of Ramanuja (Ramanuja Bhasya; Sri Bhasya)*. Translated by George Thibaut. *Sacred Books of the East*, vol. 48. New Delhi: Motilal Banarsidass.

Ranganathan, S. 2016. "Vedas and Upaniṣads." In *The History of Evil in Antiquity (2000 BCE–450 CE)*, edited by T. Angier, C. Taliaferro and C. Meister. London: Routledge.

Ranganathan, Shyam. 2017. "Three Vedāntas: Three Accounts of Character, Freedom and Responsibility." In *The Bloomsbury Research Handbook of Indian Ethics*, edited by Shyam Ranganathan, 249–274. London: Bloomsbury Academic.

Ratie, Isabelle. 2009. "Remarks on Compassion and Altruism in the Pratyabhijñā Philosophy." *Journal of Indian Philosophy* 37: 349–366.

Śaṅkara-Misra. 1923. *Vaiśeṣika Sūtra Bhāṣya*. Translated by Nandalal Sinha. In *Sacred Books of the Hindus*, edited by Nandalal Sinha. 2nd rev. and enl. edn. Vol. 6. Allahabad: Sudhindra Nath Basu, Panini Office.

Soni, Jayandra. 2017. "Jaina Virtue Ethics: Action and Non-Action." In *The Bloomsbury Research Handbook of Indian Ethics*, edited by Shyam Ranganathan, 155–176. London: Bloomsbury Academic.

Vatican Council II. 1965. *Ad Gentes*. www.vatican.va/archive/hist_councils/ii_vatican_council/documents/vat-ii_decree_19651207_ad-gentes_en.html.

Wang, Qingjie. 2010. "Virtue Ethics and Being Morally Moved." *Dao* 9, no. 3: 309–321.

White, David Gordon. 2014. *The Yoga Sutra of Patanjali: A Biography*. Lives of Great Religious Books. Princeton, NJ: Princeton University Press.

4 Logic

The nectar of immortality

Introduction

Logic is an important part of philosophical research. Just as *THE RIGHT OR THE GOOD* is the foundational concept of ethics, which competing theories of ethics differ on, in logic the leading concept is that of *VALIDITY* or (proper) *INFERENCE*. Competing theories of logic would have different things to say about this concept. These days, when students learn about logic, they typically learn symbolic logic—one of the great contributions of recent Analytic logicians. But systems we learn are always one among competing alternatives, and even the best systems can seem quirky. As an example, we could consider the truth table for the conditional: if *P* then *Q*. According to the common truth table, this claim is true, even when *P* and *Q* are false. The explanation for this calls on an account of validity.

Indian philosophers too have contributed to discussions on logic and inference (Gillon 2016; cf. Ganeri 2001). In the Hindu tradition, the salient contributors are philosophers in the Nyāya school. 'Nyāya' in one sense is 'reason,' but it can also mean 'justice.' The school itself begins with the *Nyāya Sūtra*, which outlines logic as it sees the topic. The tradition distinguishes empirical perception (*pratyakṣa*) from inference (*anumāna*), but also from verbal testimony (*śabda*). (The *Sāṅkhya Kārikā* too draws such a distinction, but calls the third variety "*āptavacana*"—authoritative testimony—(SK IV). Virtually the same three distinctions can be found in the *Vaiśeṣika Sūtra*.) All can be a source of knowledge, but they are different (NS I.1.3). This is an interesting distinction: it entails that drawing inferences is not the same as taking people's word as true, or observing how things are. One way to make sense of this distinction is to understand inference as what follows from observations, and the testimony as the endorsement of an inference. The endorsement worth taking seriously would be credible (NS 1.1.5). All are yet distinct elements in knowledge: one can have observations without further inferences, one can have inferences without credible endorsements. This tripartite distinction corresponds to a distinction between premises (observations), validity (inference), and soundness (credible testimony). Validity has to do with what follows from prior information (such as observations), and soundness has to do with the inferences that are worth repeating. Today, it is standard to define sound arguments as the valid arguments with true premises and valid arguments as those arguments whose conclusions have to be true if the premises are true.

Our topic in this chapter is logic: specifically, a representative Hindu account of logic. A representative Hindu account of logic is not necessarily what all Hindus endorse. Rather, it represents the logical disagreements of Hinduism. As it represents the logical disagreements of Hinduism, it depicts what differing Hindu parties converge on while they disagree about what is reasonable. As what we converge on while we disagree is objective, for it resides outside our minds and is observable from multiple perspectives, accounting for what we converge on while we disagree about reasons is objective: it is the objectivity of reason itself. A depiction or representation of this would be objectively true as it *reveals* what is objective. It is important to note that the objectivity so understood would transcend assumptions, beliefs, and perspectives. The representative Hindu account of logic would hence be a philosophical account of logic that is true of logic as such: something that represents what parties in philosophy converge on while they disagree about what is reasonable.

Independently of Hindu resources to depict the objectivity of reason, we can begin with the philosophical idea *VALIDITY*. We often note that valid arguments are those whose conclusion follows from the premises, or rather, arguments where if the premises are true, the conclusion must be true. Such arguments may not consist of true premises. Consider the following:

(1) *The moon is made of green cheese,*
(2) *Green cheese is tasty,*
∴ *The moon is tasty.*

This is a valid argument, as the conclusion follows from the premises, or, if the premises are true, the conclusion has to be true. You would be misguided in the assessment of this argument if you thought that reasonable arguments—the valid ones—have to have true premises and conclusions. Here is another example:

(1) *The author of this book is Shyam Ranganathan,*
(2) *You, the reader, are not Shyam Ranganathan (the author of this book),*
∴ *The moon is not made of green cheese.*

The premises and the conclusion of this argument are all true, yet the argument is not valid: if the premises are true, the conclusion does not have to be true, or, the conclusion does not follow from the premises. This is an invalid argument. It often comes as a great shock to students: validity—reason, logic!—has nothing to do with actual truth.

The valid arguments with true premises are called *sound* arguments. To identify a valid argument we do not need to agree with it. Indeed, we can converge on the validity of an argument while we disagree about its soundness—as is standard in philosophy. Given that what is objective is what we can converge on while we disagree from differing perspectives (in the way that we can disagree about how a table or chair looks from differing perspectives), valid arguments are objective. Valid arguments are what we converge on from differing substantive perspectives:

from some perspectives, the valid arguments appear sound, and from others they do not. Validity so understood is the essence of the objectivity of reason.

Once we acknowledge that validity is objective, and objectivity is like a conch—what looks different from differing perspectives—it appears that validity is a social phenomenon. When we identify a valid argument, we appreciate the force of an inference from a third-party perspective, without having to endorse it. If we try to understand a valid inference in terms of what we think is true, from our first-party perspective, we will confuse a valid inference with invalid inferences that contain true premises and conclusions—or worse, we will make the beginner philosophy student mistake of rejecting the validity of an argument because we disagree with its premises or conclusion. There really is no other way to determine whether an inference is valid except from this third-party perspective, for from here, we give up determining the credibility of an argument in terms of what we think is true, yet we are in a position to assess whether the conclusions of such perspectives follow from their considerations.

The resource that I propose to call upon that models this convergence on a third-party perspective that we do not give into is an ancient myth that appears in many sources: The Churning of the Milk Ocean. It is a famous and interesting myth in its own right (famously on display as a sculpture in Suvarnabhumi Airport, Bangkok, Thailand), as it contains characters that are the main deities of popular Hinduism. The story is on one very superficial level about candidate-gods trying to prove themselves in a world of competition. Their goal is to gain the nectar of immortality from the ocean, and they can only do that if they work against each other. This is representative of the amazing diversity of Hinduism. All Hindu options are in competition with alternatives like the various candidate-gods vying for legitimacy on that Milk Ocean. They need each other to mount their case, but none concedes that the other is correct. Given our observations about validity as the objectivity of reason, where validity is discerned by our convergence on the force of third-party perspectives that we do not give in to, this story models logical validity as what represents the logical disagreements of the various candidate options of Hinduism. The churning is the back and forth of appreciating the force of a third-party perspective, without giving in—we experience this seeming indeterminacy of the third-party perspective in the push and pull of that ocean. All Hindus can converge on this churning without having to agree, just as all philosophers can converge on the force of third-party perspectives without having to agree.

Texts, *psychologism* and the problem of logic

At the very outset I want to concede that a narrative or text can have several meanings. I came to this acknowledgment when I was working on a dissertation on the problem of translation in general. The common view is that texts are composed of sentences and words and that the meaning is holistically reducible to the meaning of its constituents. Given that we can *use* language and symbols for all manner of purpose, some literal, others ironic, I noted that bare texts can support multiple *works* depending upon the disciplinary constraints we imposed on a text. A discipline is a practice that we can undertake from differing perspectives: it is not a set of beliefs that we employ to interpret a text. Rather it is a common action that we can employ to triangulate on the objects of research from differing theoretical perspectives. And hence the kind of disciplinary concern we bring to a text renders some significances salient, and others derivative. And, moreover, I showed that once we acknowledge this, we can produce translations of original texts that were linguistically different but the same, given disciplinary considerations. This research was also where I discovered that *everyone* in the *W*estern tradition, whether in the Analytic or Continental traditions, assumed the standard linguistic account of thought, which we have and will examine further. I say this now at the outset to dismiss criticisms based on the assumption that a story such as the Churning of the Milk Ocean must have a single meaning: it depends on one's disciplinary considerations. I also want to reiterate that as we attempt to identify a representative Hindu account of logic, we are not at all interested in Hindu beliefs: no part of this analysis will depend upon the account being the substance of Hindu conviction.

We have already distinguished between beliefs and thoughts in Chapter 1. This distinction is blurred by the standard, linguistic model of thought (as we shall see in Chapter 5), and deconstructing the distinction is an important function of the practice of Yoga, as we shall see (in Chapter 5 and beyond). But our very Hindu story of the Milk Ocean gives us pause to be deeply suspicious of such critters as beliefs. "I believe that it is raining outside" explains nothing and is true in virtue of my believing it: I can't even infer from this the embedded proposition "it is raining outside." It only explains "I believe that it is raining outside." To employ belief in explanation, which is what interpretation is, is to employ a rationally corrupt device in explanation, and the result is a forced account of the world from a perspective.

It is possible to study logic as though it comes apart from philosophy but in reality, it is a result of philosophical research. In this section, I first want to review certain bizarre trends in the philosophy of logic of late as played out in the history of European philosophy, and also the story of the Churning of the Milk Ocean. The former is troubling, and the latter is dispositive. In the next section we will tie these threads together.

*Recent philosophers of logic in the W*est

Syllogisms are a very specific type of inference, characterized by: "two premises, each of which is a categorical sentence, having exactly one term in common, and having as conclusion a categorical sentence the terms of which are just those two terms not shared by the premises" (Smith 2016). Reason comes in many more forms (more premises, different types of claims) and hence the syllogistic model we learn first from Aristotle is restrictive.

In an effort to break out of the narrow bounds of reasoning on Aristotle's account, we find authors attempting to take different approaches to the topic of logic. In his day, John Stuart Mill was a leading figure in this movement.

According to Mill, deduction, epitomized by the syllogism, is indebted to induction (observations that lead to generalizations or predictions) to generate its major premises (typically concerned with generalizations) and hence induction is foundational to reasoning (Mill 1882: II.i p. 126 and iii, p. 147). Presumably, this process of induction would be applicable to the laws of logic themselves, such that we would come to understand what they are via observation. But this renders the study of logic an empirical affair concerned with the "analysis of the mental processes concerned in reasoning" (Mill 1882: p. 130, fn 51). In the final analysis, logic as induction is to be understood as a part of psychology (Mill 1882: p. 130, fn 51). This is the position of *psychologism*. The psychologistic foundations of logic would help us be more open about the varieties of inferences as they play out in our mental lives.

Edmund Husserl, regarded as the father of phenomenology and in some sense the Continental tradition of philosophy, originally took to Mill's account of reasoning as a psychological process. The reason for endorsing it is obvious: how else would we learn about the laws of logic except by observing cases of reasoning. But Gotlob Frege, commonly regarded as the father of Analytic philosophy, published a criticism of Husserl's endorsement of psychologism (1894), which resulted in Husserl changing his position. Following Frege, Husserl criticizes Mill's psychologism in the first part of his *Logical Investigations*, the series of works that set out his theory of phenomenology. According to Platonists such as the post-Frege Husserl, the problem with a psychologistic account of reason is that it cannot distinguish between how people do think, and how they ought to think: yet reason is normative (Husserl 2001: vol. 1, p. 41; cf. Frege 1980). Frege too adopts a Platonistic view about reason. Just as Plato distinguished between the normative world of objects of reason, governed by the Good, and the empirical world of the senses, so too do Husserl and Frege endorse such an approach to make sense of the objects of logic. But this leads to further questions: how can we observe rational objects?

Husserl's project of phenomenology attempts to answer this question: through a serious of reductions that serve to bracket questions of the existence of the phenomena, we come to the rational core, the intentional object (cf. Beyer 2015). It is, however, not obvious how this is itself not an example of the kind of psychologistic exercise that Mill endorsed, for it is an entirely first-person account of the objects of analysis. Frege for his part attempted to tackle the question via language. It is by understanding the meaning of what is said that we come to an appreciation of the rational objects that are invoked. To this end, Frege invokes his famous context principle: a word only has its meaning within the context of a sentence (Frege 1980: x). By understanding the meaning of a word within a sentence, we get to the corresponding object on Frege's account. Frege did not recognize that this too is not so far from psychologism, for one's interpretation of a sentence that allows us to fix the meaning of its constituent words will depend in large measure on psychological factors, such as what one believes the sentence is about. One reason Frege did not consider this is that he brought a considerable amount of logical and mathematical machinery to bear on the questions of propositional analysis. But a problem remained for Frege, however. In his attempt to show that basic rules of arithmetic are reducible to more basic logical notions, he committed himself to axioms that provide no way to answer Russell's Paradox: "does the set of all sets contain itself?" Rejecting or affirming this leads to more problems given Frege's assumptions. Frege eventually conceded and came to entertain the possibility that numbers are experienced via a type of rational intuition (Frege 1979a, 1979b). As noted, in the case of Husserl, this appears to be nothing more than psychologism.

I want to draw attention to features of this period in the history of the philosophy of logic. First, Mill defends psychologism, and Frege and Husserl unsuccessfully reject *psychologism*. Indian philosophers, I would add, have not (on the whole) endorsed such a theory. Indeed, the main thrust of much Indian philosophy is to adopt a critical attitude to our assumptions and psychology. Buddhists for instance proffer the practice of mindfulness as a means of discharging our latent psychology from having to play the role of reason (*Maha-Satipatthana Sutta* 2000). The Nyāya distinction between three contributions to knowledge (observation, inference, and testimony) already pries apart our psychology from sources of knowledge as our observations (what seems true from our perspective, replete in our psychology) are distinguished from inference and credible testimony. In the philosophy of Yoga, our psychology is our *saṃskāra* (tendency impressions) that we generate by endorsing and identifying with experiences (YS I.18, II.7–14). They are the subconscious analog of memory (YS IV.9)—also formed when people identify with experience: both are to be criticized. The trouble with them is not merely that they represent what is no longer the case. *Saṃskāra*-s, like memory, may not have even been true at the time of their formation, when we identify with experiences. If this Yoga analysis of memory and *saṃskāra* seems opaque, consider the example of a young human early in life who is bitten by another animal, say a dog. The human who is bitten can decide to identify with this experience, and this involves forming a belief or fear, something like, 'I believe that dogs bite me' or 'I fear that dogs bite me,' and this identification will thereby inform his or her interaction with future dogs, not as someone open to new experiences (and critical of the embedded proposition 'dogs bite me'), but one who defines themselves in terms of a belief or fear of being bitten by dogs. The *saṃskāra* is the subconscious memory of this event, but it may not even be true of the original event: the human in question may not have feared or believed that dogs bite at the time of the bite but only after deciding to identify the event as essential to their personal narrative. Moreover, in binding themselves to this experience as a *saṃskāra*, our human taints his or her opportunities for positive experiences with dogs: every new experience will be filtered through the *saṃskāra*, causing an experience of alarm that only confirms the prejudice. To rely upon one's psychology as the foundations of reason is to rely upon one's *saṃskāra*-s as reasonable, and this, according to Yoga, is a mistake.

Whereas Indian philosophers generally drew a line between psychology and critical thinking, it is not obvious that our philosophers in the *W*estern tradition managed such a distinction for the following reason. From the very earliest times, starting with Plato, we have the metaphor of a perspective being invoked to account for knowledge: in the *Republic* (514a–520a) he teaches us that the difference between the knowledgeable individual, freed from the cave of illusions, and the ignoramus, is that the ignoramus is tied to a bad perspective (viewing shadows cast on a wall). Plato echoes this in the *Phaedrus* (245c–249d) with the idea that the knowledgeable person transcends the bonds of Earthly perspective, and sees everything from on high. This is at the outset of a tradition of accounting for knowledge in terms of a point of view—so much so that critics such as Thomas Nagel (1986) will later attempt to motivate the objective perspective as the 'view from nowhere.' This is a reflection of the dominant approach to thought in the *W*estern tradition going back to the Greeks, which identifies thought with the perspective encoded in one's language: *logos*. The problem with the idea of thought as one's perspective (one's belief) is that it never satisfies the worry that what we are privy to is nothing more than the figment of our imagination. So if we think about thought in terms of a special perspective, we can continue to entertain the worry that the objects that we observe are nothing but phantasmal features of our perspective. *Psychologism* falls from this approach to thought as an inevitability. In short, it is the tendency to assimilate propositions to beliefs and other propositional attitudes, which are features of psychology.

There is a way around this problem: if objects are what we can see from multiple perspectives, as Indian philosophical motifs endorse (such as the Jain parable of the Elephant and Blind Men, or Viṣṇu's Conch), in identifying an object, we are not identifying something that is a feature of our thought. We are identifying what we can think about from differing perspectives, and hence the identity of the object comes apart from our psychology. This ability to triangulate on objects in a common world shows us the difference between objects and the subjective: reflections in mirrors are subjective as we can see them from only one perspective, but the mirror (though we may disagree on how it seems to us from our perspective) is what we can converge on from differing perspectives. Reason is objective because we can take differing perspectives on the soundness of an argument as we converge on its validity (or lack thereof, as the case may be).

A second problem with the *W*estern trio of logicians is their politics. Mill was a racist imperialist, who referred to South Asians as racially immature, and in need of a despot like Akbar (*On Liberty* I.10). Husserl claimed that philosophy and reason as such was a peculiar and definitive feature of Europe (1965: 159), absent in other peoples from other cultures. Everyone else wants to become European, he says (1965: 157). Not only is this racist, as it depicts critical thinking in its most general sense, philosophy, as peculiar to Europeans and absent in all other humans, it is also an attempt to depict *W*estern imperialism and cultural conversion as a gift to non-westerners. Finally, Frege was a closet Anti-Semite with fascist sympathies (Frege 1996 [1924]). The list continues. Martin Heidegger, Edmund Husserl's famous student, was a member of the Nazi party in Germany, *and* he defends *psychologism* as a truism in his *Logic: The Question of Truth*. On his account, the problem with typical accounts of psychology is that they are empirical, but ultimately psychology has to do with the mental, and it is undeniable that thinking is mental he claims. Moreover, the basic substance and topic of logic is *truth* (Heidegger 2010).

One positivistic response to the alarming observation that so many influential philosophers of logic were racists and politically naïve is that logic has nothing to do with politics, so the political views of these philosophers are not relevant to assessing their contributions to logic. Logic is about how things are—truth as Heidegger claims, or psychological laws as Mill claims, objects of phenomenological analysis as Husserl claims, or linguistic meaning as Frege claims—but ethics is about what we want or desire. There is one fatal problem with this approach known as the 'Frege-Geach problem': we can use ethical claims in arguments and reason about them as much as anything else, so it is not obvious how they are so different from other claims assessed within logic. A valid argument remains valid even if the premises and conclusion are about ethics (Woods 2017).

Another problem of course is that logic is not about truth. It is about inference, and the essence of inference is validity, and valid arguments can have false premises and conclusions. But if we think that logic is somehow about truth, the way things are, then a conclusion that we draw from our perspective about the way things are is that the alternative perspectives are false, simply because they deviate from how we see things *and* they are unreasonable because they are not true. Anyone who is not part of our chosen group, defined by its perspective, would hence seem constitutionally unreasonable. This is the seed of racism as it depicts people of other groups as constitutionally unreasonable, as groups who are the target of racist attitudes are often described. I am hence unsurprised that the likes of Mill, Husserl, Frege, and Heidegger were racists, because they identified reason with how things are—be it psychology, the objects of phenomenological reduction, linguistic meaning, or truth in its most abstract sense—though they differed on what that amounted to. The way out of this madness is simple: appreciate that reason is not about truth. It is about validity, which is the force of a third party perspective that we do not have to give in to.

As we visit the Milk Ocean, we will find that the gods are those who know how to accommodate third-party perspectives in their own exercise of rationality. The demons cannot.

The Milk Ocean

Now we can return to our journey to the Milk Ocean. In this section I will first review the figures who play a role in the story. I will then review the story. To clarify, what follows is a straightforward explication of the story and its characters, not an interpretation. If it were an interpretation it would precede from beliefs, like "I believe that Viṣṇu is *tapas*"—and as we noticed, we cannot draw any further inference from such a belief. Rather as an explication it treats the perspectives in the story, including its characters, as decomposable into propositions (not beliefs) that entail their contribution to what is controversial.

The cast of key figures

In the previous chapter, I outlined the major disagreements on dharma in the Indian tradition and noted the identity of the iconographical depictions of Viṣṇu (also known as Hari or Nārāyaṇa), Lakṣmī, and Ādi Śeṣa rising above the waves of an external ocean on the one hand and the *Yoga Sūtra* identification of yoga (meditation) in terms of three procedures on the other (YS I.2, II.1). The first is *Īśvarapraṇidhāna, or the approximation to the Lord.* The Lord as the person who is self-governing and unconservative is analyzable into the procedural ideals of *svādhyāya* (self-governance) and *tapas* (unconservativism). Lakṣmī, who sits on herself (as the Lotus) and thereby presents herself, is the model of self-governance and Viṣṇu, who objectifies himself by turning away from himself (as his disk), exemplifies *tapas*. He rests on the deity who approximates them—Ādi Śeṣa—who floats above the waves of the ocean, as he is mindful of self-governance (Lakṣmī). The added richness of this image is that *Īśvarapraṇidhāna* is able to be mindful of his own self-governance by accommodating unconservativism. *Īśvarapraṇidhāna* accomplishes Yoga here (*citta-vṛtti-nirodha*) by approximating its Lord, which are two people. We arrive at this account by treating these perspectives (the three deities) as their constituent propositional content, which explains their controversial (asymmetrical) relations.

I also noted the identity of Śiva as the benign, counterculture destroyer, who exemplifies a Consequentialist account of Mindfulness, often associated with Buddhism but also present in the Vaiśeṣika and Kaśmīrī Śiva tradition, among others. Mindfulness is the practice of merely observing mental content so it serenely flows away from motivating us to wrong doing. Mindfulness hence destroys pathologies that arise from selfish motives that bind us to suboptimal beliefs. In this case, the Consequentialist treats such pathologies as *justifying* a peaceful observational stance. Śiva, deep in this meditation of detachment from such mental content, is the epitome of Mindfulness. Śiva as mindful can enjoy the fruit of difficulty and misguided effort, and thereby take it away, without being tainted by it because he is appropriately mindful of them. His complement is Śakti, the Goddess whose emotions are her expressive range. Together they make up this first couple of Mindfulness, who can be destructive (when Śiva treats us as the mere content of his mind). This is a very different model of meditation from the Yoga/Bhakti model we find in the *Yoga Sūtra* and Vaiṣṇava lore, where yoga is depicted as supporting and constituting a world of diversity. Moreover, we come to an appreciation of Śiva's role as the archetype of mindful meditation by explicating the perspective of Śiva as the destroyer seated in meditation.

One large group in the story are the Devas, often simply called the "gods" in English. They are often identified with forces of nature. Then there are the Asuras, who are often simply vilified as demonic. One exception is the pair of Friendship (Mitra) and Justice (Varuṇa) (*Ṛg Veda* 5.63.3). Similarly, we find the case of the Asuras, Rāhu and Ketu. Rāhu is originally a demon that gets inadvertently legitimized (by Viṣṇu in our story), and to reverse the harm of this Viṣṇu has to sever the torso of Rāhu, which becomes a legitimized God. This derivative Asura is Ketu. In the subsequent tradition, Rāhu is identified with the northern node (the point from the Earth's perspective that the path of the Sun and the Moon overlap in the northern sky) and Ketu with the southern node (the point from the Earth's vantage that the path of the Sun and the Moon overlap in the southern sky). They are credited with illusions like eclipses. In the south of India, Rāhu is associated with solar eclipses, and Ketu with lunar eclipses (Allocco 2009: 44–45). Rāhu and Ketu are vilified but they are also Gods, duly worshiped and propitiated by many Hindus.

So while in general the Asuras are opposed to the Devas, it seems as though there are exceptions: Varuṇa, Mitra, Rāhu, and Ketu enjoy the status of being both. One possibility is that this classification is merely a vestige of an old language, in which "*asura*" also meant 'god' (O'Flaherty 1976: 60). But what the Asuras might share is their capacity to efface their identity: they are demons because they can possess us, but this is fine in the case of Friendship and Justice, but problematic in other cases. In Indic astrology, as attested in works such as Mantreṣvara's classic *Phaladīpikā*, weight is placed on the dignity and placement of Rāhu and Ketu in astrological charts—their influence can apparently be positive or negative.

An explanation for why Asuras are generally bad, but there are notable exceptions, is that Asuras, as we shall see in our story, do not like diversity. They like things their way or no way at all. While this is generally a bad thing, we might think that it is a requirement in the case of Friendship or Justice: Friendship should make no room for unfriendliness, just as Justice should not make space for injustice. The Asuras are, as a group, individuals who prefer the first-person perspective: they want to understand the world from their perspective only. The gods, we shall see, are quite tolerant of third-party perspectives and they become vindicated in our story.

Before continuing to the story, it is worth noting its presentations of Viṣṇu. He is always characteristically doing something different (as unconservativism himself), but he also appears in three forms. He appears early as the Turtle. Turtles are animals who can withdraw their limbs and senses. They are hence symbolic of the yogic activity of *pratyāhāra*—withdrawal of the senses (YS II.54), a condition of non-empirical enquiry, like logic! Viṣṇu also shows up as the physician, Dhanvantari, bearing the nectar of immortality (*amṛta*). This is snatched from him by demons. He has to come back as Mohinī, the enchantress, who flatters all, retrieves the nectar, but then dispenses it to whom she pleases. She also mistakenly legitimizes the demon Rāhu and must decapitate him to save Rāhu from being overbearing.

The story

The story of the Churning of the Milk Ocean (*Mahābhārata: Āstika Parva*; Vālmīki *Rāmāyaṇa* XLV; *Viṣṇu Purāṇa* IX) found in many sources represents Hinduism in one respect: it contains within it many of the main deities of popular Hinduism, but it also narrates a time when who was a god was an open question, much like the question of what Hindus should philosophically endorse is an open question. It is hence a marvelous symbol of Hinduism as a microcosm of philosophy. My narration of the story is a composite of the different versions, which keeps a core narrative that explicates itself.[1]

The story begins with the Devas (gods) being insecure with their lot. According to one version (*Bhāgavata Purāṇa*) they were cursed by a sage as a result of a perceived slight, which involved Indra's elephant dropping a garland the sage derived from the Goddess Lakṣmī and gifted to Indra. In short, the gods fall into disrepute.

The disparaged Devas meet with Viṣṇu, who advises the Devas to churn the (Milk) Ocean with the Asuras to obtain the *amṛta* (nectar of immortality). It is easy to overlook the importance of the proposal: the Asuras and the Devas are generally arch enemies. What Viṣṇu proposes (characteristically) breaks with past practice: for the Devas to regain their legitimacy, they have to cooperate with those they oppose. The Asuras for their part are in it for the *amṛta*, which is what the Devas are interested in too. As they both can only procure the *amṛta* with each other's cooperation, they agree. But the cooperation is peculiar: it involves opposing each other in a giant game of tug of war that churns the Milk Ocean. The king of snakes, Vasuki, agrees to be the rope. The churning device is Mount Meru, and it rests on the back of Viṣṇu in the form of the turtle who can withdraw his senses.

According to the version from the *Mahābhārata*, the Ocean, which starts out being rather ordinary, becomes Milky as a result of the churning, which both agitates the water but also adds the remnants of natural liquids (such as tree sap) to the water. In trying to clarify this ocean, it becomes as though opaque.

Midway through the exercise a poison is emitted that threatens the entire project. Viṣṇu advises the participants to get the help of Śiva (the destroyer) as the only one who can help: he agrees to get rid of it by drinking it. Pārvatī (Śiva's consort), concerned about the effect of the poison on Śiva's heart, places her hand on his throat to prevent it from going any further. Consequently, Śiva is called "*nīlakaṇṭha*" (blue throat) as the poison remains there.

The gods and demons can now churn the ocean. Well before the nectar appears, several objects and people—collectively, *ratna*-s (gems)—emerge. One object that emerges is Viṣṇu's conch (objectivity). Persons who appear from the churning include Śrī (Lakṣmī the Goddess of wealth and Viṣṇu's consort). In some versions of the story, Wine, or the Goddess of wine (Vāruṇī—the consort of Justice) appears too. Finally, Dhanvantari the divine physician (often depicted as yet another form of Viṣṇu) appears with the nectar. The gods and the demons had originally agreed to share the result of their work, but the demons abscond with the nectar determined to have it only for themselves. In response, Viṣṇu appears in his female form as Mohinī the enchantress. All are overwhelmed by Mohinī's beauty and agree that she will take possession of the nectar and distribute it evenly. Yet, Mohinī decides to distribute the nectar to the Devas only (Friendship and Justice are apparently not part of the demon contingent—requiring no redemption). One exception to Mohinī's plan is Rāhu, who though an Asura, assumes the form of a god to gain the nectar. As the nectar is being consumed by Rāhu, the Sun (source of light) and Moon (the reflection of light) reveal to Viṣṇu that Rāhu is actually an Asura not worthy of the nectar. Viṣṇu slices Rāhu's head (what speaks or makes claims) off with his disk, but as he had already consumed the nectar, the torso (what can assume an attitude) is immortal as a distinct demon/God: Ketu.

What is the story about?

The tug of war is identical with the appreciation of a third-party perspective—its force—without having to agree. This appreciation of the force is facilitated by the animal who withdraws its senses (Viṣṇu as the Turtle). The transitivity of Vasuki, pulled from divergent perspectives over the turtle, is a non-empirical transitivity: validity. Validity is this non-empirical transitivity of the force of an argument, which is the force of a third-party perspective to which one does not have to agree. It is third-party not because one cannot endorse it, but because in order to appreciate its force we have to treat it as someone else's perspective. And this is the universal experience of all who participate in this public event.

Validity hence has an essence: the transitivity facilitated by Kūrma, Viṣṇu the Turtle. It is unconservative, unconstrained by past actions, but it also preserves and accommodates a diversity of perspectives. Everyone can participate in this activity but only those who are respectful of the enterprise of third-party disagreement deserve to be validated as a god. The nectar that Viṣṇu dispenses is for those who know how to disagree, and that distinguishes the Devas from the Asuras, who do not know (or are not willing) to disagree. Knowing how (or willing) to disagree is about appreciating the importance of a diversity of perspectives in a rational world. The Asuras want everything their way, and hence they cannot be reasonable and are thereby not worthy of immortality. This latter component of the story adds to our usual account of reason. Usually we talk of reason, in logic, as a mere logical relationship between propositions. If an argument is valid (P), then its objectivity comes apart from the truth of the components (Q). If the objectivity of an argument comes apart from the truth of its components (Q), then we can converge on the validity of an argument from differing perspectives (R). To deny this last proposition sets up a domino effect (via Modus Tollens), which leads to the rejection of (Q) and by extension (P). But to be reasonable is to appreciate the validity of an argument. This shows that to be reasonable is to accept diversity. The gods do this: the demons do not.

The usual positivistic story we hear about reason as something divorced from morality and politics—one made famous by Logical Positivists and their followers (Ayer 1946)—is confused: it treats logic as something independent of the values that make a diverse and liberal world possible, characterized by a diversity of perspectives. The appreciation of this confluence entails the convergence of logic and political justice, captured in the Hindu term *nyāya*, which stands for both. It also sheds light on why logic is more than a mere symbolic essence, and extends to a diversity of critical thinking matters, including matters cataloged in the *Nyāya Sūtra*—matters such as how to engage in debate.

Those who claim to be studying logic but harbor xenophobic attitudes (like the philosophers of logic that we reviewed above) likely fall into this trap by adopting the procedure of the Asura: to think that the reasonable is how things appear from their perspective only. This is *psychologism*: the conflation of one's own beliefs with the thinkable. Those who fail to distinguish truth from reason are likely susceptible to this error, because to converge on the truth of a proposition is to agree with it, and hence to think that logic is about truth is to think about it as inimical to disagreement and a diversity of perspectives. The psychologism of recent *W*estern philosophy and its accompanying politics of racism are of a piece.

There are a few elements in our story that are yet to be accounted for. One is Śiva's act of consuming the poison. The other is the legitimization of Rāhu and its deflation into something that results in Ketu. This is relatively straightforward if we expect any further elaboration of the story to be consistent with the observation that the churning is the process of disagreeing about reasons.

The poison that arises mid way through the project is the fruit of the desire of the participants but not the actual nectar that they were aiming for. It is hence the apparent futility of their efforts, and this poison threatens to sap the motivation of those involved in the disagreement. Śiva can consume this as he is a practitioner of mindfulness meditation—indeed the archetype of this meditation itself. As we noted in Chapter 3, those who engage in this kind of meditation can be aware of the problems of others and not allow it to taint them as they do not allow such matters to motivate their own action: they are rather mindful of them. Such pathologies, such as anger, frustration, apathy, thrive on being endorsed for then we act in accordance with them, and then they continue by animating us. Mere Mindfulness allows us to disengage the pathologies from our motivation and hence they do not continue: they are destroyed. That Pārvatī, the Goddess of Śiva's experiences, stops the poison at the throat, is Śiva's complement in his Mindfulness not allowing the pathologies to motivate Śiva: they are rather stuck in a world of his voice, where he can refer to them without being moved by them.

Rāhu is cut down to size, and we know the head—the claim-making part—continues to be Rāhu, while the body—the part responsible for gait—becomes Ketu. We know from the story that it is Viṣṇu's insertion of himself as the disk—his triangulated self-triangulation—that cleaves the two parts. We also know from the story that it is Viṣṇu who legitimizes Rāhu. How, why, what?

Recall that Viṣṇu is giving out the nectar to those who know how to disagree when he legitimizes Rāhu. He himself is one such person who knows how to disagree, so he could form the proposition, "I deserve the nectar," which is true. But reflecting on this, and that he believes it, he can form the further belief, "I believe that I deserve the nectar." (The examples could vary: Viṣṇu might form the thought, "this person x deserves the nectar" and given that it is his choice as to who will receive it, he might conclude that x deserves it because "Viṣṇu believes that x deserves the nectar." Or, even, the thought could be "this person x is here for the nectar" and Viṣṇu may move from this to "I believe that this person x is here for the nectar.") In this case, Viṣṇu has moved from a thought to a belief, and he has done so on the basis of the evidence—innocently. We briefly reviewed the distinction between beliefs and thoughts in Chapter 1: they have differing inferential properties. One cannot infer the embedded thought ("I deserve the nectar") from a belief ("I believe that I deserve the nectar") though it seems like we can derive the belief from the thought by describing our own (or someone else's) attitude about a thought. But a belief ("I believe that I deserve the nectar") is the kind of thing that is true *merely* because of the described attitude even while the embedded thought ("I deserve the nectar") is not true. While embedded thought is objective—something we can converge on while we disagree—the belief is not. Thought is godly (tolerant of disagreement), the belief is not. So there would be no way to disagree with "I believe that I deserve the nectar" believed by Viṣṇu, for in converging on the belief, we would have to agree that yes, Viṣṇu believes that he deserves the nectar. Recall this is a context in which Viṣṇu is dispensing the nectar only to those who are tolerant to disagreement: the belief is apparently not tolerant of disagreement. Yet, it has assumed the form of a God—Viṣṇu—by being parasitic on his attitude to the thought, "I deserve the nectar." Rāhu is this demon of description: it can thereby assume the form of a god—it is a propositional attitude description that assumes the form of the proposition it describes. The proposition is a god for it allows for disagreement: the belief is not. The only way out of descriptions of such attitudes is to separate the attitudinal component from the thought: so we separate the Ketu—"I believe that"—from the claim "I deserve the nectar." Graphically, this is tantamount to severing the attitudinal component of the demon, from the head, which makes the claim "I deserve the nectar." In staring at himself as the disk rotating away from himself, Viṣṇu sees something that is true by virtue of his own attitude, but that is nothing but himself revealing himself and corresponding to himself as someone staring at himself. So Rāhu as an independent personal propositional attitude description that one has to agree to in virtue of the embedded attitude is reduced out of the picture by Viṣṇu's act of autonomy and defiance in the face of belief. What is remaining is the attitude (Ketu—"I believe that"), and the description of the embedded claim (Rāhu—"*p*").

Rāhu and Ketu are, in some sense, dead on arrival: the attitude (Ketu) needs an object, of which it is deprived, to animate our mental lives, and the claim (the Rāhu) lacks a personal endorsement that makes it true. Note, we know this by explicating the story: treating the perspectives as propositions that explain their controversial claims and actions. We cannot get there from belief: "I believe that Rāhu is first-person propositional attitude ascription" explains nothing but this belief. It is an explanatory dud: a severed head.

Rāhu as mere description (of *p*) is innocuous but when describing us (taking our form) it presents our attitudes to a thought as though a *fact* (a true thought)—and moreover it is true because of our attitude, but nevertheless, demonic as it substitutes what we can be reasonable about (*p*) with what we cannot (descriptions of propositional attitudes towards *p*). Rāhu hence would be the range of emotional presentations (attitude descriptions) that we feel compelled to endorse by virtue of the constitutive attitude, and it is likely for this reason that there is a close association between Rāhu and Durgā (Śiva's consort) in the south of India, as Śiva's consort presents the range of emotions. Rāhu is also, as noted, associated with solar eclipses, where the moon (reflection) gets in the way of light, and here in the case of the propositional attitude ascriptions, our reflection on ourselves gets in the way of the thought we are thinking. It sheds light on why Rāhu is associated with (*vimati*) logical fallacies or silly thinking while Ketu (attitude) is responsible for inappropriate attitudes (*Phaladīpikā* 14.9). But the corollary of these drawbacks is that well-disposed, Rāhu shorn of Ketu allows us to be reasonable and Ketu free of Rāhu allows us to be free of objects of obsession. Hence, they are not all bad and many Hindus propitiate them because, when you get their good side, it is good.

Returning to our comments about recent European philosophers of logic, we can note that the Churning of the Milk Ocean shows what is so wrong with their politics, and in turn their approach to logic. Logic requires a diversity of perspectives, and hence xenophobia, racism, and other isms that define the reasonable as the sole preserve of a privileged perspective are mistaken. To collapse this special perspective with reason is to commit the error of psychologism, which is the product of Rāhu describing us being reasonable as a substitute for us being reasonable.

Interpretation and explication

We have considered and reviewed the distinction between interpretation and explication but in a very general way. Explication is the explanation by way of inference and validity. Interpretation is explanation by way of belief and truth. Now that we are familiar with it, and our Milk Ocean, we can distinguish the two approaches formally.

To explicate a perspective *P*—augustly called a "philosophy"—about topic *t*, is to *E*:

- Discern the reasons of *P* that constitute *P*, which explain *P*'s use of "*t*" and to arrive at a systematization of *P*'s reasons that explains the uses of "*t*." The systematization of *P*'s reasons that entails *P*'s *t*-claims is *P*'s theory of *t*. The reasons of *P* may be what *P* explicitly says, or what is entailed by *P*.

This is the first step. This is when we look to a perspective to provide the reasons that entail its use of a controversial term, like "dharma" or "morality." Its reasons are its theory of dharma or morality. Then there is the second step:

- Compare theories of *t*: what they converge on while they disagree is the concept *T*.

We could call this second step the *consilience of entailments*. In short:

- *Explication* is the explanation of a perspective in terms of its entailed theories that entail the perspective's controversial claims.

This is the procedure of understanding that underwrites philosophical research. This allows us to understand the concept *DHARMA* or *MORALITY* in terms of the disagreement between theories of dharma or morality. Given that it is the same disagreement (about *THE RIGHT OR THE GOOD*) we know that they are the same concept. It should be salient by now, that in engaging in philosophy, we are churning the ocean of mental content. Each one of us is engaged in articulating some perspective, perhaps our own, that entails a theory that entails our controversial claims, and the object—the gems from this confluence of opposition—are the concepts we haggle over. Hence, the intelligibility of our positions in philosophy depends on the disagreements that flush out our views. What structures the possibility of this activity is the non-empirical transitivity of—Viṣṇu's back as the turtle—validity. It is at once unconservative but also supportive of a diversity of perspectives. Moreover, those philosophical positions worth considering transcend their own narrow perspective and make a claim to being taken seriously among the diversity of perspectives. Those positions that cannot make a case for themselves from a third-party perspective are not worth being taken seriously, eternally.

Then there is interpretation. To interpret some package *P* is for the interpreting subject *S* to *I*:

- Use *S*'s reasons (or if you prefer, "premises," "assumptions," "beliefs," "truths," and even "*tradition*") r_S in the explanation of *P*.[2]

In short:

- *Interpretation* is the explanation in terms of the beliefs of the interpreter.

So as we shall see in our next chapter (Chapter 5) on thought, and as we saw earlier (Chapter 2), this method of understanding falls from the standard approach to thought in the *W*est as linguistic meaning. (According to this theory of thought, thought is the meaning of what we say, which means that those who endorse this view have to believe their thoughts, lest they deny the meaning of what they say, which is absurd. It hence conflates thought and belief.) Interpretation is the standard approach to studying Indian thought in Indology: Orthodox Indologists decide whether Indians had anything to say about "ethics" based on beliefs about what ethics is. Interpretation is the process of trying to explain everything in terms of a personal propositional attitude description (Rāhu). It is a disease of reason for the reasons noted: nothing follows from a Rāhu except itself. And while explication relies upon the essence of reason, validity, entailment, interpretation puts the cart before the horse: it starts with truth but a truth that entails nothing else.

Worth noting is that interpretation violates validity, for explanations in terms of what you believe run afoul of the procedural constraints of validity: valid arguments rely upon all sorts of propositions, even the false ones, and do not essentially have anything to do with true propositions or the ones you believe. Interpretation hence is structured around a standard of explanation completely foreign to reason. Yet, it takes the form of a god, something that knows how to disagree. In describing what you take to be true, it uses these descriptions as its premises, and then derives conclusions based on these premises, but as beliefs entail nothing but themselves, interpretations are question-begging, of the form "I believe that *p*" therefore "I believe that *p*." Here too, we find an imitation of godliness, for question-begging inferences are all of them valid, and validity is the essence of reason. But interpretation is parasitic on real reason: the miscreantism of interpretation is that it violates validity by assuming that reasonable explanations have to start with the truth or what one believes. It emphasizes what follows from such an irrational starting point, which is valid if it begs questions. It is the demon that takes the form of a god: Rāhu. Explication in contrast is Viṣṇu all the way through: it facilitates and preserves a multiplicity of perspectives that can converge on objectivity while disagreeing. It is the essence of reason.

We saw in Chapter 2 and to some extent in Chapter 3 that the adoption of interpretation by Indologists results in the nonsensical conclusion that "dharma" has many meanings and that Indian philosophers were not interested in ethics. In short, this is the result of the Asuras' method. But Indologists probably do not think of themselves as demons and they will no doubt resist the notion that there is anything amiss in trying to understand Indian thought in terms of their own beliefs about ethics. One reason that interpreters might fail to appreciate the deep irrationality of their enterprise is that Justice and Friendship are Asuras. They like all Asuras are intolerant of alternatives, but we usually think this is acceptable in the case of these moral virtues. Hence, we find many interpreters arguing that we should adopt an open-minded attitude to our research subjects—that we should interpret them *charitably* (cf. Adamson Accessed 2017). But this is a perversion: it confuses moral virtues with logical virtues, and the result is that in being charitable, the interpreter tries to understand others in terms of their own perspective. This is narcissistic, but also imperialistic. With friends like that, who needs enemies?

Representative Hinduism and reason

To be clear, this story functions as a *representative* Hindu account of logical disagreements in so far as it functions as a representational account of the disagreements of reasons as such. It tells us that what we converge on when we disagree about reasons is the non-empirical foundation (the turtle) of the third party's force (their tug) that we do not have to give in to. This is what all involved in the disagreements of logic can converge on while they disagree. This is what we call "validity." To appreciate that this functions as a representational Hindu account of logical disagreement, we do not have to endorse a Rāhu of any sort: we do not have to believe that this is what Hindus endorse as their account of logic.

But as the story represents what we converge on while we disagree about reasons, it is instructive. It shows that there is a difference between reason (the Devas) and psychology (Asuras), and moreover that reason is about appreciating a diversity of perspectives locked in a disagreement, in a public world. It shows us that the path ahead in this disagreement is divided first by futility—we are not going to convince anyone of our certitude by engaging in this project of logic—but moreover that the reasonable people are those who appreciate that a diversity of perspectives is part of what it is to be reasonable. It solves a very basic problem in the philosophy of logic: what is the foundation of reason?

If we were to treat reason as some basic rule or value, we can always raise the skeptical challenge: how do we know that the proposed rule or value is the foundation of reason? The Churning of the Milk Ocean depicts reasoning in a manner that avoids this skepticism by treating reason not as something that we have to agree to (like a basic rule or value), but rather something we are free to disagree to, and that is why it is reasonable. It shows us that reason is a *thing* (something we converge on while we disagree) and not itself a claim or principle (which can be true or false). It is the force of a third-party perspective that one is free to disagree with, or perhaps more elegantly, Viṣṇu's (the preserver's) back as the turtle (the non-empirical animal) on which the transitivity of reason rests. The story is a mythological account of philosophy itself, which allows all of us to transcend our limitations and be gods, if we can appreciate the requirement of diversity and disagreement to being reasonable.

And, by way of repetition, the plausibility of this account as a representative Hindu account of reason does not depend upon Hindus believing it, or being raised to regard it as their account of logic. Rather, it represents what Hindus converge on when they disagree about reasons: the force of a third-party perspective that they do not have to agree to. It also shows us what was wrong and misguided with the thinking of our recent European philosophers of logic who managed at once to pursue the topic of reason while holding xenophobic and racist views. Their error was failing to appreciate that reason requires diversity. This failure is tantamount to conflating the reasonable with how oneself thinks, and in this move we also engage psychologism. Colonialism and imperialism are outcomes of this psychologism. Another word for it is *interpretation.*

Reading philosophy

In Chapter 1, I noted that much of what passes for research in Indology is not really research at all. Rather, it is interpretation. Having reviewed the question of the objectivity of reason via a representative Hindu account of logic—what we converge on as we disagree about reasons—we are in a position to acknowledge how to avoid the common mistakes of Orthodox Indology.

Becoming a philosopher

The reason that explication is the default method of philosophical research and understanding is that it allows us to disagree, and philosophy is a discipline and disciplines are epistemic projects that facilitate disagreement. So, of the two, interpretation cannot be the method of philosophical understanding for it makes disagreement unintelligible, and yet explication can. But why is it that these are the only two options? Could there not be others? My reason for focusing on these two is simple: the two contrasting methods of understanding disagree about the following:

- Truth is determinative of reason.

Interpretation affirms this, explication denies it. It is tempting to bring up two alternatives: induction and abduction. Induction is a kind of reasoning process that attempts to establish generalizations on the basis of the enumeration of the evidence. It is common in the empirical sciences like meteorology: generalizations about the upcoming weather are frequently based on observations of past and current weather patterns. Abduction is also called "inference to the best explanation." It is also common in the empirical sciences and often combines with induction (as when a meteorologist chooses one out of competing inductions). Explication in contrast is deduction, which relies on validity, applied to the process of understanding philosophy. Induction and abduction are alternatives to deduction. Why cannot induction or abduction be our method for studying philosophy? While interpretation rejects or runs roughshod over validity, inductive arguments are famously invalid and do not have to be valid in order to be taken seriously, and the same is apparently true of abductive arguments—which involve choosing among alternative explanations.

While induction and abduction do not treat validity as a standard of reasoning, they also do not entail the error of thinking that truth is determinative of reason—though interpreters may wish to rely on induction and abduction as nondeductive reasoning forms to bolster their project. An inductive argument can be cogent, strong or weak: the strong ones render their conclusions plausible, while the weak ones do not. The strength of an induction does not rely upon the truth of its premises: cogent arguments in contrast are not only strong, but have true premises. (Strength is like validity, and cogency like soundness.) Similarly, an inference to the best explanation does not have to be true: it merely has to be the best among alternatives. Hence neither induction nor abduction involve endorsing the fallacy of interpretation, that truth determines reason. And while induction might generate strong generalizations that fail to be deducible from the evidence via validity, the goal in induction and abduction is not to start off with the truth as a means of explanation, but to get us there, and in this respect move past imperfect states of understanding. All which recalls a quote from the Vedas:

> *asato mā sadgamaya*
> *tamaso mā jyotir-gamaya*
> *mṛtyor mā amṛtam gamaya*
> from falsity lead us to truth
> from darkness lead us to light
> from death lead us to immortality
> (*Bṛhadāraṇyaka Upaniṣad* I.iii.28)

Inferences that take us from the false to the true do not in and of themselves violate validity. (Invalid inferences proceed from the true to the false.) Indeed, explication helps us with this too, as it allows us to appreciate the disagreements of philosophy (which include false claims) and arrive at a big picture of the facts of philosophy. And as the Churning of the Milk Ocean myth shows, along with this quote from the *Upaniṣads*, we are in a position to transcend the limitations of our perspectives when we allow for disagreement, and this involves moving from the partial and false accounts of the way things are from our various perspectives, to a synoptic understanding—the understanding of the gods. So interpreters cannot look to induction or abduction in hopes of a defense, for their project is about arriving at the truth and leaving behind the false: yet interpretation is about starting with the truth as the grounds of explanation.

Reasonable people do not have to reject induction or abduction but it is unreasonable to expect that they will shed light on philosophical matters for the following reason: philosophy is a discipline, disciplines are concerned with disagreement and what we need to participate in philosophy is a method that reveals the disagreements of philosophy. Explication reveals the disagreements of philosophy. Induction and abduction in contrast make the case for something being true (whether it is the inductive generalization, or the chosen abductive explanation). So while philosophers might seem to make inductive arguments or abductive arguments, the only way to understand the disagreements of philosophy is to explicate them. And as a discipline such as philosophy is concerned with disagreement, it is concerned primarily with explication. The reason that induction and abduction can function in the empirical science is that the discipline of science is itself concerned with empirical disagreements, which is why *testing* is central to empirical investigation. Testing in the sciences plays an analogous role to explication in philosophy: it makes the disagreements of the discipline intelligible.[3] To value testing is to understand empirical hypotheses in terms of their conflicting predictions while explication allows us to understand the competing logical implications of competing philosophical theories. In both cases, there is something objective that is being tracked: what we can disagree about.

From these considerations, we can note the following.

(1) Reading philosophy is about *explicating* the perspectives expressed in a text.
(2) As explication sheds light on the disagreements of philosophy, the merits of a philosophical text consists in how much we need explication to make sense of it, and thereby how much it sheds light on the disagreements of philosophy.

Good philosophy is hence not philosophy you necessarily agree with. Good philosophy is the philosophy that makes you work philosophically to make sense of it. Working philosophically is explicating, and thinking philosophically is explicating: a skill, a yoga. Good philosophy may hence come in all sorts of forms. It could be an essay (like the various mediaeval commentaries and tracts of Indian philosophers), it could be aphoristic (like the *sūtra* texts of early Indian thinkers), it could be a story (like the Hindu epics, or the *purāṇa*-s, where we find the

Churning of the Milk Ocean story) or perhaps even a poem (as we find in the *Upaniṣads* or Vedas). Good philosophy is often not easy philosophy for what makes philosophy good (that it requires philosophical thinking on the part of the reader) and what makes a text easy to read, are really different characteristics. Two factors bear upon the easiness of a text, for the interpreter.

First, for interpreters, the easiness of a philosophical text is a function of the subjective similarities between the reader and author of the text. In this case, the interpreter will read the contents of her own beliefs in the text by another author, and what is said will not only be readily intelligible but seem obviously true. And as interpreters confuse truth with reason, they will think that what they are reading is paradigmatically rational. Proportionally, if a philosophical text draws from resources that are alien to the interpreter, such texts will appear to deviate from the rational, as it does not rely on their beliefs, which they confuse with reason.

Second, since philosophy is about explication, for interpreters, texts that render their content explicit (which in this case is whatever they as interpreters believe) will seem like the paradigm cases of philosophy (easily read as philosophy) for it does the work of explication (that is, instead of the interpreter doing explication, the text seems to be doing it). But what seems explicit will depend in large measure on what is intelligible to the interpreter, and what is intelligible to the interpreter is what expresses their own beliefs. So philosophy will seem like easily expressed beliefs to them—what anyone can do, if they have these same beliefs.

In both cases, ease of comprehension is conflated with the content of the interpreter's beliefs.

For the explicator, as explication has to help us with shedding light on the disagreements of philosophy, the familiar and explicit may fail to do this. For the explicator, the value of philosophy will hence come apart from its ease and clarity. Bad philosophy can be clear: clearly bad. Bad philosophy can be easy: easy to determine as bad. While what counts as rational and philosophical is a subjective matter for the interpreter, dependent on their beliefs, good and bad philosophy is objective for the explicator as the value of a philosophical text and contribution is judged independently of one's perspective and beliefs. Bad philosophy will require very little philosophical thinking to understand, and it will fail to elucidate the disagreements of philosophy. Bad philosophy is interpretation.

Becoming a philosopher is very much about mastering the skill of explication as a method of research. It takes time and practice. Like music, it is something we can learn, though some have the gift. It is invaluable as it constitutes the practice of reason in its most basic form: understanding the force of a third party without having to give in. Interpretation in contrast, anti-philosophy, is about imposing one's view on others, so they give in.

The West *in philosophy*

At the undergraduate level of philosophy instruction, interpreters and explicators will mingle and probably not be able to tell each other apart *if* the majority of philosophy being taught and discussed hails from the culture of the student body and if the interpreters identify with this cultural background. In this case, the explication of philosophical theory will coincide with the beliefs of the interpreters. While explication sheds light on the disagreements of philosophy, that is often not apparent at first (but only after much study) and hence at this early stage, the difference between interpreters and explicators will not be apparent. Throw in some foreign philosophy, and there will be cracks. Interpreters who identify with the domestic culture will have trouble seeing this material as philosophy, which means what they believe. In our world, the proliferation of interpreters has to do with the *W*est: the linguistic account of thought with a European origin. This account of thought conflates what we say in language with the thinkable. Denying a thought on this model is denying the meaning of what we say, which is absurd. So in the context of the *W*est, the *W*esterner (one who endorses the *W*est) will be led to interpretation because they will conflate belief and thought to avoid this absurdity. But as explanation on their account primarily relies on their own beliefs, which are true by virtue of their attitude, easy interpretations will seem to be *sui generis*—not relying on tradition, or enculturalization, but obviously true and doxographically inescapable. Here *W*esterners will not see themselves as cogs in the wheel of *W*estern imperialism, lacking individuality and endorsing all of a *W*estern provenance, but will likely feel like Hegel's thought thinking itself—understanding all, while subsuming the alien and the foreign within a synthetic, master understanding. Here, cases and thought experiments designed to elicit the beliefs of the interpreter—often called "intuitions"—pass as the paradigms of rationalist philosophy (cf. Cappelen 2012). Philosophy is not only psychologized via the conflation of thought and belief but also anthropologized: widely shared beliefs that facilitate social interaction are taken to be a background standard of reason (cf. Wolf 1987). The case of the foreign philosophy that cannot be explained by the contents of reason as the interpreter sees it will seem non-rational, but obviously traditional. In this context, for the *W*esterner, philosophy is about celebrating European culture as the content of reason (for an explicit example of this, see Rorty in Balslev and Rorty 1991).

Some of these interpreters might resist the easy identification of foreign ideas with tradition but domestic ideas with reason. They may be influenced by the philosophical writings of interpreters, such as Gadamer, who argue that understanding requires tradition, and hence the seemingly obviously true ideas that we intuit through reason, are really, on this account, the ideas made obvious by our tradition (Gadamer 1996: 270–293). But this is not an improvement. First, far from criticizing the identification of philosophy with the European tradition, it excuses all bias as a necessary feature of reasoning, and hence a Eurocentric bias in one's understanding of philosophy is par for the course (Gadamer 1990). Stranger still, this theory of interpretation (all understanding is understanding by way of some background set of traditional beliefs) is presented as though it is one truth that transcends time and place and is true for everyone: it is "ontological" to use Gadamer's words. For the interpreter, it appears as the *sui generis* content of reason, which (because it is believed) escapes being treated as a mere consequence of a specific tradition (the *W*est). It hence encourages and instantiates a mode of a-historical, armchair intellectual history where the peculiarities of the *W*est, namely an obsession with language and interpretation, are taken to be everyone's faults (such as we find in Orthodox Indology).

Of course, if one pursues philosophy to the graduate level, then there is increasing pressure on students to shed light on the controversies of philosophy as their contribution to the field and this requires explication. This is a difficult environment for an interpreter to survive in. Die-hard interpreters—die-hard *W*esterners—will tend to duck out. Yet they—committed *W*esterners—will not see not pursuing philosophy further as a loss: for them, philosophy is just about their beliefs of a European provenance and they already have those—nothing new to acquire from further study. Indeed, in general, an entailment of the *W*est is that there is nothing new to learn or discover in philosophy because it is merely about the celebration of European beliefs, which the *W*esterner believes they have. Yet, the entire process of doing philosophical research, and putting together a contribution to the philosophical literature, involves explication. If interpretation and its major vehicle, the *W*est, survives here, it survives as a theory of understanding that many entertain, quite at odds with philosophy—a theory we can disagree with, even if it is the dogma of the day. So, the *W*est survives in academic philosophy not as the basic practice of philosophy but a dominant but poorly understood philosophical movement animating work in the Continental and Analytic traditions—poorly understood because if one endorses it, objectivity is obscured. It shows up not in how academic philosophers attempt to catch up on the literature, or new research, but in their theories of thought (it is language) and the interpretive insularity (focused on all things *W*estern) this brings. It survives as a fuzzy haze obscuring the yoga of philosophy, which nevertheless survives because unlike interpretation, philosophy tracks what is objective.

As an example of philosophy poorly understood and aborted under the *W*est, let us consider the interpretation of Jonathan Edelmann, as provided in his "Hindu Theology as Churning the Latent" (2013). Edelmann draws a distinction between philosophy and theology, and argues that Hindu thinkers are better understood as theologians, not philosophers. After providing such a distinction he defers to Viśvanātha Cakravartin's (eighteenth-century Caitanya Vaiṣṇava-Hindu) analysis of the 'churning of the ocean of milk.' The act of churning on this account is a metaphor for coming to understand the latent content of a *purāṇa.* He further argues for a definition of a Hindu theologian as someone trained in a disciplinary tradition, who seeks knowledge of ultimate reality (Brahman), and who seeks to follow the ethical requirements of a Hindu tradition.

Here are his distinctions:

> *Philosophy* engages argument, reason, and logical analysis, without assuming in the process of argumentation the authority of a particular religious or revealed text, even though the philosopher may believe in the authority of a sacred text, and may even seek to establish its truth through rational argumentation.
>
> (Edelmann 2013: 429–430)

And:

> *Theology*, however, presupposes the value in providing a rational interpretation and explication [(Edelmann does not seem to draw a distinction between the two as I have)] of a sacred text as a self-sufficient means of understanding the truth. For theology, it is a legitimate form of argumentation to use scripture and tradition as a premise in an argument, but that is not how philosophers argue today.
>
> (Edelmann 2013: 430)

Providing some anecdotal support for this distinction, he notes that his past pursuit of an undergraduate degree in western philosophy threw authors like "Śaṅkara into sharp relief." Śaṅkara, like Rāmānuja, was a Vedāntin who takes the end of the Vedas, especially as summarized in the *Vedānta Sūtra*, to be the final philosophical word on a variety of issues spanning metaphysics and epistemology to values. But as the *Vedānta Sūtra* and many of the basic texts of the Vedānta tradition were ambiguous, defenders had to take a stab at explicating it while defending its content—that is, they had to render explicit what they took to be the content of these texts while shedding light on disagreements. They were successful to varying degrees in their task of explication but what is noteworthy was that they, like Abhinavagupta (a Kaśmīrī Śaiva thinker), were not claiming to start from scratch but to improve upon something already known—but often using this as an opportunity to make novel arguments. (Indeed, it seemed to be a norm in India that one could not claim to be original without being rude, so there was a widespread practice of commenting on authoritative texts as a means of providing novel arguments.) Edelmann reports being disappointed with their work as it was preoccupied with "scriptural interpretation" rather than "rational argument." He continues:

> I recognized it as skilled reasoning, but not philosophy, at least not the sort of philosophy I was reading in Plato, Descartes, Kant, or Quine, who for the most part left the minutia of scriptural interpretation to others . . . Hindu thinkers such as Śaṅkara, Rāmānuja, Abhinava, etc. are often said to be doing an odd or atypical form of philosophy, rather than doing a normal form of theology. In my view, they are normal theologians, not odd philosophers.
>
> (Edelmann 2013: 434)

Methodologically, if one were committed to explication—the yoga of philosophy—one would not treat one's undergraduate degree in philosophy or the highly selective samples of philosophy that one studied as definitive of philosophy. One would have regarded it as evidence towards the disagreements of philosophy, but also as an opportunity to practice one's own skill at being a philosopher. Explication, like all disciplines, hence serves as a *prāyaścitta*—atonement, expiation—for the bias and unrepresentative samples that one learns from, for explication and disciplines in general will not let us draw conclusions on the basis of such a biased sample.

Explication, philosophy, like all other disciplines guides us to what is objective and away from bias. But if one interprets, one will treat the propositions with which one is presented as the content of one's beliefs, and hence the propositions about philosophy one learns in one's undergraduate degree will come to be set in one's beliefs about philosophy, and this is then used as a standard of explaining what philosophy is. Induction, which can be empirically respectable, is corrupted to draw conclusions on the basis of a biased sample (what the interpreter is aquatinted with by happenstance not via a systematic, global survey of philosophy), and the conclusion is then treated as the premise in further arguments. For the interpreter, they have learned everything there is to know about philosophy by way of the biased samples with which they are familiar. Edelmann shows himself here to have not opted for becoming a philosopher by adopting explication. (Indeed, Edelmann's formal study of philosophy ends with an undergraduate degree in the topic.) What strikes me about Edelmann's description of his trajectory is that in it, he assumes that thinkers of the European tradition are doing philosophy (the ones his professors chose for their pedagogical merits) and this sets the standard against which non-western thinkers are to be appraised: this move is classic *W*est and Edelmann is showing himself to be operating within the ideological boundaries of the *W*est. Accordingly, to 'study' non-western thinkers is not to learn something new about philosophy (hence, when Edelmann discovers that Śaṅkara is doing something different from Quine, he does not take this as an opportunity to revise his understanding of philosophy, but to decide that Śaṅkara is not doing philosophy because Śaṅkara is not doing what Quine is doing). The point of this narrative is to figure out whether non-western thinkers talk and act like western thinkers. There is nothing objective about this project: nothing to discover. It is about comparing the paradigm European cases with everything else, as a potential deviation, and the project rests on the subjective elevation of the European as arbitrator of everything.

There are problems with Edelmann's distinction between philosophy and theology, and his choice of paradigm philosophers from the *W*estern tradition. The first problem is the question-begging use of the term "scripture." This is a word used for texts with a religious connotation. So to understand its relevance we need to understand what religion is. And if religion, as I noted in Chapter 1, is whatever cannot be interpretively derived from the *W*est, then of course: all Indian and Hindu texts and matters of importance will be scriptures, not because of their content, but because of their racial categorization as Indian. If defending scripture is characteristic of theology then all Indian intellectual work will be theological.

The next problem is that Edelmann in his example of the contrast between *W*estern philosophers and Indian theologians is that he has chosen to contrast Indian philosophers who are exponents of a tradition, with *W*estern philosophers who are for the most part system builders (Quine being an exception). If Edelmann chose to compare Plato, Descartes, and Kant with Patañjali, Īśvarakṛṣṇa, Gautama or the authors of the Vedas (the legendary authors respectively of the *Yoga Sūtra*, the *Sāṅkhya Kārikā*, the *Nyāya Sūtra* , and the source of the Vedas) it would not only be harder to motivate any sense that Hindu and Indian thinkers were not philosophers but theologians, it would certainly seem implausible to suppose they were all or mostly behind the idea of Brahman (a central concern of Hindu theology according to Edelmann). (With respect to Quine, a survey of his publications, and not merely the famous highlights, show that he thought that science was the source of all truth. He appears far more like Edelmann's theologist than philosopher.) Similarly, if he had compared Platonists, Kantians, and Quineans with Vedāntins and Kaśmīrī Śaiva-s, it would be harder to motivate the idea that philosophy does not involve appeal to *scripture* and *tradition* as a premise in the argument—Platonists would rely on Plato's 'scriptures' and a Platonic 'tradition,' just as Vedāntins rely on the *Upaniṣad*-s and the subsequent Vedānta tradition, as premises in their arguments.

But the deeper and irreparable problem with Edelmann's argument is that it is an interpretation: an explanation in terms of what he takes to be true—specifically his descriptions of philosophy and theology. Interpretation is Rāhu run amuck. The only reason interpretations seem reasonable is the conflation of thought and belief, which makes what we believe to be true the unavoidable reasonable conclusion. The problem is that thoughts and beliefs are not the same, and hence the resulting necessity of an interpretation is based on an illusion. Like all interpretation, it constitutes an imposition of a bias on others, as though they have to agree simply to participate in a conversation of philosophy. If we were to treat Edelmann's paper as a contribution to a disagreement about philosophy, we would have to explicate it and competing options—and the objectivity of philosophy is what we would converge on as we allowed for this disagreement. What we would find is that we do not need to agree with Edelmann: the objectivity of philosophy is explication.

It is worth concluding this section on reading philosophy with two further points, one regarding the motivation for Edelmann's gloss, and whether there is anything objective about Hindu theology that could be elucidated by Viśvanātha Cakravartin's analysis of the 'churning of the ocean of milk.' One of the reasons for Edelmann's project of re-branding Hindu philosophy as Hindu theology is to address a concern raised in *The Journal of the American Academy of Religion* (December 2000): "Who speaks for Hinduism?"—a question posed because, as Edelmann puts it, "there seemed to be a crisis of authority in the academic teaching of Hinduism" (2013: 435). The observation that there is a crisis of who speaks for Hinduism assumes that Hindus, in sharing a religious identity or thoughts, share a perspective that must be represented—and the fact that Hindus seem to say very different things violates this expectation of unanimity. This, as we shall see in Chapter 5, is reducible to the linguistic account of thought characteristic of the *West*. If thought is the meaning of what we say (an essential element of the *West*), then in entertaining a thought, we are entertaining shared meanings, and this constitutes a common perspective. A representative Hindu account of thought shows something very different: that thinking with others is not about agreeing with them or sharing a perspective, and hence the objectively accurate account of Hinduism is not an account of the common perspective of Hindus but their disagreements—which are coextensive with the disagreements of philosophy.

Edelmann's project of elucidating a Hindu theology that is organized around commitments to Brahman fails to get Hinduism right as not only is it dependent upon a meta-narrative about thought that is characteristic not of India but of the *W*est, but because there is nothing about Hinduism that entails that Hindus share a perspective by way of being Hindu that has to be represented by way of Hindu theology. Someone who can speak for Hindus has to be able to speak about their disagreements, not their agreements. For that, we need philosophy, not theology. For Edelmann, Hindus need their own space to articulate their religious worldview, and theology is where this should happen (Edelmann 2013: 436). But the truth is Hindus have all the space in the world they need to articulate their perspectives—the disagreements of philosophy. The freedom they need is to challenge the dominant *W*estern narrative that Indian reasoning is chained to tradition and not philosophical and the bizarre incursion of the *W*est into philosophy that swaps reason with the celebration of European beliefs—a destabilizing force that corrupts philosophy by replacing it with the auto-ethnography of the *W*esterner. As we shall see in Chapter 5, a representative Hindu account of thinking takes us away from such parochialism, unlike the standard model from the *W*est, which cements reactionary conservativism. Contrary to the usual narrative, the source of tradition bound, anti-philosophical thinking is not Hinduism but the *W*est.

Finally, there is the matter of Hindu theology: is it anything objective to be discovered? This depends upon the objectivity of theology. Is it really anything that different from philosophy? Certainly within the context of the European tradition, there was a concerted effort to distinguish theology from philosophy and to put philosophy in its place: it was to be the handmaiden to theology (Henrichs 1968). Theology in turn was the discourse of committed Theists whose views have non-European origins (as we find in Judaism, Christianity, or Islam), and Theists are Virtue Ethicists who believe that God is the paradigm virtuous agent. Except for proponents of the Nyāya-Vaiśeṣika tradition in India, it is difficult to find Hindu Theists. Certainly, we find discussions like theology in the Indian tradition, among Vaiṣṇavas who discussed the properties of the Lord that Edelmann references (with a catch—Vaiṣṇavas were typically not Theists as noted in Chapter 3, but rather Bhaktas). But if we were to categorize the activity of such thinkers as theology on the basis of our familiarity with the western tradition, we would be interpreting. And if we need explication in order to understand the disagreements of people engaged in what is often called theology, then the distinction between theology and philosophy is artificial, and nothing we discover if we merely read texts explicatively. The distinction between theology and philosophy appears rather the attempt to normalize the *W*est's account of the world, where philosophy is reserved for European contributions rooted in the European tradition, and theology (religion) is that other stuff: when Plato and Descartes talk about god without non-European references, that's philosophy—when it is the discourse of Christians, or Muslims, who have Middle Eastern sources for some of their ideas, that's theology. Of course, in the interpretive context of the *W*est where beliefs of a European provenance are treated as the content of reason, the European sources will seem rational, and the extra-European sources traditional, and committed not to truths that can be intuited, but scripture. That is not evidence of the difference between philosophy and theology: that is an implication of the *West*.

Objections

I shall consider four objections.

Tu quoque

One objection that I want to simply avoid taking too seriously is the idea that the above explication is actually an interpretation, because, all explanation is interpretive. Unless one disavows interpretation, this criticism is an example of an informal logical fallacy: *tu quoque*, or the appeal to hypocrisy.

Defense of the inside perspective

The idea of validity as what we converge on while we disagree about reasons entails that there is nothing private or special about any perspective. We understand the reasonableness of a perspective from the third-party perspective. That means that even in our own case, the reasonableness of our perspective is something that is determined from the third-party vantage, from this third-party vantage can anyone appreciate the force of our perspective without having to agree. So, the idea that we have to be an insider within a perspective or worldview to understand it is a mistake. But one might object that there is something special and privileged about an inside perspective, such as the inside perspective of being Hindu.

According to this (nationalist) proposal, those inhabiting a perspective occupy a position of epistemic privilege, and moreover should be taken seriously. Hence, we should not allow the idea that there are third-party perspectives on Hinduism for us to evaluate it. Rather, we have to begin with the internal perspective of the Hindu and understand the unity of this Hindu vantage. This position has become popular in extra-academic accounts of Hinduism from Hindus who complain that the academic study of Hinduism is biased and fails to give due credit and importance to the Hindu vantage. (Many of these folks thrive on Twitter and blog wars, so I am intentionally not citing examples.) But if this is true, then we should look acceptingly at Hindu beliefs, and not do anything to bring them into disrepute.

There are two problems with this. First, if it is true that there is some type of unity to a Hindu perspective, this cannot be assumed *a priori* but has to be shown enumeratively by being open to disagreement and then finding that there is none. But the only way to do this is via explication, which assumes that the objectivity of a perspective is something known from a third-party perspective. But, even if one does not agree to this, there is something fundamentally misguided about assuming the vantage of the insider as privilege: all one sees from here is one's opponent, looking disapprovingly at you. But then, one conflates one's own perspective with a third party trying to understand you from their vantage. We could call this *other-mediated self-understanding*. Hindus, when asked to speak about their religion, often do not claim that it is the South Asian equivalent of moral philosophy but rather profess Hindu beliefs—itself a sign of *W*esternization, as the conflation of belief and thought is a product of the *W*est's linguistic account of thought. But more often than not I find, anecdotally, the tailoring of Hinduism to meet interpretive assumptions of the *W*est and religions imagined or associated with the *W*est. Hindus will hence often profess to endorse monotheism (though they recognize many gods, and are often endorsers of Bhakti, which is the opposite of Theism's Virtue Ethics), and down play idolatry (even deny that "idol" is an appropriate term for objects of worship for very confused reasons, like "no one looks up to or tries to emulate an idol!" or "'idol' is known by native English speakers to be a term of criticism"—never mind "Indian idol," or "teen idol," or "idolizing" someone). The idea that we should identify with a vantage is Rāhu: it (the propositional attitude description) takes the form of a god (the thought). It results in the confusion of self and other.

This account does not do justice to Indian logic

A third complaint is that in an account of a representative Hindu account of logic, we have not surveyed the diversity of Hindu and Indian views on logic. Certainly this is true, but it is important to be mindful that any survey of actual Hindu views on logic would be incomplete, and would fail to truly represent the topic. If the essence of logic is objective and this objectivity is what Hindus converge on when they disagree about reasons in general, then a representative Hindu account of logic just has to shed light on what that is like. That is about becoming a god.

*Criticisms of the W*est *are unfair*

Authors operating in the contemporary academy who are interested in India and Hinduism are motivated by an interest in the topic, and on the basis of their learning, they come to proffer theories and explanations—much like the author of this book. So it seems to be unfair to criticize them as engaging in the imperialist project of the *W*est, especially because imperialism is not a motivation or commitment of such scholars. By parity of reasoning, it is unfair to criticize Husserl, Mill, Frege, Heidegger, and others as racists, especially if they did not explicitly endorse racist beliefs (they did, but let us assume they did not).

Having distinguished between thoughts and beliefs, it should be clear that this defense (call it the *I don't have the bad belief* defense) is a failure. Interpreters will always claim to be innocent because they lack a certain guilty belief. Sexist interpreters will claim not to be sexist because they have no explicitly misogynistic beliefs about women. Racist interpreters will claim to not be racist because they have no explicitly racist beliefs. But the problem is their reliance on belief as a tool of explanation: that's the source of the imperialism. Beliefs take the form of a god: they are parasites. Explanation in terms of such parasites is a disease. The *W*esterner does not have to hate Hindus or have a negative belief about Hindus to participate in a political project of imperialism and colonization of India just as the misogynist or racist does not need to have misogynistic or racist beliefs to be misogynistic or racist. They merely have to use beliefs that marginalize Hindus, women, and members of certain racial categories from public participation in disagreement as the standard of everything. Such a marginalization serves to impose an external perspective on Hindus, women, and racial groups: that is objectively malicious. That is enough to objectively injure Hindus, women and members of racialized groups. What is being injured is not their feelings, but their freedom to resist external incursions into their space, their freedom to disagree, and hence their freedom to contribute to our understanding of objectivity. Moreover, as the Churning of the Milk Ocean teaches, it is irrational. All of this is easily avoided by explication.

Conclusion

Our goal in this chapter was to identify a representative Hindu account of logic, which accounts for what disagreeing parties of Hindus can converge on while they disagree about reasons. As Hinduism is the microcosm of philosophy with a South Asian twist, this depiction would model what is objective about logic—what we can converge on while we disagree about logic. I have argued that the myth of the Churning of the Milk Ocean fulfills this objective. It teaches us that we need variety and diversity in order to protect reason, for reason takes this diversity of perspectives as its object. Being reasonable is not the same as what one believes. Reason is the capacity for self-transcendence that respects first- and third-party distinctions and thereby protects the autonomy of the critic. It is not a special perspective: it is the capacity to appreciate the force of third-party perspectives, without having to give in and collapse the distinction between first- and third-party reasons. Hindus can converge on this event of the Churning of the Milk Ocean, while they disagree about what constitutes reason. Moreover, Hindus do converge on this, while they disagree. Not all options of Hinduism are worthy of the nectar, just like not all options of philosophy are worthy of immortality. But all are required for us to understand the essence of reason as objective.

The chapter also brings to the fore the anatomy of irrationality: interpretation. Interpretation is an explanation in terms of a perspective. Why interpreters fail to appreciate that interpretations are fundamentally unobjective is Rāhu:

- As the attitude of the believer makes the belief claim true, it is not possible to doubt it.

Not only is this true for the believer whose attitude makes the belief true, but also for the third party who converges on the belief.

- As the belief is not possible to doubt, it seems certain—beyond doubt.

Certainty in this case is an experience of intransigence, which psychologically (from one's own vantage) is indistinguishable from the intransigence of an external object. If we could examine a proposition from differing perspectives, then its objectivity would be salient, and indeed, if we understand objects from multiple perspectives they cease seeming and being intransigent relative to our perspective as we can do something to change our relationship with the object. But when we evaluate everything from a first-person vantage, all we have is the intransigence of conviction by virtue of belief. And hence:

- The truth of the belief is confused for an insurmountable objectivity.

This is the model of irrationality: in this case, people are unable to evaluate whether their propositions are worth taking seriously because of this self-generated sensation of certainty. One way that this irrationality is furthered is by scholars trying to account for Indian texts, and philosophy by way of Indian beliefs. But explanations in terms of Indian beliefs are no more objective, and in philosophy we are interested in the objectivity of perspectives, their theories and claims. Explication, as what allows us to evaluate the content of a proposition independently of a perspective, avoids this problem. It is the Churning of the Milk Ocean. Like Rāhu sneaking into the line, once we have identified these independent propositions, we can identify candidate Indic beliefs, but these would be parasites.

Notes

1 Amy L. Allocco narrates a slightly different amalgamation in her dissertation that helps shed light on a connection between Rāhu, a main character in the myth, and the Goddess Durgā (Allocco 2009: 44–45). Further versions can be found narrated by Doniger (O'Flaherty 1976).

2 For defenses of this procedure, see Gadamer (1990, 1996), early Davidson on Charity (Davidson 2001: 101; 1986: 316) and Quine (1960: 59). My colleagues, Robert Myers and Claudine Verheggen, remind me that the full and mature Davidson moves to an externalist semantics and moreover triangulation (Myers and Verheggen 2016)—an idea that I have stressed is a basic theme in the Indian tradition. It is true, that Davidson moves away from characterizing understanding as interpretation, in his later works.

3 For an interpretive account of science, according to which scientific disagreement is opaque, and testing plays little role, see Kuhn (1970).

References

Adamson, Peter. Accessed 2017. "Rules for History of Philosophy." *History of Philosophy without Any Gaps*. https://historyofphilosophy.net/rules-history-philosophy.

Allocco, Amy L. 2009. *Snakes, Goddesses, and Anthills: Modern Challenges and Women's Ritual Responses in Contemporary South India*. Ph.D. Dissertation, Emory University.

Ayer, A.J. 1946. *Language Truth and Logic*. New York: Dover Publications.

Balslev, Anindita Niyogi, and Richard Rorty. 1991. *Cultural Otherness: Correspondence with Richard Rorty*. Shimla: Indian institute of Advanced Study.

Beyer, Christian. 2015. "Edmund Husserl." In *The Stanford Encyclopedia of Philosophy*, edited by Edward N. Zalta. Summer 2015 Edition. http://plato.stanford.edu/archives/sum2015/entries/husserl/.

Cappelen, Herman. 2012. *Philosophy without Intuitions*. Oxford: Oxford University Press.

Davidson, Donald. 1986. "A Coherence Theory of Truth and Knowledge." In *Truth and Interpretation: Perspectives on the Philosophy of Donald Davidson*, edited by Ernest Le Pore, 307–319. Cambridge: Blackwell. Original edition, read at a colloquium organized by Richard Rorty as part of the 1981 Stuttgart Hegel Congress.

Davidson, Donald. 2001. "On Saying That." In *Inquiries into Truth and Interpretation*, 93–108. Oxford: Clarendon Press.

Edelmann, Jonathan. 2013. "Hindu Theology as Churning the Latent." *Journal of the American Academy of Religion* 81, no. 2: 427–466.

Frege, Gottlob. 1894. "Rezension von: E.G. Husserl, Philosophie der Arithmetik I." *Zeitschrift für Philosophie und philosophische Kritik* 103: 313–32.

Frege, Gottlob. 1979a. "A New Attempt at a Foundation for Arithmetic." In *Posthumous Writings*, 278–281. Chicago, IL: University of Chicago Press. Original edition, 1924.

Frege, Gottlob. 1979b. "Numbers and Arithmetic." In *Posthumous Writings*, 275–277. Chicago, IL: University of Chicago Press. Original edition, 1924.

Frege, Gottlob. 1980. *The Foundations of Arithmetic: A Logico-Mathematical Enquiry into the Concept of Number*. Translated by J.L. Austin. 2nd rev. edn. Oxford: Basil Blackwell. Breslau: W. Koebner.

Frege, Gottlob. 1996 [1924]. "Diary: Written by Professor Gottlob Frege in the Time from 10 March to 9 April 1924 (translated by R. Mendelsohn)." *Inquiry* 39: 303–342.

Gadamer, Hans-Georg. 1990. "Culture and the Word." In *Hermeneutics and the Poetic Motion Translation Perspectives V*, edited by Dennis J. Schmidt, 11–24. Binghamton, NY: State University of New York Press.

Gadamer, Hans-Georg. 1996. *Truth and Method*. Translated by Joel Weinsheimer and Donald G. Marshall. 2nd rev English language edn. New York: Continuum, 1996. Originally published Tubingen: J.C.B. Mohr (Paul Seibeck).

Ganeri, Jonardon. 2001. *Indian Logic: A Reader*. Richmond, Surrey: Curzon.

Gillon, Brendan. 2016. "Logic in Classical Indian Philosophy." In *Stanford Encyclopedia of Philosophy*, edited by Edward N. Zalta. https://plato.stanford.edu/entries/logic-india/.

Heidegger, Martin. 2010. *Logic: The Question of Truth*. Translated by Thomas Sheehan. Studies in Continental Thought. English edn. Bloomington, IN: Indiana University Press.

Henrichs, Albert. 1968. "Philosophy: The Handmaiden of Theology." *Greek, Roman and Byzantine Studies* 9: 437–450.

Husserl, Edmund. 1965. *Phenomenology and the Crisis of Philosophy: Philosophy as Rigorous Science, and Philosophy and the Crisis of European Man*. New York: Harper & Row.

Husserl, Edmund. 2001. *Logical Investigations*. Translated by J.N. Findlay. International Library of Philosophy. 2d edn. 2 vols. London; New York: Routledge.

Kuhn, Thomas S. 1970. *The Structure of Scientific Revolutions*. 2nd edn. Chicago, IL: University of Chicago Press.

Maha-Satipatthana Sutta. 2000. Translated by Thanissaro Bhikkhu. *Access to Insight*. www.accesstoinsight.org/tipitaka/dn/dn.22.0.than.html, Accessed September 23, 2013.

Mill, John Stuart. 1882. *A System of Logic, Ratiocinative and Inductive, Being a Connected View of the Principles of Evidence, and the Methods of Scientific Investigation*. 8th edn. New York: Harper & Brothers.

Myers, R.H., and C. Verheggen. 2016. *Donald Davidson's Triangulation Argument: A Philosophical Inquiry*. New York: Routledge.

Nagel, Thomas. 1986. *The View from Nowhere*. New York: Oxford University Press.

O'Flaherty, Wendy Doniger. 1976. *The Origins of Evil in Hindu Mythology*. Berkeley, CA: University of California.

Quine, Willard Van Orman. 1960. *Word and Object*. Cambridge, MA: MIT Press.

Smith, Robin. 2016. "Aristotle's Logic." In *The Stanford Encyclopedia of Philosophy*, edited by Edward N. Zalta. Winter 2016 Edition. http://plato.stanford.edu/entries/aristotle-logic/#SubLogSyl.

Wolf, Susan. 1987. "Sanity and the Metaphysics of Responsibility." In *Responsibility, Character, and the Emotions: New Essays in Moral Psychology*, edited by Ferdinand David Schoeman, 46–62. Cambridge: Cambridge University Press.

Woods, Jack. 2017. "The Frege-Geach Problem." In *The Routledge Handbook of Metaethics*, edited by T. McPherson and D. Plunkett. New York: Routledge.

5 Subcontinent Dharma, the global alt-right, and the philosophy of thought

Introduction

In this chapter, I want to move to a topic that we have been dancing around: thoughts, propositions. On one account, thought is linguistic meaning—this is the standard account of thought. In contrast to this view, Yoga, a representative Hindu account of thought, depicts thought as what we converge on when we disagree about a thought. It plays a central role in explaining Hinduism as the microcosm of philosophy. We will explore these two options via a (semi) fictional geography: Subcontinent Dharma. On Subcontinent Dharma there are differing communities distinguished by their view of dharma, and these differences are linguistically encoded such that "dharma" in a speaker's idiolect is just their communal moral theory. We shall see that when the standard model of thought is introduced in to an environment, people become defined by their communal identity, and moreover colonized. Religious identity is an example of this colonization. The results are anachronistic nationalisms, which are depicted as indigenous and ancient but are a fabrication of colonialism.

Like most readers of this book, I once thought that yoga was this peculiar activity that one undertakes in studio classes, lead by a teacher, and it involves putting your body into unusual postures. Moreover, like many, I was once under the impression that yoga has something to do with traditional teachings—all the people that I knew who were big on yoga had a guru, and were proud of the lineage and supposed antiquity of the teachings. For me, this view changed, over night, when I agreed to teach a philosophy class on the *Yoga Sūtra* and noticed that all the available translations were interpretations. This led me to a project of explicating and translating the *Yoga Sūtra* while I was working (coincidentally) on the philosophical problem of thought in translation. On the other end, I am impressed by the richness of the ideas of Yoga, and that conventional views about the topic are at odds with what is in the text. The conventional approach is to treat the *Yoga Sūtra* as a text to be interpreted. The philosophy of Yoga vitiates against interpretation. Conventionally, Yoga is seen as a traditional and ancient teaching of India, and to be valued as such. Philosophically, Yoga is about being critical of memory, prejudice, and tradition. The goal is not our bondage to a guru or a tradition: it is our own unconservativism and self-governance in a public world.

The linguistic account of thought is the most basic philosophical commitment of the *W*estern tradition. This is the standard account. It connects authors in the Analytic and Continental traditions back to their Greek origins in the idea of *logos*. We shall see that as an account of thought it creates a historical rupture. Those who operate with it operate within a world defined by their linguistic perspective, which means that they have no access to antecedent culturally encoded linguistic frames, and no appreciation for alien linguistic frames. Worse, they treat their perspective as *sui generis*—as though it itself is not a consequence of past choices (karma).

I shall argue that Yoga constitutes a representative Hindu account of thought—not because it is right, or because Hindus believe it, but because it is what we (Hindus and everyone) converge on when we are free to disagree about thought. This freedom to disagree made possible by Yoga represents Hindu disagreements about thought. Thought so depicted is objective. Usually, when I explain a representative Hindu account of a topic, I stress that such a representation of Hinduism is not the same as what all Hindus believe. In this case, the representative Hindu account of thought is a criticism of belief. So it would be quite an accomplishment to believe it.

Earth and taking off to outer space

This section is split into two parts. The first part concerns an explication and contrast between the standard account of thought and Yoga. In the second, we take a trip to Subcontinent Dharma.

*Theory: the W*est *vs. Yoga*

There are at least two versions of the linguistic account of thought: linguistic particularism and linguistic internalism.

If you are a linguistic particularist you deny that "it is a good day" in English shares the same meaning as "c'est une bonne journée" in French (cf. Wittgenstein 1958: I §241; cf., McDowell 1998b: 61–63; 1998a: 128; cf. Lance and O'Leary-Hawthorne 1997: 20; Derrida 1981; Gadamer 1996, 1990) and you thus deny that they express the same thought. If you are a linguistic internalist, you are inclined to see "it is a good day" and "c'est une bonne journée" as expressing the same thought because you take them to share a sentential meaning. Linguistic internalists are hence open to the possibility that speakers of English and French can, via their own languages, engage in a cross-linguistic agreement or disagreement on the goodness of the day (cf. Hare 1952: 146–149; cf. Horgan and Timmons 1991, 1992a, 1992b, 1996, 2000; cf. Boyd 1988: 210; cf. Dreier 1990: 8; cf. Wedgwood 2006; cf. van Roojen 2006; Henning 2011). What is essential to the linguistic internalist idea is that *if* two words have the same meanings in differing languages, the two words bear the same concept in both languages and hence it is possible in differing languages to entertain questions about the same idea.

Linguistic particularists deny that any two languages can share the same meanings and concepts, but agree that the meaning of our words in our language is just their conceptual content.

Philosophers in the Continental and Analytic traditions assume this account of thought and hence understand problems of philosophy. One of the outcomes of this approach to philosophy is the *anthropologization* of philosophy: philosophy as something that tracks and deals with linguistic meaning has to do with being human, but also human as understood by some paradigmatic cultural commitment. In the Continental tradition, since Hegel, this expresses itself in a brooding over the history of the European *W*est as central to philosophy (a theme carried through in the work of Husserl, Heidegger, Gadamer, and Derrida). In the Analytic tradition, this usually shows up in thought experiments, which assume facts about English as a conceptual constraint on what anyone could intelligibly be thought to say. So when we find philosophers in the *W*estern tradition thinking about translation and understanding across linguistic boundaries, we find that diversity is treated as a threat to cross-linguistic understanding (cf. Quine 1960; Derrida 1981). A vivid example of this is the recent Moral Twin Earth thought experiment. This is an experiment based loosely on an earlier thought experiment by Hilary Putnam, who asked us to imagine two distinct but superficially identical worlds, where people speak interintelligible languages. Yet, on one world, 'water' is understood as a clear, odorless, tasteless liquid and refers to H_2O, and on another, Twin Earth, 'water' is understood as a clear, odorless, tasteless liquid yet there it refers to XYZ. The question posed is, can we understand Twin Earth talk of water and our talk of water as commensurate, and Putnam's claim is that we cannot for the meaning of "water" is not psychological but rather what the term picks out. So their "water" does not mean what our "water" means and we cannot translate their water talk as our water talk (Putnam 1975).

Terrance Horgan and Mark Timmons (cited above) adopt this experiment to dharma (they use "good" and other English language terms, but we will Indianize our narration). Imagine the same two superficially identical worlds. When speakers of these two worlds meet, they seem to be able to have a conversation about "dharma"—they can ask whether it is dharma to always tell the truth, or to wear shoes in the house, or whether animal sacrifices are dharma or not. Yet, when we examine the behavior of these terms in their respective worlds, the Earth term "dharma" seems to be causally responsive to a certain physical property that gives rise to Consequentialist-type claims, while on Twin Earth, "dharma" seems to be causally responsive to certain alternative physical properties that give rise to Deontological claims. Can we understand these people as having a conversation about dharma?

The hidden assumption in both Putnam's and the latter experiment is linguistic internalism, and given this assumption, "water" is not translatable straightforwardly on Earth and Twin Earth. "Dharma" can be understood as having the same meaning on both planets but *only* if the *right* semantics for "dharma" in both worlds is some type of internalism such as Expressivism: accordingly the meaning of moral terms like "dharma" is to express one's mind. If we adopt a kind of naturalism, which identifies the meaning of "dharma" in terms of its referent, "dharma" cannot have the same meaning on both planets as they have different world indexed references. Given linguistic internalism, an Expressivist account of "dharma" would confirm that speakers of languages on Earth and Twin Earth can entertain the same concept of *DHARMA*.

Linguistic internalism and linguistic particularism are both versions of the linguistic account of thought. Linguistic particularism denies the possibility of cross-linguistic communication. Linguistic internalism, as we see in the Twin Earth experiments, places a constraint on possible explanations of cross-linguistic communication. It entails that if it is possible, it is possible because the languages share a semantics for the relevant discourse. In other words, scratch the surface and there can be no deep linguistic diversity if cross-linguistic communication is possible. So linguistic internalism hence encourages a kind of armchair linguistics, where philosophers stipulate what sentences mean across languages in order to explain cross-linguistic communication.

What is certainly worth observing is that a linguistic account of thought blurs the distinction between beliefs and thoughts for the following reason.

- If one endorses the idea that thought is *the linguistic meaning of what is said*, then to deny a thought, is to deny *the linguistic meaning of what is said*, but this is to deny that the thought is meaningful, which is absurd.

So, to avoid absurdity:

- For every thought one has, one believes it.

Hence:

- For every p I entertain, "I believe that p."

Further:

- For others to share a thought with me, they have to share my beliefs because there is no way for anyone to entertain a thought without believing it!

So to even have a conversation with others, to communicate with them and to relate to each other as thinkers, there has to be some type of common agreement and shared worldview, otherwise we are not sharing thoughts on this account.[1] We saw this inclination in the literature of Orthodox Indology, where Indologists assume that in order for Indians to talk about ethics, they have to say the kinds of things that Indologists believe about ethics. Orthodox Indology with its emphasis on philology, linguistics, the study of India and interpretation—explanation by way of beliefs—is no accident: it falls from a commitment to the linguistic account of thought characteristic of the *W*est. Rare indeed is an appreciation of the problems associated with this approach. If all thoughts have to be the same as beliefs, what about false propositions: are there any at all, for to recognize a false proposition on this account is to acknowledge the meaning of what one says that one denies (cf. Russell 1938: §54)?

I think it is worth emphasizing how *prima facie* irrational these conclusions are, and if we reject them we have to reject the linguistic account of thought. They are irrational for the truth conditions of a proposition and a belief are distinct and as noted at the start of our investigation, any theory of thought that leads us to conflate a thought and a belief is thereby irrational: it is committed to entailments (*p*, therefore "I believe that *p*") that are not valid. But if we put aside these criticisms we can understand (as we just now saw) how the Greek *logos* ranges not only over thought and language (words) but also opinion: these become logically conflated on the linguistic account of thought. Yet, there are important logical distinctions to be drawn between a belief and a thought: 'I believe it is raining outside' (or, 'I believe *IT IS RAINING OUTSIDE* is my thought'), is true by virtue of my attitude of endorsement, but it does not follow from this that it is raining outside. The thought 'it is raining outside' entails that it is raining outside, and the truth of the claim depends upon it raining outside. If I know that it is raining outside, I know I should take an umbrella. If I know that 'I believe that it is raining outside' (or, '*IT IS RAINING OUTSIDE* is my thought') I do not know that I should take an umbrella. In the *W*estern tradition, we find G.E. Moore identifying 'It is raining outside but I do not believe it' to be an absurdity, which Wittgenstein later called "Moore's paradox" (*Philosophical Investigations* II.190c). This is not a paradox (an apparent contradiction). A contradiction is the affirmation of a proposition and its denial. 'It is raining outside' and 'I do not believe that it is raining outside' are not the affirmation and denial of the same proposition. They are two differing claims. The first is true if it is raining outside. The latter is true if I believe it.

Yoga (Patañjali 2008) defines its project as the normative (*vṛtti*) control (*nirodha*) of thought or mentality (*citta*) (YS I.2). This is to explicitly criticize thought as the object of belief: for to control one's thought is to reject a passive approach to thinking where thought is treated as a mere object of one's attitude. It is hence the crucial logical contrary to the linguistic account of thought, which conflates belief and thought.

This is a project of *tapas*, or anti-conservativism. When we ethically control thought, we are free (YS I.3). This realizes our *svādhyāya* or self-governance. When we fail to engage in the responsible control of our thought, we *identify with it* (YS I.4). To identify with a thought is to treat the thought as the subject of attitudes, so that to think is to believe, or perhaps fear or loathe. It is a short step from this to forming memories and *saṃskāra*-s. A *saṃskāra* is a 'tendency impression,' or a subconscious first-person propositional attitude ascription—what we might call a prejudice. It leads us to interpret experiences by way of our *saṃskāra*-s, and the difference between a *saṃskāra* and a memory (*smṛti*) is negligible (YS IV 9): the latter tends to be conscious while the former operates subconsciously. But in each case, we have undermined our freedom to think critically by an identification with thought, or such identifications—propositional attitudes—are true by virtue of our attitudes. The entire practice of Yoga, including *Īśvarapraṇidhāna, tapas*, and *svādhyāya* (reviewed in Chapter 3), is geared toward supporting people to transition from an attitudinal approach to life, to *samādhi*—absorption. To be in a state of absorption is to be engaged in critical thinking. The reason that absorption is critical thinking is that in identifying a thought (*dhāraṇā*) being moved by its propositional implications (*dhyāna*) we move past seeing the thought as opaque and rather see it analyzed into its objective implications—which we can inhabit as we take divergent perspectives in the matter (*samādhi*). As Patañjali notes in Book III of the *Yoga Sūtra*, this process of thinking in terms of an understanding of objective implications gives rise to powers (what we might call prediction and control): this is no doubt an essential part of empirical and technological research. The ultimate absorption is the absorption in the cloud of dharma (*dharmameghasamādhi*), characterized by a lack of selfishness in all contexts. The final *samādhi* must be an ethical *samādhi* for to think critically is to appreciate that there are no privileged perspectives, as we require a diversity of perspectives to be reasonable (Chapter 4), and that the project of thinking is about engaging in thinking. This results in our own autonomy (*kaivalya*). These three last limbs of Yoga (called together "*saṃyama*"), which comprise critical thinking (I translated this as "perfect constraint of thought" but perhaps the literal meaning of *saṃyama* is better put as "with the Yama Rules" [YS III.1–4], which we shall examine in Chapter 6), are preceded by several moral and epistemic limbs, including *pratyāhāra* (the withdrawal of the senses, limb 5)—which we investigated in the previous chapter on Logic. Once we master logic, we hence think clearly by focusing on a thought, being moved by its implications, and thereby immersing ourselves in thinking.

The essence of yoga is disciplinarity for discipline facilitates objectivity, while deflating the importance of our own perspective and attitudes. Analytically, we can specify that:

- A yoga, or disciplinary practice, is some practice that we can engage in differing relative positions.

The *Yoga Sūtra* is an elaboration the idea of a yoga. We can individuate yogas (such as mathematics and philosophy) in terms of the practice they require across contexts. Any yoga has the following benefit:

- The yoga allows us to triangulate on objects of interest.

To make room for yoga is to transcend particular perspectives and hence to transcend selfishness. This paradoxically brings about our own autonomy in a public world by freeing us from being defined by a perspective. But with this freedom from perspective and selfishness comes a freedom from understanding in terms of attitudes that always references ourselves relative to what we investigate.

Can we attempt to run the idea of triangulation without yoga? If we do, we will not be able to account for how it is that people who are independent of each other can be said to be observing the same object from differing perspectives. We would have to take it as an article of faith that independent observers are observing the same thing. But if we allow a discipline—a yoga—then independent researchers can employ the same yoga and investigate the same objects from differing locales and perspectives: the discipline calibrates observers and renders their observations comparable to other similar observations from differing perspectives. Mathematicians can hence triangulate on numbers and derivations from differing locales, scientists can engage in the same experiment at different times and places, and philosophers can examine the same theory, argument, and concept from differing theoretical perspectives.

To compare the Yogic account of thought, it is useful to introduce a distinction relied upon for some time in philosophy. This is the distinction between the *intension* of a proposition, and its *extension.* The intension is something like the definition or mode of presentation of a thought, while its extension is the objects that the thought is true about. Given a linguistic account of thought, there are many ways to make sense of this distinction: Fregeans affirm the reality of intensions, and treat the extension of a thought as its truth value. Expressivism as a kind of Fregean model of thought would treat the meaning of a moral claim, "it is dharma to sacrifice animals," as the expressive abilities of this sentence to voice the mind of the speaker, and the extension as what this evaluation tracks. Millian naturalists deny that there are intensions, but rather extensions that are the objects of which language is true. So naturalists on Moral and Twin Earth would treat the extension of this sentence as whatever "dharma" refers to in the relevant natural environment.

If we adopt a Yogic approach to thought, we could understand the intension of a thought as the common disciplinary purpose of differing linguistic, semantic, or mental representations (*citta*), and the extension as the collection of such *citta.* So in thinking, we are normatively constraining representation (*citta*) according to disciplinary considerations. Like a *dharmameghasamādhi*, constraining mental representation allows us to transcend the selfishness of perspective and to appreciate what is objective—what can be known from differing perspectives. On this approach, there would be no need to oppress or deny the relevance of contrary approaches within the same thought. We transcend the selfishness of each of the constituent *citta*-s via this disciplinary constraint. And we might further appreciate a thought to be true when, having duly constituted it by our discipline, the various elements of the extension of a thought *triangulate* on a common object. This adaptation of the intension/extension distinction to yoga entails that there can be multiple *kinds* of thought, and they will be distinguished by the governing yoga. So propositions of mathematics would be different from those of philosophy, for instance. The same sentences can comprise distinctive thoughts on the basis of distinctive disciplines. Whether a thought is true has to do with whether its extension reveals its object, which it triangulates on from differing perspectives, and this is to be determined by comparing differing perspectives that constitute a thought unified by a common disciplinary purpose.

In summary, the difference is thus:

Linguistic Model of Thought

- Intension: a sentence's definition
- Extension: what the sentence is true of

Yogic Account of Thought

- Intension: common disciplinary use of meaning (in service of an inquiry)
- Extension: collection of meaningful devices (such as sentences) that share the intension

We could likewise identify a yogic account of *thinking*:

- Intension: a common disciplinary purpose (determined externally)
- Extension: competing perspectives that share the common disciplinary purpose

When we talk about thought, we think of the extension in terms of semantic content. When we talk of thinking, it is the actual perspectives that matter. The semantic content of the extension of a thought (barks, chirps, sentences) are treated as representations of perspectives, calibrated by the governing disciplinary purpose. Thought is a nominal representation of thinking, the more basic activity. Thinking is something we do from a perspective, but as it is defined by the common disciplinary purpose, it allows us to transcend our perspective, and contemplate intentional objects of thought. True thoughts are the project of thinking that reveal a common object of inquiry.

Full disclosure: I defended this kind of view as a philosopher in my dissertation on translation and semantic content (Ranganathan 2007, 2011). One of the advantages of thinking of meaning and content in terms of disciplinarity is that it allows us to work around linguistic and cultural differences. So for instance, differing languages do not have to have words or sentences with the same meaning in order to express the same thought: they need only have resources that have the same *disciplinary* use, and this disciplinary use is something determined not internally by a culture, but externally by the discipline. This is a form of *externalism*, which we could call *linguistic externalism*. It is externalist because a discipline is never reducible to our particular practice, but has to do with possibilities across contexts. It is an externalist position, for whether you express a certain thought has nothing to do with your perspective or that built into your language, but an external disciplinary criterion that correlates your semiotic activity (bark, chirp, linguistic utterance) or epistemic activity (smelling, hearing, looking) with other such semiotic activity (other epistemic activity) in other contexts. Whereas on the linguistic account there is a one-to-one relationship between the meaning of what one says and its propositional and conceptual content, on this Yogic account, there is not. (Those who endorse the linguistic account of thought might endorse speech act pluralism—the idea that one sentence can express many propositions given contextual factors—but they would be committed to reducing each proposition to a sentence that is its meaning [Cappelen and Lepore 2005]). So one and the same sentence, symbol, sign, bark, chirp, or sigh can express differing thoughts relative to differing disciplinary interests. Moreover, to think is not on this account to have an attitude to a proposition but to be absorbed (*samādhi*) in the public activity of thinking. On this account, thinking is not about the meaning of what you say: it is about your semiotic participation in a wider project of research, whether one knows it or not. All makers and users of meaning, all who track objects from differing perspectives, animals in general, can hence participate in thinking.

So whereas the linguistic account of thought defines thought agent relatively (by way of the meaning of what you say), the Yogic account does not reference the thinker as an observer of thought. So at no point can one infer from a thought an attitude to the thought, such as a belief. Put another way, to entertain a thought is not to commit one to believing it. Thoughts are hence a lot more like questions, which we explore, than claims we can have definite attitudes toward. The detractor might point out the following: given that the Yogic account of thought provides a definition of a thought, we can take this definition to be an account of the meaning of what you say when you express a thought. This is to reduce the Yogic account of thought to the linguistic account of thought—it is a bit like endorsing a Rāhu when one is thinking (as Viṣṇu did as discussed in Chapter 4). As the linguistic account of thought apparently commits one to believing a thought one endorses, so too the Yogic account. The problem for this rebuttal is that on a Yogic account of thought, thought is the disciplinary use of a semiotic resource, so the only way we could treat any linguistic representation or meaning as thought is if we use it to think: but this prevents us from conflating the meaning of what we say with our thought: it is the use that is the thought. This account frustrates the idea that a thought is the same as a belief, for whether semantic activity counts as thinking depends on disciplinary considerations that transcend our attitudes. Any attempt to reduce a thought to one's belief would be a failure to think on this account. It would be a Rāhu, not a Viṣṇu.

Subcontinent Dharma

Imagine a subcontinent where there are several communities, all speaking inter-intelligible languages, *but* the meaning of "dharma" in each language is the community's governing theory of dharma. We could call each such community a nation as they differ as to basic questions of how to live, and answers to such questions define their national identity. Nation Pūrva Mīmāṃsā holds that "dharma" is what is given in intuition (*śruti*) and consistent with tradition (*smṛti*) and it is defined as a beneficent command. Dharma includes animal sacrifices, and other practices revealed in what they call intuition. Next to them are a series of Nation Vedānta-s, each different. Nation Advaita Vedānta agrees with Nation Pūrva Mīmāṃsā in practice, but holds that ultimately, even "dharma is an evil for one who desires *mokṣa* (freedom)." They hence take an anti-realist view of their own national identity. Nation Dvaita Vedānta rejects the idea that all traditional practices given are correct: animal sacrifices are incompatible with bhakti, which pleases Viṣṇu. But they also believe that each one of us is defined by a distinct character (except for Viṣṇu) and those with an evil character are eternally damned, those with a fantastic character are eternally liberated, and the middling varieties have to experience a purgatory forever. Then there is Nation Viśiṣṭādvaita Vedānta: they technically endorse the Pūrva Mīmāṃsā story about the content of dharma but supplement it with a philosophy of bhakti to Lakṣmī and Viṣṇu, and in practice they abhor violence to animals as incompatible with a devoted life to Lakṣmī and Viṣṇu. They believe that the content of dharma is Deontological (*karma yoga*) but one can practice it as a means of worshiping Lakṣmī and Viṣṇu (*bhakti yoga*). Those who for reasons of birth or station are not able to conceptualize their dharma as a means of worship are encouraged to surrender (*śaranāgati*) to the Lord, which results in the inculcation of virtues such as: *śama* (egalitarianism), *dama* (self-restraint), *tapas* (unconservativism), *śauca* (integrity, purity), *kṣamā* (patience), *arjava* (rectitude), *bhāyabhayasthānaviveka* (prudence), *dayā* (compassion), and *ahiṃsā* (non-harm) (*Vedārthasaṅgraha*, van Buitenen trans. p. 129). These are the inculcation of the virtues of the Lord. Then we find further east the Nation Gaudiya Vaiṣṇavas. They believe that the content of dharma is revealed in the *Bhāgavata Purāṇa*, in addition to other Vaiṣṇava sources, and they define the essence of dharma as *bhāgavata dharma*:

> They do not look upon or utilize their Svadharma [personal dharma] as a means for attaining self-centered objects like power, pleasure and heavenly felicity. Being devoid of desires for worldly pleasures and attainments, they work without attachment, dedicating the fruits of their actions to the Lord. They are calm and pure-minded. They are devoted only to spiritual values, having abandoned all self-centered and egoistic objectives. Through the performance of Svadharma with detachment and dedication, they attain to purity of being.
>
> (*Bhāgavata Purāṇa* III.32.5–6)

Then there is Nation Jainism: they regard "dharma" to be the dispositionality or motion actualized by the free individual who relies not on their action (karma) but virtue. They regard the *deontic* content of dharma as inconsistent with any harm of any other being who is essentially virtuous. On their account, this extends not only to animals but to plants and differing kinds of things. Quite unrelated to them are the Nation Buddhist Theravada. On their account, dharma is a Consequentialist affair geared toward minimizing suffering. Dharmas come in two varieties: some ends are worthy of emulation (such as moral teachings) and others are not, and they justify Mindfulness. Next to them are the Nation Buddhist Mahāyāna, who understand dharma to be a social affair and hence emphasize the importance of minimizing suffering not for the individual but for all.

Not entirely different are two Śaiva nations. One, Nation Kaśmīrī Śaiva, are Consequentialist but also monists: we ought to minimize the suffering and maximize the bliss of our experiences, which include the experience of others on their account. The other is Nation Vaiśeṣika, who like the Buddhists and Jains adopt a teleological approach to dharma, which for them consists in many categories that the virtuous individual appreciates. They idealize their practice as Śiva, the archetype of mindful meditation.

Let us add to this two communities that were created by migration. One is Nation Muhammad: for them, dharma is what Muhammad said (Hadit). Then not too far from them is Nation Jesus: for them, dharma is what Jesus taught. Finally we shall include an anomalous group: Nation Thems. The Thems view of dharma is that it is cashed out in terms of Ten Commandments and their holy book, presented to their ancestor by their God. But whereas the other nations have their own jurisdictions, the Thems are split up and inhabit various cultures where they have two linguistic identities: on the one hand they speak and endorse the language of their host community and its account of dharma, but they also endorse the language and account of dharma of their ancestral language.

The historical explanation for these communities may differ. Some communities arise because of the migration of ideas, and perhaps even people, such as Nation Muhammad, Nation Thems, and Nation Jesus. The other communities are descended from antecedent peoples who may not have differed so sharply on dharma, but as time went on, and the communities became increasingly distinct, each evolved their own theory of dharma as their lives adapted to their geographical environment and the social realities of their part of the world. But, the problem that all such communities face is the same: can these folks understand each other as agreeing or disagreeing on dharma when they, in their respective languages, entertain the sentence-form: "eating meat is not dharma"?

At the outset it is worth noting that on a Yogic account, the answer is a resounding "Yes"! The proposition *EATING MEAT IS NOT DHARMA* will be the common philosophical use of the diverse sentences-forms "eating meat is not dharma" on Subcontinent Dharma and the common philosophical use is to claim that meat eating does not fall into the ideal theory of *THE RIGHT OR THE GOOD*. Speakers of each language hence employ their own sentences to entertain this proposition, which is not the same as the meaning of what they say. Hence, in entertaining the proposition they are not committed to believing it. They may if they wish fall back on the theory of morality encoded in their language to assess this proposition, or they may adopt the posture of the philosopher who is critical of the values that underwrite their community. Moreover, all will be able to understand the historical origins of their culture and language as a result of a philosophical shift and commitment to a particular moral paradigm, and they will recognize the contingency of such a paradigm—history could have been different and the values that underwrite their culture and community could be different. Hence, no one will be inclined to draw any conclusions about values simply from historical precedent that underwrites their community's ethos, and each is free to engage in a philosophical reflection on what values we should endorse. We would correlatively have no reason to define others in terms of their cultural or linguistic origins: we treat each as free to engage in the appropriate philosophical activity that leads to an understanding of common questions.

A representative Hindu account of thought would depict thought as what we converge on while we disagree about thought. Speakers of various cultures on Subcontinent Dharma would converge on a Yogic account of thought as the common philosophical use of their diverse sentences, while they disagree about a thought, such as *EATING MEAT IS NOT DHARMA*.

As G.E. Moore noted, moral questions are open ended, and cannot be solved simply by bringing up definitions (1903). But, contrary to Moore, we know that this is not because it is a fallacy to try to define *THE RIGHT OR THE GOOD*. Anyone can adopt their favored moral theory as the moral semantics of their idiolect, and can thereby define moral terms. This is not a fallacy. But because we are all free to simply define what our words mean, in isolation or as a group, then philosophical questions and ethical questions cannot be reduced to questions of the meaning of our terms, for the meaning of our terms is a result of philosophical decisions. Rather, we have to look to the content of the disagreement to explain what is true when we think critically about ethics. This is the objectivity of thought. True thoughts reveal some object of disagreement that we see from differing perspectives, the false ones do not.

Colonialism, nationalism, and anger

> A taste for one's own sentiment flows also in the learned and arises from a commitment to one's vantage.
>
> When these are traced back to their source, their subtle form can be abandoned.
>
> (Fortunately) future suffering can be prevented.
>
> The *cause* to be abandoned is the tying of seeing with what is seen.
>
> (*Yoga Sūtra* II.9–10, 16–17)

If we adopt linguistic particularism, no speaker of any language shares a thought with linguistic others when they use the same sentence form about dharma. But given the contingencies of linguistic diversity on Subcontinent Dharma, linguistic internalism entails that speakers of differing languages do not mean the same thing by "meat eating is not dharma" and they entertain differing thoughts. But stranger still, in each language the right answers to ethical questions will be linguistically encoded. It will be a matter of the definition of "dharma" in a particular language whether meat eating is dharma, and correlatively it will be a contradiction in terms to deny whatever is encoded linguistically. So one cannot critically engage the moral theory encoded in one's language on this account: to do so would be to transcend the bounds of meaning. But this is strange as the definition of "dharma" is a historical and cultural contingency: not a moral fact.

Given that the linguistic account of thought undermines criticizing one's own moral theory, how would speakers of languages on Subcontinent Dharma view each other? Either they could import everyone else's notions of "dharma" into their own language (so every language would have several different terms, such as "dharma$_{\text{Mīmāṃsā}}$" and "dharma$_{\text{Hadit}}$") or treat their own term, in their language, as the default concept, and regard everyone else as mistaken. Either way, speakers on Subcontinent Dharma would not be able to understand a disagreement about the dharma of meat eating for either way there will not be a single thought that speakers from differing communities could disagree about. In each case, the right answer will be determined analytically by definition, leaving no room for disagreement. But as all people must primarily get along in their own community, each community will be chauvinistic with respect to their governing dharma theory—they will treat it as the presumptive theory and employ it in practical reasoning. But in so far as they use their native definition to understand what is required by dharma they would have to interpret alien cultures accordingly. As we have seen in previous chapters (such as Chapters 2 and 4), interpretation renders aliens mysterious and inexplicable when they depart from one's own norms and beliefs and as a result everyone who adopts a linguistic approach to thought will be inclined to view others as inexplicable, irrational, but also substantively mistaken by virtue of their ethnicity. Plato is to be given credit for clearly seeing the implications of this theory of thought. In the *Republic*, Plato reasons that after intellectuals of a community clearly understand *logos* (reason, thought, but also the meaning of what they say), there can be no room for dissent, and certainly nothing to be learned from outsiders. Plato depicts this as a consequence of the work of the philosopher who through *logos* is able to discern meanings (the forms or essences). But what this is, is how things look from within a culture. From the outside it is pretty clear that "philosophy" is reduced to linguistic anthropology, and criticism is replaced with a participant observation. Far from protecting the role of the philosopher, it reduces philosophy out of the picture. Anyone who wishes to question the values encoded in one's language becomes a threat.

To the extent that each community chauvinistically employs their definition of dharma as a matter of community identity, then any contrary approach will seem like a threat, not merely to them politically but to dharma itself. So speakers of the various languages will be inclined to xenophobia and paranoia. And as the aliens that one fears do not understand what is reasonable or dharma by one's own lights, then it would seem like one is doing them a favor by proselytizing but also by colonizing others so as to impose one's worldview on others. So the linguistic account of thought will hence incline individuals to become imperialists, not only to protect one's own view of reason and dharma, but also as an act of beneficence. It creates both imperialists and missionaries!

What is apparent here is that communities whose account of dharma is nonviolent and perhaps pacifistic will become colonial aggressors. We know for instance that while Jesus taught that we ought to turn the other cheek (Matthew 5:38–42), historically, Christians were among the most enthusiastic of colonial aggressors in the Americas and elsewhere. Today in India, while many Hindus object to meat eating on the grounds that it constitutes a type of violence to non-human animals, like cows, many are motivated to engage in acts of violence against perceived eaters of beef (Khan 2015). The linguistic account of thought explains how there can be this apparent disconnect between the substantive ethical theory, say Christianity or some variety of pro-*ahiṃsā* Hinduism, and imperializing actions. On the one hand, in conflating thought with one's beliefs, it renders the possibility for philosophical disagreement on moral questions unimaginable. So, in so far as others break one's own moral code, they appear to be beyond the pale of reason itself. Second, it creates a sense of paranoia and urgency in depicting aliens as morally deficient and one's own essential morality as imperiled in a public world of those who do not believe. Third, as the linguistic account of thought conflates belief and thought, there is no way to entertain disagreement except as an oppositional attitude toward one's own belief, which is really just one's positive attitude toward a proposition: disagreement is hence made into a personal threat, not a mere logical difference about what truth value to assign a thought. In short, it undermines the philosophical content of theories that people profess, and thereby its rationality and practical consistency. People within these communities who buy the linguistic account of thought will be inclined to endorse politicians who profess their beliefs, which is not the same as leaders who are reasonable in theoretical and practical matters. Ordinary citizens will renounce their own interest as critical thinkers, and act as a mob, driven to protect their community behind leaders who articulate the shared ethos.

The community that will likely get the brunt of the xenophobia are the Thems. The Thems will seem like double agents, as they have allegiances to more than one linguistic orientation with differing encoded theories of dharma. And hence, communities that adopt the linguistic account of thought will give rise to Anti-Thematism.

What is most important for us interested in a representative Hindu account of thought is that any moral outlook can be switched into something narcissistic, xenophobic, and imperialistic merely by endorsing the linguistic account of thought, and this same vice disappear if we adopt a Yogic account of thought. As noted earlier, and certainly worth repeating, yoga is a *prāyaścitta*—it is an expiation that reduces fault, blame, and badness. It turns anything that could seemingly be partial, and imperialistic, into a benign participant in a public world of diversity.

Ancient Jewish communities have existed in India without Anti-Semitism for centuries. This might seem to entail that the cultures of dharma in India are more tolerant and that the cultures of dharma from the *W*est are not. But this is inaccurate. What creates colonialism, imperialism, and mistrust is not any particular account of dharma: it is the linguistic account of thought, and more specifically its conflation of belief and thought with linguistically encoded values. So to the extent that traditional India and Hinduism has been open and tolerant, it has managed this by not endorsing the linguistic account of thought. And as India today slides toward Islamophobia and violent intolerance for minority practices, it slides in this direction because of the tacit adoption of the linguistic account of thought.

Any value system is benign if we treat it as a contribution to philosophical disagreement, and this is what the representative Hindu account of thought does.

But it is a historical reality that the linguistic account of thought comes to us mainly from the *W*est, where it originated in ancient Greece. To be clear, we find this account of thought entertained elsewhere. It seems to be assumed by Confucius in the *Analects* (III, 3 4–7), in his famous *doctrine of the rectification of names*. According to this doctrine, the meaning of our words are values that we ought to adhere to. But China also had Taoism (*Tao Te Ching* 80), which is fiercely critical of taking language as thought seriously. But in the *W*est, there is no historical counterbalance to the idea of *logos*. So with the transmission of the *W*est, we find an uncritical acceptance of its governing theory of thought. As this xenophobic account of thought spreads, it keeps with it beliefs and attitudes of its origins. Hence, Europe remains the archetypal frame of reason as this theory of thought spreads. And the result is that everything it comes in contact with, as it moves toward the east (first Judaism, then Christianity, and later Islam,[2] and finally the various philosophies of South Asia and East Asia) are treated as religions, and hence not philosophy. One of the outcomes of this spreading of the linguistic account of thought is nationalism. What one sees in South Asia—the movement both toward nationalism and irrational oppression of perceived outsiders—are all signs of *W*esternization.

On Subcontinent Dharma, if everyone assumes yoga, they can maintain their cultural differences but yet engage in critical reflection on questions like whether dharma permits meat eating. If meat eating is permitted by dharma, the common philosophical *use* of the various sentences with their different meanings "meat eating is permitted by dharma" will triangulate on meat eating by treating the discipline that holds the thought together as the common platform for triangulation. This allows us to generate an ideal theory of *THE RIGHT OR THE GOOD*. As this is a central concept of philosophy, it would be yoga of philosophy that would constrain our inquiry, and if meat eating is dharma, it would show up in the ideal theory. Understanding whether this is so will involve an amount of philosophical research, but it would not be impossible by virtue of the nature of thought. But if we assume the linguistic account of thought, each nation's theory of dharma will appear beyond reproach and chauvinistically identified as what all within a nation must adhere too. This is nationalism, but also populism, which conflates the right answer to a philosophical question with the common opinion of individuals defined by a national identity.

Hindu nationalism (cf. Sharma 2011), a contemporary phenomenon, would be unintelligible without the linguistic account of thought and its genealogy. The genealogy allows Europe to be an archetypal frame which then renders things Indian (Hindu) a religion. Hindus by virtue of endorsing the linguistic account of thought from Europe would thereby be committed to a comprehensive view of Hinduism as something culturally encoded. Hindus will then confabulate and demand that their dharma be understood as the *ancient dharma*, and that Hinduism itself is a religion stretching back in an unbroken continuity to antiquity, save for the interruption of foreigners. It is a most *deep version* of colonization by the

*W*est. There are other versions of nationalism that are also unintelligible without the linguistic account of thought. The primary example is the bifurcation of a common north Indian language into Urdu (a Muslim language) and Hindi (a Hindu language), a phenomenon chronicled in the book *One Language: Two Scripts* (King 1994).

A seemingly alternate route to defending Hindu nationalism that does not involve identifying a Hindu state with Hinduism is to claim as V.D. Savarkar (Accessed 2017) has that "Hindu," or some cognate, such as "Sindu," is an ancient device that Hindus have used to refer to themselves, that it is false that it is a *W*estern imposition on India, and hence Hindus have always been a people or nation from the earliest times. This argument also relies heavily on linguistic internalism or linguistic particularism, and more generally a linguistic approach to thought, for it assumes that to translate and understand how Hindus have thought about themselves, you have to either endorse their linguistically encoded worldview (linguistic particularism) or have a linguistically encoded worldview that is isomorphic in this way (linguistic internalism). Take away the linguistic account of thought and one no longer can motivate either view about content, but then the supposed linguistic history of Hindu self-reference becomes indeterminate in significance. And rightly so: that there is a history of talking about unicorns does not mean there are unicorns, even if everyone believes it.

The phenomena of nationalism, chauvinism, and xenophobia are relatively new to India. In the *W*est there are jurisdictions that claim to be secular (like France and much of Europe) that object to Muslim coverings for women (*hijabs, burkinis*), or Sikh turbans, but are quite alright with discrete displays of religious sentiment. This will certainly favor people whose religious observances do not involve headgear, which in Europe will include Christians, and exclude Jews, Muslims, and Sikhs. In Quebec, Canada, we find the same obsession with religious identity and concern about Muslim identity in particular—though a prominently displayed crucifix behind the speaker's chair in the National Assembly is protected and widespread sentiment has kept crucifixes hanging in hospitals (Peritz 2017).

In the U.S., the lines between the Judeo-Christian ancestral religion of many Americans and the operation of public institutions are blurred ("Official Prayer, Religious Displays and Ceremonial Religion" Accessed 2017). What is peculiar here is not that Judeo-Christian prayers, ideas, or symbols are invoked to solemnize and legitimize American institutions, but they are done so to the exclusion of contrary religions fulfilling the same role (NBC 2007).

"Alt-right" is a term that has been coined for nationalist, populist ideologies that reject political conservativism in the U.S. and elsewhere. These groups share xenophobic views (now especially against Muslims) that echo previous Anti-Semitic positions of Europe. Scholars of India cringe in seeing many of these same elements in contemporary Indian politics. What these positions share is a commitment to a xenophobic platform that is immune to the evidence (such as, there are terrorists who are not Muslim, and most Muslims are not terrorists). We have an explanation for this: what characterizes these far right positions is not their culture, or even ideology, but rather the conflation of belief with thought, along with a chauvinism about their own culture. This leads to the demonization of aliens (outside of the culture of the chauvinist) and the concomitant commitment to beliefs about the chauvinist's culture—beliefs that are true by virtue of the attitude of the believer, but beliefs that also reveal to the chauvinist the precarity of his position: if it is true merely by virtue of the chauvinist's attitude, then the chauvinist will resist and oppose people who do not share his views. They will hence demonize scholars as liberal elites or biased interlopers. There is a fragility in this paradigm, and it goes back to the linguistic account of thought. By way of this paradigm, the far right, anti-research conservative conflates his idiolect with the content of thought.

If we were to adopt a Yogic account of thought, people would be free to inhabit a pluralistic society with multiple and competing philosophies and citizens would be free to use those resources they are raised with to engage critically in philosophical inquiry. So Christians could rely upon their resources to critically investigate their own background philosophies, for instance, and no answer would be understood as settled as a matter of definition. In a secular India or U.S., citizens would be free to make use of ideas drawn from multiple sources, some Christian, some Jewish, some Muslim, some Hindu, some Buddhist, some Jain, some Sikh, to engage in public participation. No person's idiolect would be conflated with the content of thought, and thought would rather be investigated by disciplinary research. Far right advocates often paint such scholarship as an elitist perspective, and those who operate within the paradigm of the *W*est are powerless to respond to this criticism for according to this paradigm, that is correct. But a Yogic approach shows that this is a mistake: those who engage in yoga, disciplined research, are not members of an elite perspective. They transcend perspective by tracking objects of research from differing perspectives. And when they come to a conclusion, it is not because of their perspective or a final perspective, but as a synopsis of what we can disagree about, which is objectivity (YS IV.15). Those who inhabit *W*estern far right, anti-research paradigms often claim that the consequence of such research is that their views are no longer welcome and their freedom of speech is hindered. But this is a bit of a confusion: the findings of research that summarize what we can disagree about take into account dissenting perspectives. The critics of research do not see things this way because they confuse thought with belief. They think that free speech is the freedom to express their beliefs. Society has no use for that. Free speech serves to protect thinking, and that is not the same as the freedom to say whatever one wants.

Before closing this section it is worth noting the crippling implication of belief. As beliefs (I believe that it is raining outside) are true by virtue of the attitude of the believer and not by virtue of the embedded thought (it is raining outside) believers tend to be immune to the evidence. So while believers will have the company of fellow believers—those who share a linguistic culture that they treat as the content of thought—they will be handicapped in addressing pressing problems that call for hitherto unknown solutions. Research, professors, international scholarship and universities will seem like a threat—"liberal elites." But certainly a Yogic account of thought would not only be preferable, it is also the representative Hindu account of thought: it is the account of thought that we would have to converge on while we disagree about thought. So if you want to disagree with others, you have to endorse it!

It is worth noting how the *opposite* of the representative Hindu account of thought cuts us off from history. Because the linguistic account of thought treats the meaning of what you say as your thought, it treats the historical contingency of your culture and language as the *sui generis* content of thought, and as a result deprives you the opportunity to critically examine the origins of these values. Correlatively, it leads to the identification of people with the theories and values encoded in their language and culture. Worse, because everyone will regard their own language as providing the *sui generis* content of thought, the identification of others in terms of the historical values encoded in their culture and language will be mediated through the interpretive biases of the native speaker using their language as the frame of thought. So not only will others be defined by their contingencies—a fault Patañjali calls "*asmitā*," or 'selfishness' (YS II.6)—it defines them in terms of everything that is inexplicable by the interpretive resources of the chauvinist. This is how racism is sustained in our world. All the while the linguistic account of thought renders this reasonable as it identifies people with their language and culture. It is, however, a mistake for we can use our language and culture, via the representative Hindu account of thought, to engage in critical debate, even about the values encoded in our own language and culture.

In exploring Subcontinent Dharma, we have come back to the *W*est: the linguistic account of thought with a Eurocentric backdrop. The problems on Subcontinent Dharma arise from the linguistic account of thought—the Eurocentric origins of this account of thought is not a problem in and of itself, but given that the account treats the meaning of what we say as the *sui generis* content of thought, Eurocentric linguistically encoded assumptions are treated by this account of thought as the *sui generis* content of thought—as though there is not an entirely political history to the formation and development of the encoded assumptions. The farther off an alien culture is from its Eurocentric values, the less it will be able to intellectually understand the alien, and the more it will be inclined to treat the alien as the appropriate object of social scientific research, while treating the native Eurocentric commitments as philosophical and not in need of social scientific inquiry. As we see on Subcontinent Dharma, this yields nothing but acrimony and misunderstanding. All of this can be avoided by adopting Yoga.

Finally we come to some appreciation of why the dominant *W*estern tradition has emphasized the *right* perspective as central to knowing (as noted first in Chapter 2). If thought is the meaning of what we say, then the possibilities of truth are constrained by the right perspective and the right perspective is informed by *logos*: our language, and treating it as the content of our beliefs and thought. But as each linguistic orientation is historically arbitrary—a function not of some *a priori* insight but prior sociological phenomena that give rise to languages with their semantics—the search for the right perspective is futile, but it is also undermotivated if true thoughts track the objective. A representative Hindu account of thought will help us with that.

Objections

In this section I will consider four objections.

Doniger, anti-research, anti-higher learning

Wendy Doniger, a famous Indologist I cited earlier, has claimed that Hinduism is a series of shifting overlapping circles (Doniger 1991). Such an account, like Kant's notion of religion as what overlaps on a core center of morality, requires interpretation: one has to define the circles in such a way so as to allow only those to count that overlap and use this definition in an explanation of the phenomenon! Doniger is more famous in recent times for her controversial book, *The Hindus: An Alternative History* (Doniger 2010). It is a historian's book, in which she makes the claim that: "Placing the *Rāmāyaṇa* [one of the stories of Viṣṇu's incarnation as Rāma with Lakṣmī as Sītā] in its historical contexts demonstrates that it is a work of fiction, created by human authors, who lived at various times" (Doniger 2010: 662). This hit a nerve. Many Hindus were upset at this, and argued that the book violated a colonial era rule (295A of the Indian Penal Code) that prohibits hurting religious sentiment. The rule stipulates that one is guilty of a crime for the "deliberate and malicious intention of outraging the religious feelings of any class," and many will dispute that Doniger had such an intention. The controversy climaxed with Penguin, the Indian publisher, being forced to withdraw the book from publication over fear of threat and violence. Doniger publically defended Penguin who she said tried to defend the book in court and that the real problem is the penal code law.

Many Hindus are suspicious of academics because they do not account for Hinduism the way Hindus see it, but from an outside perspective that is skeptical. It seems that academics pass off their outsider's bias as "learning" and this is offensive. The appropriate response it would seem is for Hindus to engage in a scholarship from the inside, and this involves assuming some common inside Hindu perspective. But then, answers to such questions about Hindus will be settled by the cultural resources of Hindus, like the meaning of their words. But this opens the door to taking a Hindu nationalism seriously, where answers to questions about the significance of Hindu ideas is determined not from the outside, but from a unified inside comprehensive perspective—that is culturally and linguistically encoded.

I want to clarify that I think that much of what is written about Hinduism (to date) is nonsense but our investigations to this point do not legitimize the idea of a privileged insider perspective. One problem is that Orthodox Indologists—and most people—employ interpretation in the study of India, and not explication: they hence assume their naïve views about morals or controversial claims as a theoretical frame and Indian and Hindu ideas have to fit the mold. There are some obviously offensive examples of this, such as Paul Courtright's interpretation of Gaṇeśa in terms of psychoanalytic theory as the frustrated Oedipal son who wants his father (Śiva) dead and to have sex with his mother (Pārvatī) (Courtright 1985).

Courtright acknowledges now that he overstepped the bounds of interpretation (2003). The problem is, however, that there are no acceptable bounds of interpretation: interpretation is congenitally irrational (Chapter 4). In the case of the reaction to Doniger, it seems that there are two sides to a Yogic response to the controversy that followed her book: one brings to light disciplinary constraints on research, the other criticizes "hurt feelings."

In our account of yoga, thinking is an exercise in disciplinarity and what it aims at is the content that explains the possibilities of disagreement: true thoughts reveal such content. A genuinely true thought is hence a nuanced thing, which does not reject controversy but rather reveals it. So if we have absolute claims being touted by scholars, as though the matter is beyond being revisited, or as though the content itself is indubitable, we should have grounds for pause to wonder if what we are getting is the truth, or something else: interpretation. But truth is not absolute for a different reason: it is always relativized to a discipline as propositions are relativized to disciplines. So there is not a single truth about a topic, but many relative to distinct disciplines. So while perhaps history the discipline cannot reveal Rāma as an explanation of historical disagreement about what happened (and so it may be false that Rāma existed as a historical human), we need only remember: our explorations in Chapter 3, where we saw that many Hindu deities function as moral abstractions and regulative ideals of practice (in Bhakti) and hence we have philosophical reasons to countenance their objectivity (as what we can philosophically disagree about); and Chapter 4 when we looked to reason, we found that the gods are what we discover when we are open to disagreement about reasons. The gods here are indispensable in explaining philosophical disagreement (they, unlike the Asuras, know how to disagree) and hence are revealed to us by philosophical truth (which like all truth reveals the content of disagreement). Moreover, most Hindu deities, including Rāma, are not creator gods, and hence Hindus should not be fussed about what historians have to say about them—as they do not play a role in creation, we should not expect that they existed in the past. Theists, who are Virtue Ethicists, who take a paradigm powerful agent(s), God(s), to be the source of right action, take God(s) to be an actual good thing(s): they seem to have to square their Gods with history, as the Theist's God(s) seems to entail its own historicity as an actual good agent, and not a mere procedural abstraction of right action. Whatever your moral theory, it seems that keeping in mind the disciplinary foundation of truth gives us reason to deflate the pronouncements of historians: they are not talking about everything, just history, so we should not treat it like it is the final word on everything. It is less important than it might first appear.

Second, the very matter of "hurt religious sentiments" depends upon the linguistic account of thought that conflates thought and belief: when others reject our beliefs, they reject our positive attitude toward a thought. In essence, if you confuse belief and thought, disagreement seems like personal marginalization, as it marginalizes your attitude. The Hindu nationalist sensitivity to having feelings hurt is nothing peculiar about Indians or Hindus: get rid of the linguistic account of thought as the uncontroversial, default account, and no one has to conflate their belief with their thought, and then no one has to have their feelings hurt simply because others disagree—and there will also be no real grounds for the nationalism too. But as the linguistic account of thought as something beyond controversy is a product of the *W*est, this hypersensitivity to have one's sentiments hurt is a sign of *W*esternization.

As a nuanced response, there is this objection: offensive scholarship on Hinduism arises not merely because people exceed their disciplinary expertise: it arises out of a lack of respect for the material being studied.

Given our previous investigation into a Yogic approach to thought, we are in a position to observe that the problem with so much scholarship on India is that there is a lack of symmetry between the topics explored, and the disciplinary interests of scholars. This is most blaring in the case of philosophy, where Indian thought and ideas that are native to philosophy are studied by historians, linguists, and social scientists. The problem is that since thought itself is *defined* by a disciplinary interest, scholars have to be careful to study texts as though authors of such texts are peers, working in the same discipline. The discipline employed in research by a scholar doing fitting research is the same discipline that structures the thoughts that the scholar explores: this procedural commonality allows for the vantage of the researcher and their historical subjects to triangulate on common topics and thoughts, which they are free to disagree about. Hence, a philologist studying India who follows this rule would study Indian philologists as peers (as an example, consider Rao 2015). Historians would do well to study the work of Indian historians. Literary scholars would do well to study literature or perhaps native literary theorists. When we fail to employ this disciplinary parity (when for instance we find linguists and historians publishing on Indian philosophy) there is an absence of collegiality that would normally characterize serious scholarship and the result is an uncollegial atmosphere that characterizes Orthodox Indology. This strikes a lot of Hindus as offensive and imperious. Moreover, the common Hindu perception that most Indologists and academic scholars of Hinduism are know-it-alls out of touch with the reality of Hinduism is understandable and partly true. The error is not merely a violation of manners, as though it is merely rude that a philologist studying an Indian philosopher does not treat her as a colleague because she does not regard the Indian philosopher as a colleague in philology: it consists in a violation of disciplinary boundaries, which is masked by drawing inferences about a discipline such as philosophy written by an Indian, by way of what seems true from research in some extraneous discipline, such as philology or Sanskrit studies. This violation is interpretation, explanation by way of what one takes to be true. That the study of Sanskrit, a language, is the primary tool of Orthodox Indology seems to settle the question: it is the *W*est and its linguistic account of thought that licenses the prioritization of the study of Sanskrit and philology, not to mention interpretation. The resulting violation of collegiality and disciplinary boundaries is *W*estern imperialism. We come to this diagnosis not by rejecting the academic study of India and Hinduism, but by a rigorous defense of thought as discipline relative. An inside perspective does not reveal the truth to us about these matters: it is yoga, discipline, that gets us there, and that vitiates against interpretation *and* imperialism. An atmosphere that was more attentive to disciplinary difference would help defuse the notion that academia is a monolithic outside perspective that demeans some common insider Hindu perspective. It is not a perspective: it is a bunch of disciplines.

Why not relativism?

Given Subcontinent Dharma, and the linguistic account of thought, why could not people merely assume relativism instead of chauvinism and xenophobia? This seems like a reasonable response: if the meaning of "dharma" is culturally encoded, then it seems that the appropriate response to cultural variations on dharma is moral relativism: each culture defines what dharma is and what dharma is not and there is no fact of the matter above this.

What is not usually observed is that this is not really an option given the linguistic account of thought. In order for moral relativism to get off the ground, we need a common proposition about values, such as "meat eating is wrong," across cultures, whose truth conditions change depending upon local custom and expectations. But the linguistic account of thought denies this on Subcontinent Dharma: each culture operates with its own proposition that sounds like other propositions about dharma in other languages. But when we move to the representative Hindu account of thought, we have a common proposition that everyone can endorse across cultures, but the same considerations that lead us here undermine the idea that the truth of the proposition is determined by local values, for these are deflated in order to appreciate the common proposition. Moral relativism relies upon imagining a very strange option: that the real moral semantics across cultures is really something like an Expressivism, but the cultural forces constrain what one can claim in each locale (Dreier 1990). It is to dream imperialism into existence. This is to avoid the challenge of diversity as present on Subcontinent Dharma—and the challenge of Hinduism and India.

Is not Subcontinent Dharma about our intuitions?

In Chapter 4, I noted that one of the ways that the *W*est presents itself in philosophy is by the gratuitous invocation of cases, with the sole purpose of eliciting intuitions. The problem with this practice is that the intuitions are beliefs, and reflecting on cases to determine one's beliefs is not philosophy: it is introspective psychology. The Moral Twin Earth thought experiment is an example: Horgan and Timmons present us a case, and we are supposed to identify the solution on the basis of what seems intuitive. But is not Subcontinent Dharma more of the same?

There is an important distinction here. While Subcontinent Dharma is a case, and a thought experiment, it is not designed to elicit our intuitions but to track the logical entailments of competing philosophical proposals about thought. Entailment, as we learned in Chapter 4, has to do with reason, and this is quite the opposite of belief.

The criticism of the West is unfounded

In Chapter 4, I examined the suggestion that what we find in India and Hinduism is not philosophy but theology and that theology is crucially tied to tradition, in a way that philosophy is not. Accordingly philosophy appears to be uniquely western while what we find in India is religion or theology, which is tied to a tradition. But on Subcontinent Dharma, we find the opposite: the *W*est is the paradigm that ties us to tradition, and constitutes a reactionary conservativism. It is a paradigm where tradition (in so far as it is linguistically encoded) and thinking are collapsed. The representative Hindu approach to thought in contrast celebrates the ideals of yoga, namely the Lord: unconservativism and self-governance. Each of us is free to either endorse or criticize the outlook of our background as we understand the content of thought as what transcends our perspective. The *W*est's inability to disentangle belief from thought renders it a force of imperialism: interpretation is its default mode of understanding, and disagreement is hence unintelligible. But then it seems like all western philosophy is imperialistic. But this is absurd.[3]

Nothing in our analysis commits us to viewing western philosophy as *ipso facto* imperialistic. As noted in Chapter 4, whether a perspective is imperious or godly has to do with whether it is tolerant of disagreement, and whether a perspective can tolerate disagreement has nothing to do with the perspective but the background account of thought. So Indian perspectives can be imperious by the adoption of a linguistic account of thought, and western perspectives can be accommodating if they adopt a yogic approach to thought. Philosophy as a yoga, a discipline, is a *prāyaścitta*—an expiation—that turns the bias of any perspective into a contribution to our understanding of objectivity. So western philosophy by definition is non-imperialistic as it is philosophy. *W*estern philosophy is the very strange leftover, and even a contradiction in terms. In Yoga we find the basis for a criticism of all prejudice that tries to define us by way of our background. Not only does it lead us to renounce xenophobia and conservativism while recognizing diversity and disagreement as constitutive of thinking, it leads us to disentangle thinking from the natural characteristics of persons. Your biology, your culture, do not define you. You as a person have an interest in transcending these limitations by disciplined thinking.

Tradition and thinking

In a very influential book, *Ethics and the Limits of Philosophy*, Bernard Williams argues that hyper-traditional societies provide their members a means of participation in a moral landscape and moral knowledge, and this moral knowledge is an appreciation of how to correctly participate in the culture's linguistic culture. When people leave this culture and enter a multicultural world, they come to doubt morality as such for they lose the tools they had to engage in moral reflection. While he rails against the linguistic account of thought (Williams 1985: 127), this story requires it. We saw this on Subcontinent Dharma. It is also simply implausible, for thought—unlike belief—is what we can disagree to, and a linguistic approach to thought renders disagreement on thought, when we understand what we mean, a contradiction in terms. A Yogic account of thought in contrast depicts thought as what we converge on while we are free to disagree. It is hence a representative Hindu account of thought, for it is what Hindus would converge on while they disagree about thought and particular thoughts. It teaches us something surprising: we only begin to think clearly when we are willing to leave the perspective of our background as a *frame of thought*, and engage in the activity of thinking. Thinking, according to this account, is an engagement with the public world from differing perspectives united in a common practice—the common practice that we can undertake from differing perspectives is the discipline, or yoga. But thinking so understood does not require linguistic competence: any being who continuously tracks objects from differing perspectives while engaging in the same practice thinks. This is to deflate the importance of symbols and semiotic devices in service of an inquiry: yoga. So animals certainly think as they can and do track objects while engaging in the discipline of observation, but so too do macroscopic objects in orbit, such as the Moon, the Earth, and other celestial objects, who track objects they rotate around. Given the Yogic account of thought, it is unsurprising that Hindus are inclined to attribute thoughtfulness to beings of diverse biological constitution, such as planets and non-human animals. The obstacle to this liberal approach to thinking is the linguistic account of thought. One reason to endorse it is that it apparently makes humans special: we as linguistic beings are the only ones who think accordingly. But, as we have seen repeatedly, the linguistic account of thought causes problems for humans. It undermines our ability to get along with each other in a public world and that is because it is irrational. It confuses thought and belief. Those who endorse it expect the Earth or non-human animals to have beliefs in order to think, but this is irrelevant to thinking. This suggests the following: that the interests we have as thinkers are not reducible to linguistic competence, but to our interests in being unconservative and self-governing in a public world.

Notes

1 Husserl was famous for a phenomenological reduction that is at times described as suspending belief and this might sound a bit like the yogic alternative (Husserl 2001). Yet Husserl's project was quite firmly within this tradition of *W*estern theory as it avoids prying apart the meaningfulness of what you say from the propositions you inspect.
2 See Chapter 2, note 2.
3 I would like to thank the series editors, Chad Meister and Charles Taliaferro, for sharing this objection with me.

References

Boyd, Richard N. 1988. "How to Be a Moral Realist." In *Essays on Moral Realism*, edited by G. Sayre-McCord, 181–228. Ithaca, NY: Cornell University Press.

Cappelen, Herman, and Ernest Lepore. 2005. *Insensitive Semantics: A Defense of Semantic Minimalism and Speech Act Pluralism*. Malden, MA: Blackwell.

Courtright, P.B. 1985. *Ganesa: Lord of Obstacles, Lord of Beginnings*. Oxford: Oxford University Press.

Courtright, P.B. 2003. "Silenced for Hinting at an Indian Oedipus." *Times of Higher Education*. www.timeshighereducation.com/features/silenced-for-hinting-at-an-indian-oedipus/181462.article.

Derrida, Jacques. 1981. "Plato's Pharmacy." In *Dissemination*, 61–172. Chicago, IL: University of Chicago Press.

Doniger, Wendy. 1991. "Hinduism by Any Other Name." *Wilson Quarterly* 15: 35–41.

Doniger, Wendy. 2010. *The Hindus: An Alternative History*. Oxford: Oxford University Press.

Dreier, James. 1990. "Internalism and Speaker Relativism." *Ethics* 101: 6–26.

Gadamer, Hans-Georg. 1990. "Culture and the Word." In *Hermeneutics and the Poetic Motion Translation Perspectives V*, edited by Dennis J. Schmidt, 11–24. Binghamton, NY: State University of New York Press.

Gadamer, Hans-Georg. 1996. *Truth and Method*. Translated by Joel Weinsheimer and Donald G. Marshall. 2nd rev. English language edn. New York: Continuum. J.C.B. Mohr (Paul Seibeck). Originally published Tubingen.

Hare, Richard M. 1952. *The Language of Morals*. Oxford: Clarendon Press.

Henning, Tim. 2011. "Moral Realism and Two-Dimensional Semantics." *Ethics* 121, no. 4: 717–748.

Horgan, Terence, and Mark Timmons. 1991. "New Wave Moral Realism Meets Moral Twin Earth." *Journal of Philosophical Research* 16: 447–465.

Horgan, Terence, and Mark Timmons. 1992a. "Troubles for New Wave Moral Semantics: The Open Question Argument Revived." *Philosophical Papers* 21, no. 3: 153–175.

Horgan, Terence, and Mark Timmons. 1992b. "Troubles on Moral Twin Earth: Moral Queerness Revived." *Synthese* 92, no. 2: 221–260.

Horgan, Terence, and Mark Timmons. 1996. "From Moral Realism to Moral Relativism in One Easy Step." *Critica* 28, no. 83: 3–39.

Horgan, Terence, and Mark Timmons. 2000. "Copping Out on Moral Twin Earth." *Synthese* 124, no. 1: 139–152.

Husserl, Edmund. 2001. *Logical Investigations*. Translated by J.N. Findlay. International Library of Philosophy. 2nd edn. 2 vols. London; New York: Routledge.

Khalidi, Muhammad Ali. 2005. *Medieval Islamic Philosophical Writings*. 4. Vol. 81. Cambridge: Cambridge University Press.

Khan, Sophie. 2015. "Hindu Nationalist Violence Increasing in India." *Berkeley Political Review*. https://bpr.berkeley.edu/2015/11/18/hindu-nationalist-violence-increasing-in-india/.

King, C.R. 1994. *One Language, Two Scripts: The Hindi Movement in Nineteenth Century North India*. Oxford: Oxford University Press.

Lance, Mark Norris, and John O'Leary-Hawthorne. 1997. *The Grammar of Meaning: Normativity and Semantic Discourse*. Cambridge Studies in Philosophy. Cambridge; New York: Cambridge University Press.

McDowell, John. 1998a. "Aesthetic Value, Objectivity, and the Fabric of the World." In *Mind, Value, and Reality*, 112–130. Cambridge, MA: Harvard University Press.

McDowell, John. 1998b. "Virtue and Reason." In *Mind, Value, and Reality*, 50–73. Cambridge, MA: Harvard University Press.

Moore, George Edward. 1903. *Principia Ethica*. Cambridge: Cambridge University Press.

NBC. 2007. "Hindu Prayer in Senate Disrupted." *NBC News*, December 7, 2007. www.nbcnews.com/id/19729245/ns/politics/t/hindu-prayer-senate-disrupted.

"Official Prayer, Religious Displays and Ceremonial Religion." *Americans United for the Separation of Church and State*. www.au.org/issues/official-prayer-religious-displays-ceremonial-religion, Accessed 2017.

Patañjali. 2008. *Patañjali's Yoga Sūtra: Translation, Commentary and Introduction by Shyam Ranganathan*. Black Classics. Delhi: Penguin Black Classics.

Peritz, Ingrid. 2017. "Debate over Wearing Religious Symbols Returns to Quebec One Week after Mosque Shooting "*The Globe and Mail*, February 7. www.theglobeandmail.com/news/national/debate-over-wearing-religious-symbols-returns-to-quebec-one-week-after-mosque-shooting/article33948284/.

Putnam, Hilary. 1975. "The Meaning of Meaning." *Minnesota Studies in the Philosophy of Science* 7: 131–193. Quine, Willard Van Orman. 1960. *Word and Object*. Cambridge, MA: MIT Press.

Rāmānuja. 1956. *Rāmānuja's Vedārthasaṅgraha*. Translated by J.A.B. van Buitenen. Pune: Deccan College Postgraduate and Research Institute.

Ranganathan, Shyam. 2007. *Translating Evaluative Discourse: The Semantics of Thick and Thin Concepts*. Ph.D. Dissertation, York University, Department of Philosophy. www.collectionscanada.gc.ca/obj/thesescanada/vol2/002/NR68573.PDF.

Ranganathan, Shyam. 2011. "An Archimedean Point for Philosophy." *Metaphilosophy* 42, no. 4: 479–519.

Rao, Ajay K. 2015. *Re-figuring the Rāmāyaṇa as Theology*. Routledge Hindu Studies Series. Abingdon: Routledge.

Russell, Bertrand. 1938. *Principles of Mathematics*. New York: W.W. Norton & Company.

Savarkar, Vinayak Damodar. Accessed 2017. *Essentials of Hindutva*. http://savarkar.org/en/encyc/2017/5/23/2_12_12_04_essentials_of_hindutva.v001.pdf_1.pdf.

Sharma, Jyotirmaya. 2011. *Hindutva: Exploring the Idea of Hindu Nationalism*. Delhi: Penguin.

Srimad Bhagavatam (Bhagavata Purana). 1981. Translated by Tapasyananda. Madras: Sri Ramakrishna Math.

van Roojen, Mark. 2006. "Knowing Enough to Disagree: A New Response to the Moral Twin Earth Argument." In *Oxford Studies in Metaethics*, edited by Russ Shafer-Landau, 161–193. Oxford: Oxford University Press.

Wedgwood, Ralph. 2006. "Meaning of 'Ought'." In *Oxford Studies in Metaethics*, edited by Russ Shafer-Landau, 127–160. Oxford: Oxford University Press.

Williams, Bernard. 1985. *Ethics and the Limits of Philosophy*. Cambridge, MA: Harvard University Press.

Wittgenstein, Ludwig. 1958. *Philosophical Investigations*. Translated by G.E.M. Anscombe. 2nd edn. New York: Macmillan.

6 *Jñāna*

Pramāṇa, satya and *citta* (not: justified, true, belief)

Introduction

Indian philosophy presents us with several differing terms to talk about knowledge. They range from the theoretical to the factive: such as, "*śāstra*," "*vidyā*," "*veda*," "*jñāna*," "*vijñāna*," "*prajñā*." "*Jñāna*" is the term that Indian philosophers use for factive states, and *prajñā* is a virtual synonym. In this chapter, I will identify the representative Hindu account of knowledge. This is what Hindus (and all of us) can converge on while they disagree philosophically about knowledge. It would hence tell us something objective about knowledge for objectivity is what we converge on while we disagree. This is not an account of what Hindus believe about knowledge for several reasons. One reason we shall see is that a Hindu representative account of knowledge would itself be an example of knowledge, and knowledge is not a kind of belief for reasons we have examined in the previous chapter. Beliefs are duds in the world of reason, but knowledge is not a dud. Second, it depicts what Hindus (and all of us) converge on while they disagree about knowledge and hence this convergence is not the same as any belief they could endorse.

I will explore this topic by a preliminary review of a classic kind of problem in epistemology—Gettier problems—and its ancestral relationship to Plato's account of knowledge. In the course of exploring this issue, we are in a position to observe that the concept of knowledge is *THE TRUE OR THE JUSTIFIED*, as theories of knowledge disagree about truth and justification. I will then move to an account of a representative Hindu account of knowledge by way of an account of four possible epistemic theories. The Indian *Mahāvrata*-s (Great Vows) capture this objectivity of knowledge. We will also revisit what we acknowledged in the previous chapter: that thought requires disciplinarity in order for it to be objective, and that knowledge as a thoughtful activity is hence yogic, which is to say disciplinary. This nicely squares with our epistemic practices that prize higher education, deflate, and criticize the easy conflation of belief, tradition, and knowledge. This account makes room for research. However, knowledge as revealed by clear disciplinary thinking is objective, which is to say what we converge on while we disagree—a disagreement made possible by a common practice, which is the discipline. Such an account of knowledge not only points us in the direction of research, but it also shows that knowledge is not the peculiar preserve of humans.

Belief and the objectivity of knowledge

In this section, I want to outline standard problems in contemporary epistemology and how they connect with our investigation into a representative Hindu account of knowledge. Next, I will consider the question of the objectivity of knowledge. In the third main section, we will talk about Indian philosophical resources that model this objectivity and hence count as a representative Hindu account of knowledge.

Belief and Gettier problems

In what has come to be counted as a classic paper of epistemology, Edmund Gettier derived from Plato three conditions of knowledge. Knowledge is a belief *with* justification *and* which is true (hereafter: JTB). Gettier (1963) further identified counterexamples that have come to be known as Gettier counterexamples. They have a standard form: they identify a belief that is justified and true, but somehow fails to count as what we would intuitively call knowledge. For instance, you hear that Daśaratha's son is going to be the king. You come to believe this as it was proclaimed in the court that Daśaratha has decided to retire and pass along the crown to his son. So your belief here is justified. And, it turns out that, Daśaratha's son is going to be king. So your belief is true. But it is not Rāma (the eldest son) who is to be crowned king (the son you assumed would be king), but his younger son, Bharata. Did you know in this case that Daśaratha's son was going to be king?

The scenario in question arises in the *Rāmāyaṇa* due to the temporary mental illness of Kaikeyī—Daśaratha's wife, Rāma's stepmother, and Bharata's birth mother. The king promised Kaikeyī two boons, and she decides to use them on this occasion to get Bharata crowned and Rāma exiled to the forest. The king cannot bring himself to execute the boon, but Rāma decides to voluntarily exile himself to the forest to save his father from being in a dilemma of reneging on his promise to Rāma to make him king. Rāma's decision served to render the king's utterances all true—his son would be made king, and moreover that Kaikeyī's boons were good. Philosophers in the *W*estern tradition, certainly around the time that Gettier was writing, agreed with Gettier that in cases such as this, it seems that you did not know even though your justified, true belief fits the criteria of knowledge. (All of Rāma's actions in contrast seemed to be geared to saving you from having to agree with these *W*estern philosophers.) Decades later, Stephen Stich and philosophers, inspired to take an empirical approach to such questions, surveyed university students in the U.S., and discovered that students of South Asian heritage were less likely to have Gettier's intuitions (Weinberg, Nichols, and Stich 2001: 444). I myself must confess to have never had very strong intuitions of the sort that Gettier relies on.

Gettier derives his account of knowledge from Plato, as noted, who through the character of Socrates makes a case that knowledge cannot merely be a judgment that is true, or one that is justified. Rather, it has to be not only one that is true, but also one that comes with a *logos* (*Theaetetus* 208c)—a verbal account. Justification, in Gettier's case, is the modern retelling of this discursive requirement from Plato. Many argued after Gettier's paper that the trouble with the scenario is that it assumes that justification has to be verbal or somehow accessible to the agent. Many suggested that we ought to think of justification as a causal relationship between what we know and the knower, or as a reliable connection between the two. The former approach came to be known as *internalism*, and the latter *externalism*. Early on, internalism was identified with discursive accounts of justification that were accessible to the agent. Externalism was associated with causal processes of reliable belief forming mechanisms. The thought was that if we could pin justification on this causal relationship, our beliefs would always be formed in relationship to what is true, so that we would have less grounds for being surprised when there is a drift from our beliefs and the facts.

Over the years, the distinction has become less clear in some ways. The internal/external distinction depends upon some boundary between the knowing agent and the external world, but then what counts as internal or external hinges on how one draws these boundaries. For instance, if we think of justification as depending upon the truth or propriety of rules of knowing, then a theory of justification that appeals to epistemic principles can be externalist if the truth of such principles is external to the agent, or internalist if the plausibility of the principles rests on the agent's grasp of the principles (Littlejohn 2012). Another problem is that the distinction does not appear to solve Gettier problems. Gettier problems arise from the apparent independence of the truth and justification conditions. If what makes our belief true is not connected to why we are justified in believing it, Gettier problems seem ineliminable (Zagzebski 1994). One way to solve such problems is to come to terms with this independence and accept that our justification may be misguided—fallible—and yet fulfill the justification requirement for knowledge (Hetherington 2012). Another way to apparently solve it is to try to perfect one's account of justification that avoids such problems—a task that may be impossible if the truth and justification conditions are separate. Yet in light of these two options, it is not surprising that the bulk of what one finds under "epistemology" in a database resource such as PhilPapers (Accessed spring 2017) is on justification.

Another possible means of avoiding these issues is to follow Timothy Williamson who draws a distinction between knowing and believing—a distinction that is parallel to our distinction between thought and belief that we explored in the previous chapter. According to Williamson, belief is a kind of "botched knowledge"—"belief aims at knowledge (not just truth)" (Williamson 2002: 47). Knowledge on the other hand is a factive mental state (a mental state that is true):

> A propositional attitude is factive if and only if, necessarily, one has it only to truths. Examples include the attitudes of seeing, knowing, and remembering. Not all factive attitudes constitute states; forgetting is a process. Call those

> attitudes which do constitute states *stative*. The proposal is that knowing is the most general factive stative attitude, that which one has to a proposition if one has any factive stative attitude to it at all.
>
> (Williamson 2002: 34)

Williamson agrees that knowledge is the best kind of believing, but really, knowledge is very different for in the case of knowledge, one *knows that p*, and this knowing is appropriate because *p* is true. So this shows that knowing is the primitive idea, and that it should not be explained as a kind of belief.

In our investigation into a representative Hindu account of thought, and earlier in our review of a representative Hindu account of logic, we distinguished between a thought and a belief, and a belief, it was observed, is a claim that is true in virtue of its propositional attitude. If this is so, then belief does not merely aim at truth: it is true, but for a very bad reason. A thought on the other hand could be true or false, and it is not made true by one's attitude. But a thought so understood is not a mental state. It is what we can identify when we deflate the significance of mental content by disciplinarity. Thinking is hence not a state of mind. It is a state of disciplinarity in a public world. Our investigation hence gives us reason to deny that any state of thought is a mental state, such as a propositional attitude. Williamson's solution to avoid Gettier problems by merely identifying knowledge in terms of a distinct propositional attitude (knows that *p*) from belief (belief that *p*) is nothing we will be able to make use of: it is more of the same.

Reflecting on the Gettier counterexamples, in light of our investigations into Yoga and the representative Hindu account of thought, it is rather obvious that the problem arises because the *belief that p* is agent relative, and because one's *belief that p* not only tracks *p*, but is an attitude toward *p* that may be far wider than *p*. When I believe that Daśaratha's son is going to be king, and I am surprised that the king is going to be Bharata, I am surprised because my attitude of belief aimed at a proposition "Daśaratha's son will be king" and Rāma, though I did not describe Rāma as what I believe. Put another way, my attitude was that this proposition is about Rāma, and that is *how* I believed it. This attitude that relates a proposition to a person or thing is quite separate from the justification condition of a proposition (for instance, that I heard the news from the court). It is nothing separable from the attitude of belief itself. But now we see that the Gettier problems arise when we take belief to be the object of knowledge, for belief smuggles into knowledge claims all manner of assumptions. So to avoid such problems, we have to get rid of belief from our account of knowledge. Yet, for the same reasons, we have to banish Williamson's idea that knowledge can be accounted for as a propositional attitude: so long as our attitudes play a role in knowledge, we leave room for our *saṃskāra*-s (tendency impressions, assumptions, prejudices) and *smṛti*-s (memories) to cloud our efforts to know.

Given our explorations of a representative Hindu account of thought, and our insight into the conflation of belief and thought that comes with the standard account of thought from the *W*est, we should not be surprised by our diagnosis: it is the belief criterion that gives rise to Gettier counterexamples. This diagnosis entails that Gettier problems are created from the belief-thought conflation, and that they will be unsolvable by the *W*est.

In transitioning toward an Indian account of knowledge, and more importantly for us a representative Hindu account of knowledge, it is worth noting that after "*jñāna*" (knowledge) the main term of Indian epistemology is "*pramāṇa*." It is often depicted as "knowledge source" and as Stephen Phillips notes, terms such as this "are commonly used such that the truth of the resultant cognition is implied" (Phillips 2015). Justification of course makes a case for the truth of a thought and so the failure to simply treat this ubiquitous Indian term as "justification" shows a disconnect between Indology and work in epistemology, in a way not dissimilar to the disconnect between Indology and moral philosophy (as reviewed in Chapter 3). We can yet agree with and appreciate Philips' further observation that "A knowledge episode—to speak in the Indian manner—is a cognition generated in the right fashion." The unstated qualification of course is that the cognition is true. Then, we find, we are at something very much like the JTB account—without the belief.

One of the essential elements of the JTB account is that the truth and justification requirements are distinct. In so far as *pramāṇa* was thought generally to imply the truth of the relevant cognition, the Indian way of thinking about knowledge distinguished, implicitly, between *pramāṇa* and truth (*satya*): we could acknowledge that perception or inference is *pramāṇa* without having to agree that every example of perception or inference was true. Indeed, Indian philosophers often loved to talk about perceptual illusions, like a rope being mistaken for a snake. Some, such as Rāmānuja, noted in his commentary on the *Vedānta Sūtra* that such mistakes do not entail that perception is to be abandoned. Indeed, if we were to really push the idea that error entails that we lack justification, then we land in an error theory about all knowledge (for any putative *pramāṇa* can lead to erroneous judgments), but Rāmānuja notes that it follows from such an error theory that there is no justification for the error theory.

This deserves a little attention. We might reason that if perception is a *pramāṇa* (*p*) then it will lead to true observations (*q*). False observations (not *q*) would entail the rejection of perception as a *pramāṇa* (not *p*)—*modus tollens*. But we cannot reject inference for analogous reasons. Good inferences lead to errors all the time: for this reason there is a difference between valid and sound arguments. If we were to reject perception because it leads to error, we should also reject inference because it leads to error. But then we have no way to make sense of the *modus tollens* in favor of an error theory for this requires reason (that leads to error). Worse, we would have no way to even formulate skeptical arguments against putative means of justification for these too would be susceptible to error. Rāmānuja's point is that global error theories are nonsense for considerations like this—carried to their extreme, they are self-defeating (*Śrī Bhāṣya* I.i.1; "*Great Siddhānta*" p. 53 and pp. 74–78). But the lesson that such a criticism shows is that there is always a distinction between justification and truth.

Similarly according to the eleventh-century commentator on Mīmāṃsā philosopher Kumārila, Pārthasārathi Miśra, Mīmāṃsā epistemology allows for the possibility of perceptual defeaters, which bring into question prior perceptions, and none of this brings into question perception itself. Others in this tradition, such as Uṃveka Bhaṭṭa disagreed, and desired to keep a closer tie between truth and perception. But there is enough room in Indian epistemology to entertain the distinction between *satya* and *pramāṇa* (Arnold 2014). Kumārila and Rāmānuja are just two Indian and Hindu examples of epistemologists that draw this line, but this is enough to show that the disagreements of Hindu epistemology were wide enough to accommodate the *satya* and *pramāṇa* distinction.

If we get rid of belief from our account of knowledge, especially inspired by Gettier problems and our arguments for a representative Hindu account of thought in the previous chapter, we can restate knowledge without a belief requirement, and this would be most Indian. Knowledge (*jñāna*) would be analyzed into *pramāṇa* and *satya*, and as truth is the property of propositions, then our representative Hindu account of thought would be part of our account here as the thinking that is the substrate of truth. On this account, knowledge would not be a mental state: it would be the constraint of mind itself so as to allow for justification and truth. This would allow us to acknowledge that *jñāna*, knowledge, is factive: it is a true thought. Against the backdrop of traditional Indian and Hindu images, we can appreciate how *jñāna* was often associated with the sage as someone who transformed themselves so as to think (as opposed to merely believe) and this thinking is further legitimized by *pramāṇa* and *satya*. But given our previous exploration of a representative Hindu account of thought—yoga—as applicable to research-driven, disciplinary avenues of knowledge, then this account can help us make sense of knowledge as something that involves unusual procedures of epistemic specialization that characterizes the modern academy.

Just to review what we have noted, a representative Hindu account of knowledge is not in any way what Hindus believe. It is rather what they have to converge on while they disagree about knowledge. So in our exploration we are not committed to the idea that Hindus believe knowledge along the representative Hindu lines. Rather, we are exploring how they discover this as they disagree about knowledge.

Knowledge: THE JUSTIFIED OR THE TRUE

Our survey in the previous section of dissenting accounts of knowledge points to the following: that theories of knowledge, whether internalist or externalist, or whether Williamson's knowledge first account, or the standard JTB account, converge on the disjunctive concept of *THE JUSTIFIED OR THE TRUE*. In other words, theories of knowledge are disagreements about justification and truth.

In Chapter 2, we investigated another disjunctive concept of *DHARMA/ETHICS*, which decomposes into *THE RIGHT OR THE GOOD*. We observed that there are four possible basic theories given this disjunction: The good *causes* the right, the good *justifies* the right, the right *justifies* the good, and the right *causes* the good. What made this explication of the four basic theories of ethics possible is that we relied upon the metaphysical notion of *causality* and the epistemic notion of *justification* to flush out the theoretical possibilities. This allowed us to explain the differing perspectives in a manner that was uncircular: it did not merely reduce to the basic concept of *THE RIGHT OR THE GOOD* that was under dispute. Rather causality and justification stood in to shed light on differing perspectives on this concept of *DHARMA/ETHICS*.

In the case of knowledge, or the concept of *THE JUSTIFIED OR THE TRUE*, we similarly need to flush out the theoretical options by way of something external to the concept. As we used metaphysical and epistemic notions in the case of ethics, moral and political notions can similarly help us here—we could call upon the procedural notion of a condition or *requirement*, and the teleological notion of *maximization*. Hence, we can distinguish between four basic epistemic theories. The first two are *alethic*: they prioritize truth over justification:

(1) Truth conditions justification.
(2) Truth maximizes justification.

The second two theories are juristic: they prioritize justification:

(3) Justification maximizes truth.
(4) Justification conditions truth.

The two alethic theories are mirror images of the two juristic theories. Truth is the property of thought that reveals its content: false propositions reveal nothing. Justification is the property of a proposition that shows how it is properly founded or supported. Perception reveals content, and reason supports conclusions. The distinction between the alethic and the juristic theories is commensurate with the distinction between empirical theories of knowledge and rationalistic theories of knowledge.

(1) *Truth conditions justification.* Truth is a property of thought that reveals its content—false propositions reveal nothing. For truth to condition justification is for the revelatory character of true thought to reveal justification. We could call theories that fit into this category *foundationalist theories of justification*, for justification is not founded on further justification on this account, nor is it based on multiple truth claims. It is founded on a single truth: each truth reveals its own justification. The most obvious version of this theory is the idea that knowledge is self-justified. The motivation for this kind of view is to avoid an epistemic regress, where a thought is said to be justified only in so far as it is supported by another thought. If the truth of a thought reveals its justification, then the thought justifies itself. "Mīmāṃsā and Vedānta philosophers argue that such a threat of regress shows that knowledge is self-certifying, *svataḥ prāmāṇya*" (Phillips 2015).

Rāmānuja is especially salient, for on his account, all knowledge (*jñāna*) consists in directly grasping particular things (*bhūta*) distinguished by normative traits (*dharma*). On this account, first-rate knowledge (*jñāna*) consists in a perceptual relationship between a knower and an object of knowledge—knowledge *de re* (cf. Rāmānuja I.i.1, p. 32; cf. Śrīnivāsadāsa 1978: VII.1). To grasp something is to understand its rightness or goodness, which is its justification.

This general account of knowledge allows Rāmānuja to argue more specifically for special cases of knowledge: bhakti (love, devotion). He identifies *bhakti* as having the "same meaning as 'meditation' or approximation (*upāsana*) and is marked by the character of immediate interaction (*sākṣātkara*), and which itself is dear above all things since the object known is such" (Rāmānuja, *Śrī Bhāṣya* I.i.1. "*Small Pūrvapakṣa*" pp. 15–17). Further, "bhakti is a particular kind of knowledge (*jñāna*)" (Rāmānuja, *Vedārthasaṅgraha* §238). Because in bhakti we grasp the exemplary normative properties of the thing we are knowing (its superlative dharma), it is the same as joy. But this is because Development (Brahman) is the proper object of love:

> Entities other than Development can be objects of joy only to a certain extent and for some time. But Development is such that cognizing of It is an infinite and abiding joy. Since the form of cognition as joy is determined by its object, Development itself is joy.
>
> (Rāmānuja, *Vedārthasaṅgraha* §§239–241)

While *dharma bhūta jñāna* is the general account of knowledge, it allows us to appreciate that some objects are especially worth knowing.

Vedānta and Mīmāṃsā authors also take the lead, in the Indian tradition, in championing this account of knowledge as they identify the Vedas (which means "knowledge") as the content of *śruti* or what is heard, intuited, or observed. They do not believe that everyone has the capacity to observe this content, but in so far as it is known, it is observed. This content in turn functions to justify further claims, including moral claims.

Jain epistemology has a footing in this category too. As we noted in Chapter 3, according to the Jains, our intrinsic omniscience is clouded by action. So the truth of ourselves—that is, a revelation about what we really are, shows ourselves to be intrinsically virtuous (Jaini 1998: 102–106). So knowledge about ourselves is self-justified. But this self-justified knowledge is our omniscience. Hence we are not characterized by action, but dharma.

(2) *Truth maximizes justification.* As truth is the revelatory property of thought, for truth to maximize justification is for truth to be the best means to justification. Thought, and knowledge, is not all-things-considered self-justified on this account. Rather, it is by putting together differing truth claims that we are able to come to an all-things-considered appreciation of what is justified. We could call this type of epistemic theory a *coherentist theory of justification.* Theories of knowledge that blend empirical, rational and testimonial justification provide resources for understanding how knowledge is a cumulative product of (true) thinking. The obvious Indian example of this approach to epistemology is Nyāya, and its cosmological argument for the existence of God: "Things like the Earth have a maker as their cause, because they are products (*kāryatvāt*)" (Udayana, *Nyāyakusumāñjali* Fifth Chapter). Arguments like this rely upon a backdrop of observational data, inferences from such data, but also the idea of the reliable witness or testimony, to motivate the idea that

God, the ultimate reliable individual, has to be called in to explain how things are (Dasti Accessed 2017).

The idea that a proposition *p* is justified if it arises from a reliable process might belong here or in the previous category. On most accounts of reliabilism, the justification is not reducible to the truth of any one claim (as in the previous epistemic theory) but truth nevertheless reliably maximizes the justification of the claim. In so far as one requires a host of truths to maximize reliable justification, it is a version of a coherentist *theory of justification.* Nyāya presents us with an early version of reliabilism centered on its account of *pramāṇa* and "a conception of epistemic responsibility which allows for default, unreflective justification accorded to putatively veridical cognition" (Dasti Accessed 2017).

(3) *Justification maximizes truth.* Theories of this third variety take *pramāṇa* as the means to truth. This is the inverse of the previous theory, the coherentist account of justification. Hence, we could identify this third variety of theory as the *coherentist account of truth.* In the Indian tradition, the Buddhist idea that the Buddha's experience and reason lead to the acknowledgment of the famous four noble truths (which we reviewed in Chapter 3) is an example of this kind of theory. Theories of knowledge of this third sort adopt an experimental attitude toward truth: it is to be derived from justification but it is only by playing around with justification that we are in a position to derive the truth. The experimentation that is relevant here is not primarily or essentially empirical.

In the later tradition, we find a move to a deconstructive argument, where conventional truths are treated as determined by a host of justifications, but the ultimate (coherent) truth is treated as empty (*śunya*). It is common to see this as an anti-epistemic movement (Phillips 2015). This is to fail to see the dialectic. In the works of Nāgārjuna, the most famous philosopher to defend this view, there is an explicit defense of the first order atomic truths of conventional Buddhist life and the cumulative coherence of truth all-things-considered. And we get to the all-things-considered position by appreciating that the justifications (*pramāṇa*) that follow from the first order truth lead to the cumulative conclusion that truth as such, on the grand scale, is empty and lacks content. It lacks content because it lacks autonomy, own-being, an essence: *svabhāva.* And the ultimate truth on Nāgārjuna's account does not justify nihilism. It rather shows us the unrealized possibilities of convention, which we can only come properly to capitalize on when we are sensitive to the implications (justifications) of the first order Buddhist truths (*Mūlamadhyamakakārikā* XXIV). So Nāgārjuna is not part of an "anti-epistemology" movement, and it is incorrect to call him a skeptic. Like all epistemologists, he works with the disjunction of *pramāṇa* and *satya.* However, if one takes the alethic theories of knowledge as foundational and basic to epistemology, many theories of knowledge that move from justification to truth (theories within the meditational wing of Indian philosophy) will seem beyond the scope of epistemology—clearly a mistake.

In this category, we might also place the Vaiśeṣika school. In time, it becomes syncretized with Nyāya. While Nyāya acknowledges perception, inference, and testimony as justifications, and Vaiśeṣika does too, the opening lines of the

Vaiśeṣika Sūtra paint the project of its philosophy as leading to the ultimate Right, via knowledge of dharma (normativity) and this in turn is reduced to knowledge of several categories. This too is aided by the Vedas, which it identifies as the testimony of God (*Vaiśeṣika Sūtra* I.i.16). We observed in Chapters 3 and 4 about the similarities between the Vaiśeṣika outlook and Buddhism, as far as liberation is depicted as a function of the awareness of dharmas but also as early Vaiśeṣika authors identified Śiva as their God, and Śiva is the archetype of a mindful meditator and Mindfulness is essential to the Buddhist project too. Śiva or the Vaiśeṣika God merely observes creation once in motion. The very project of Mindfulness is an example of this third variety of epistemology where experiences act as justifications for an all-things-considered truth and the impartial observer is best placed to find it.

(4) *Justification conditions truth.* This is the mirror opposite of the first variety of epistemic theory, the foundationalist theory of justification. We could hence call this variety of epistemic theory a *foundationalist theory of truth.* Justification on this account leads to true propositions, which by virtue of being true reveal their content. Justification hence facilitates the transparence of thought, and it does this by weeding out false thoughts. This is in some ways a very Indian approach to knowledge in so far as Indian epistemologists often thought that *pramāṇa* entails truth. But to acknowledge this last epistemic theory is not to collapse the distinction between justification and truth. It is rather to acknowledge knowledge as those truths and only those truths we get to via justification, or *pramāṇa.* In order to maximize knowledge, on this account, we have to become ourselves justified in our approach to truth. This requires our own self-transformation from reliance upon lucky devices of knowledge to justification. A lucky approach to knowledge confuses knowledge with devices that are true by fluke, such as a broken clock that tells the correct time twice a day, or a belief (I believe that *p*), whose imbedded proposition (*p*) happens to be true, and which is *in toto* true by virtue of attitude. But this involves transcending perspectives for when we transcend perspective as such we leave behind lucky devices, for these devices are only ever lucky in particular contexts. Patañjali's Yoga stands out as the exemplar of this variety of theory. Patañjali's Yoga acknowledges three basic *pramāṇa*-s: *pratyakṣa* (perception), *anumāna* (inference), and *āgama*—this last term can hastily be translated as "scripture" but an *āgama* is an authoritative text (YS I.7). Philosophically understood, it is broad enough to encompass what scholars call "the literature." The three together help us in our quest for truth, but only in so far as we take responsibility, as knowers, to adopt an attitude of responsibility to mental representations—which are true by luck, namely what is outside of their control. Hence, what flows from this attitude of responsibility is that we deflate the importance of devices of luck (such as mental representations or propositional attitudes), and rather engage in the project of critical thinking that relies upon discipline—a practice we can undertake from opposing perspectives. And the result is that we no longer take the attribution of truth to a proposition as constitutive of knowing (belief) but rather discover the truth (*Ṛta*) as we know (YS I.47–49). As Patañjali notes, knowledge is not *pramāṇa* such as inference or

perception, for it relates to the essence of things that we discover from employing discipline from multiple perspectives.

In defense of this approach, I think it is an essential part of how we do research in the academy: truth is something we discover but we get to it via disciplinary research that justifies our findings. The truth we discover, though constrained by our justification, is not reducible or defined by our justifications: rather, it is what we discover by research that we can undertake from differing perspectives. So while it may not be a traditional option in the *W*estern tradition, it is the option that we gravitate to when we want to push the boundaries. This is a realist approach to knowledge in so far as reality has to do with the facts about objects, and facts in turn are true thoughts, which have nothing to do with our beliefs. (More on reality in Chapter 8.) Anti-realism in contrast denies that there is any distinction between justification and truth and reduces knowledge to belief.

The *Mahāvrata*-s

> If mind had to know itself in order to be known, then the second instance of mind knowing the first would require a third, leading to an infinite regress. When mind is stilled, it assumes the shape of the knower and is thereby known.
>
> (*Yoga Sūtra* IV.21–22)

The very concept of *KNOWLEDGE/JÑĀNA—THE JUSTIFIED OR THE TRUE*—represents what Hindus have to converge on while they disagree about knowledge, and hence it would do as a very brief account of the representative Hindu account of knowledge. As noted, to get a fuller account off the ground, we have to migrate from thinking about knowledge in terms of belief to knowledge in terms of thought in order to make room for disagreement. That is fine, as the basic concept of *KNOWLEDGE* does not rely upon belief: it relies on truth and justification, which are properties of thought. Our analysis of knowledge via explication and the consilience of entailments as the concept of the *THE JUSTIFIED OR THE TRUE* facilitates an explication of four possible basic epistemic theories. To understand the options we had to rely upon moral notions to elucidate the options, just as in the case of elucidating the basic theories of ethics, we had to rely upon epistemic and metaphysical notions. This switch allowed us in each case an account of the basic theories of morality and epistemology that were not circular: ethical concerns were reducible to metaphysical and epistemic concerns of causality and justification, and epistemic concerns were reducible to the ethical considerations of conditions and maximization. The latter shows that there is a close connection to normative considerations we usually think of as characteristic of ethics and politics to epistemology. So we should feel comfortable looking for moral and political models as our representative Hindu account of knowledge.

Just as in the case of moral theory, we find here too that there is no common epistemology of Hinduism. Hindu epistemologies are to be found in all four of the basic theories we identified. This stands in contrast with alternate religions that are kinds, and not a class like Hinduism. In these cases, the defining texts or figures that constitute the category definition of the religion as a kind will certainly play a role in the relevant epistemology because the epistemology is a member of the kind that is the religion. In this case, the kind essence is downward transitive to its members. Not so with Hinduism. Hinduism's disagreements on epistemology are coextensive with the philosophical disagreement on the topic.

One commonality across many Indian philosophies is a *prima facie* endorsement of five political goals, called the Great Vows (*Mahāvrata*-s). They are *ahiṃsā* (non-harm), *satya* (truth), *asteya* (not stealing), *brahmacarya* (sexual restraint, research), and *aparigrahā* (not being acquisitive). We find this in the *Yoga Sūtra* (II.30), but also in Jainism. According to tradition, the ancient Jain *Tīrthaṅkara* (Fordmaker) Pārśva, only recognized four of the Yama Rules. The Fordmaker Mahāvīra is said to have added *brahmacarya* to the list (*Uttarādhyayaṅa* XXIII.12). In the *Nyāya Sūtra*, we find *brahmacarya* and *aparigrahā* (NS IV.ii.46) but indeed, the entire list of the Great Vows is not incompatible with the Nyāya doctrine (Chakrabarti 2017: 207) and is included in the later tradition. But it is difficult to find salient examples that do not give lips service to these values in the Indian tradition. Even ritualists, such as the defenders of Pūrva Mīmāṃsā and their Vedānta counterparts who defend the propriety of animal sacrifices do so not because violence is permissible, but because ritual is a moral exception (cf. Śaṅkara and Rāmānuja on *Vedānta Sūtra* III.i.25, *Manusmṛti* V). The Cārvāka school of hedonism, for instance, is reputed to have identified dharma (morality) with *kāma* (pleasure) (Guṇaratna 1990: 276), and while this is a minority view with philosophical difficulties, it does not in and of itself entail that we should not respect each other's sexual boundaries. Indeed, if one endorses an ethics of pleasure, the mutual pleasure of lovers would demand such respect. In keeping with such a respect, we would have not to steal each other's personal property required for our own health and wellbeing, and no one will be injured by hoarding.

Any creature that can converge on THE JUSTIFIED OR THE TRUE cashed out in terms of the *Mahāvrata*-s is aware of the objectivity of knowledge, and as this is something that most well behaved animals (and the Earth) do, they know, not just piece meal, but the objectivity of knowledge as such. Here we continue a line of thought. In the previous chapter, in our representative Hindu account of thought we had to reject the linguistic account of thought for it undermines the capacity of humans to get along and understand each other in a diverse world, and it cannot explain what we converge on while we disagree, for an implication of this theory is that disagreement is impossible. Our way of getting rid of the linguistic account of thought was to endorse thought as disciplinary practice—thought so understood is what we converge on while we disagree. However, we noted there that thinking on a disciplinary model is not a peculiarly human affair. Anything that can engage the same practice from differing perspectives while tracking objects thinks. Our representative Hindu account of knowledge is hence unfettered by the representative Hindu account of thought: it entails no restriction on what kind of creature could be engaging the concept of knowledge. But it shows us also how thoughtful creatures that track objects from differing perspectives think, which is part of knowing. When they restrain themselves so as to allow for their own and other's personal boundaries and requirements, they converge on the objectivity of knowledge! This is coextensive with the diversity of perspectives that are unharmed in knowing.

The objectivity of knowledge cashed out by these five values goes beyond the mere concept of knowledge, which is also objective. What it elucidates is the deflation of ignorance or epistemic progress. Given a representative Hindu account of thought, which we converge on when we disagree about thought, thoughts contain within them a diversity of perspectives, bound by a common disciplinary purpose. True thoughts reveal their contents. A true proposition (*satya*) is hence something we can only come to appreciate once we have appreciated and permitted the diversity of perspectives. To this end, the true ones will contain perspectives that reveal the content of disagreement—and such thoughts will hence be characterized by values that do not deprive knowing its full range of diversity (*ahiṃsā*). In this case, such perspectives will not attempt to deprive other perspectives what is theirs (*asteya*) (as we find in the imperialism of interpretation) but in revealing the content of disagreement, it will also not hoard (*aparigrahā*). In the process we can study what the content of disagreement is about (*brahmacarya*). Knowing, *jñāna*, is hence a matter of appropriate public participation in a world characterized by disciplinarity. In short, justification is at the very least *ahiṃsā*: it does not harm the objects of knowledge or the various perspectives that get us to know. What this non-harm leads us to is the truth (*satya*), which reveals a diversity of autonomous perspectives that neither deprive themselves of their requirements (*satya*) nor conflate themselves with others (*aparigrahā*), and within all of this is research and an increase in knowledge, made possible in part by the stringent respect of personal boundaries (*brahmacarya*).

Of course, if we wanted to disagree, we could revise the order of explanation: justification (*ahiṃsā*) is not what takes us to truth (*satya*): rather, it is the truth of a diversity of distinct perspectives that neither steal from each other nor clutter their own views and that makes research possible that further reveals justification, namely non-harm. As this is a list, which we can collapse into a disjunct, namely justification (*ahiṃsā*) or truth (*satya*, which reveals *asteya, aparigrahā*, and *brahmacarya*), we can converge on it from differing perspectives, including the four basic theories of knowledge identified above.

Objections

I shall consider two objections.

Theories of knowledge might make use of belief

Our investigation into a representative Hindu account of knowledge relied on criticizing the notion that belief has anything to do with knowledge. But surely if we are open to epistemic disagreement, we have to make room for theories of knowledge that take belief seriously. And yet, nothing of the sort has been defended. In response to this worry it is worth noting that the account of the concept of knowledge as THE JUSTIFIED AND THE TRUE does not rule out models of knowledge based on belief. So in a disagreement of epistemic theories, some which rely upon belief, some which do not, THE JUSTIFIED AND THE TRUE will be what they have in common as they disagree about knowledge.

As a rejoinder we might be concerned about the generalization that the entire Indian and Hindu tradition rejects the importance of belief to thought and knowledge. Surely in an ancient tradition as this, there will be exceptions. I can think of one obvious example of a philosopher who thinks that belief plays a part in ordinary accounts of knowledge. This is the famous Advaita philosopher Ādi Śaṅkara who (in the preamble to his commentary on the *Vedānta Sūtras*) argues that the first order truths about the world, as we know them, arise from the superimposition of the subjectivity (I believe that) on the objects of experience (*p*) and the result is a world of belief (I believe that *p*). And as such, a world of various 'facts' are generated but these are facts by virtue of attitude and not at all anything else. So ultimately they are false, though conventionally true. Included in our conventional beliefs are faith and devotion to deities. Yet, so long as we are under the sway of such beliefs, there are certain normative regularities (such as karma) and morality, which hold sway over us for the normative truths help us deal with our desires—the attitudes that create our conventional world (Ranganathan 2016). So for those who want to look for an Indian criticism of what is often called religious belief, we can look to this theory. But it is an interesting error theory for it claims that the reason that our ordinary beliefs are *ultimately* false is that they are beliefs: they come about by this superimposition of our subjectivity on what we can know and understand—the same kind of superimposition that occurs when we build our attitude into our claims about the world. In a *W*esternized world where belief is taken to be the object of knowledge, Advaita Vedānta will seem like a friendly addition, and Hindus who want to present themselves in conformity with the *W*est tend to adopt this (especially educated Hindus, as has frequently been observed). But, it is an ironic endorsement of the belief model of thought.

The representative Hindu account of knowledge ignores the knower

The representative Hindu account of knowledge treats it as the disjunctive concept of THE JUSTIFIED OR THE TRUE and this in turn suggests that knowledge is about mediating these disjuncts. Moreover, given the representative Hindu account of thought it would seem that astronomical bodies that are engaged in some type of disciplined orbit know as the disciplined behavior reveals content, which can be and is tracked from differing perspectives via the discipline, namely the orbit. The discipline hence allows us to engage in true thinking that is justified. But this ignores the subjective aspect of knowing: astronomical objects are not subjects.

If objectivity is what we can track from differing perspectives, the subjective is the opposite: it is what we can know from one perspective. So how things seem to us from our vantage is subjective, but what we are viewing is objective. Illusion, confusing the subjective and objective, is one way to blend the subjective and the objective but in error. When I look in the mirror and believe that there is a second person who looks like me staring at me, that is not knowledge but illusion. That confuses the subjective (my reflection in a mirror) with the objective. When we know we do not confuse the subjective and the objective. Moreover, the concept of knowledge, *The Justified or the True*, does not explicitly call upon subjectivity as a primitive notion, and hence we do not need to call upon subjectivity to explain knowledge. It is because subjectivity plays no part in the concept of knowledge that we can share knowledge and know the same things from differing subjective perspectives. While knowledge is not elucidated by subjectivity, subjectivity (what we know from one perspective) is elucidated by knowledge. So if we want to know something about subjects, we have first to come to terms with knowledge. And if a thing knows, then we have grounds for claims about how things seem to a knower from their vantage, which is an account of its subjectivity (YS III.19–20). And there may even be true thoughts about such matters, that we can think by engaging in the appropriate discipline (psychology). But this is downstream from knowledge.

As a follow-up to this objection, one might rephrase it thus: in the Subcontinent Dharma example, speakers were able to engage in thinking about a common proposition because they used their linguistic meaning in service of a discipline. Knowledge, in so far as it requires thought, would require some type of mental representation, like linguistic meaning. But many beings, whether animals or planets such as the Earth lack this. This objection confuses the direction and thrust of the representative Hindu accounts of thought (yoga) and the correlative account of knowledge. The discipline serves to deflate the importance of mental representation so that we can think, for all such representations are at best fluky truths from some perspective. If we fail to deflate its importance we treat mental representation as thought, and then we are in the realm of belief, which is true in virtue of an attitude. Mental representations have an attitudinal component in so far as they are intentional, and they point to what they represent. Failing to deflate its importance gets us back into the belief paradigm, which is a mistake. There is nothing rational about beliefs, as we have seen, for nothing follows from them. As Ādi Śaṅkara notes, they are *avidya*—nescience.

Conclusion

A representative Hindu account of knowledge is what we converge on while we disagree about knowledge: *The Justified or the True*. It is the objectivity of knowledge as such, but is also what we have to contend with as philosophers disagreeing about knowledge. What makes our account 'Hindu' is that we have used Indian resources to think about the topic. What we see through our exploration of various topics is that a representative Hindu approach to philosophical issues, whether it is logic, thought, or knowledge, liberalizes the world, and moves us away from thinking that there is something especially special about us humans, to thinking about what we share with beings that share our public world. While Hindus certainly do not agree on very much, and they do not have to agree on anything to be Hindu, we see that through our exploration of these various topics, a representative Hindu answer to philosophical questions explains an openness to thinking about knowledge and people in very broad terms. We shall explore this topic in greater detail in our next chapter on moral standing.

References

Arnold, Daniel. 2014. "Kumārila." In *The Stanford Encyclopedia of Philosophy*, edited by Edward N. Zalta. Winter >2014 Edition. https://plato.stanford.edu/archives/win2014/entries/kumaarila/.

Chakrabarti, Kisor K. 2017. "Nyāya Consequentialism." In *The Bloomsbury Research Handbook of Indian Ethics*, edited by Shyam Ranganathan, 203–224. London: Bloomsbury Academic.

Dasti, Matthew R. Accessed 2017. "Nyāya." In *Internet Encyclopedia of Philosophy*, edited by James Feiser. www.iep.utm.edu/nyaya/.

Gettier, Edmund. 1963. "Is Justified True Belief Knowledge?" *Analysis* 23: 121–123.

Guṇaratna. 1990. *Tarkarahasyadipika*. In *Carvaka/Lokayata: An Anthology of Source Materials and Some Recent Studies*, edited by Debiprasad Chattopadhyaya. New Delhi: Indian Council of Philosophical Research in association with Rddhi-India Calcutta.

Hetherington, Stephen. 2012. "The Gettier-Illusion: Gettier-Partialism and Infallibilism." *Synthese* 188, no. 2: 217–230.

Jaini, Padmanabh S. 1998. *The Jaina Path of Purification*. New Delhi: Motilal Banarsidass.

Littlejohn, Clayton. 2012. *Justification and the Truth-Connection*. Cambridge; New York: Cambridge University Press.

Phillips, Stephen. 2015. "Epistemology in Classical Indian Philosophy." In *The Stanford Encyclopedia of Philosophy*, edited by Edward N. Zalta. https://plato.stanford.edu/entries/epistemology-india/.

Rāmānuja. 1996. *(Śrī Bhāṣya/Brahma Sūtra Bhāṣya) Vedānta Sūtras with the Commentary of Rāmānuja*. Translated by George Thibaut. Sacred Books of the East, vol. 48. New Delhi: Motilal Banarsidass.

Ranganathan, Shyam. 2016. "Vedānta, Śaṅkara and Moral Irrealism (Ethics-1, M10)." In *Philosophy, E-Pg Pathshala*, edited by A Raghuramaraju. India, Department of Higher Education (NMEICT). http://epgp.inflibnet.ac.in/ahl.php?csrno=27.

Śaṅkara (Ādi). 1994. *The Vedānta Sūtras with the Commentary by Śaṅkara (Brahma Sūtra Bhāṣya)*. Translated by George Thibaut. Sacred Books of the East, vols. 34 and 38. www.sacred-texts.com/hin/sbe34/sbe34007.htm.

Śrīnivāsadāsa. 1978. *Yatīndramatadīpikā*. Translated by Svāmi Ādidevānanda. Madras: Sri Ramakrishna Math.

Weinberg, Jonathan, Shaun Nichols, and Stephen Stich. 2001. "Normativity and Epistemic Intuitions." *Philosophical Topics* 29: 429–460.

Williamson, Timothy. 2002. *Knowledge and Its Limits*. Oxford: Oxford University Press.

Zagzebski, Linda. 1994. "The Inescapability of Gettier Problems." *The Philosophical Quarterly* 44, no. 174: 65–73.

7 Moral standing

Who counts, gods, and the afterlife

Introduction

Our topic in this chapter is moral standing: the status belonging to what should be considered in ethical deliberation. Our aim is to discern a representative Hindu account of moral standing, which is what we converge on as we disagree about moral standing—using Hindu resources to model the debate. Such an account is *objective*—philosophically objective—as it is the object of philosophical disagreement.

In the next section I will review the disagreements over moral standing, East and *W*est. In the third section I shall examine the representative Hindu account of moral standing: what we converge on while we disagree about moral standing. It, unlike the well known theories of standing, plays a role in explaining many common Hindu conclusions about who counts, the gods, and the afterlife. I will then review some objections before concluding.

Moral standing East and *W*est

The *W*est and its tradition of identifying thought with language, along with the empirical generalization that (human) language is a human matter tends toward anthropocentrism. People who buy into the *W*est will tend to treat the category of "person" and "human" as interchangeable, assume that humans have standing, and expect that the moral standing of non-humans has to be proved by way of the anthropocentric criterion that entails that (only) humans count. When we move to Chinese philosophy, we find the focus on the human in Confucius's *Analects*, but this is contrasted with the radical naturalism of Taoism such as in the *Tao Te Ching*, which identifies the *Tao* (the ultimate normative principle) with nature. For its author, Lao Tzu, the prioritization of humanity over the Tao is an error.

Hindus, and Indian philosophers overall, tolerate a very wide idea of moral standing. Buddhists tend to identify moral standing with all sentient beings, as do Jains. In the wider Hindu world the gods such as Viṣṇu take on many animal forms as incarnations, and his closest devotees include an eagle (Garuda) a monkey (Hanuman), and he resides on a cosmic snake (Ādi Śeṣa) while cavorting with his partner, Lakṣmī, who is a Lotus and the Earth. Śiva likewise is depicted with Nandi (the bull), his son, Gaṇeśa, is half elephant (Gaṇeśa also rides a mouse). Śiva's other son Kārttikēya is associated with a peacock, and the popular stories of Hinduism (the *purāṇa*-s) depict beings with standing from diverse species. A fact worth noting is that India, along with other South Asian countries, consistently rank among the lowest per capita consumers of meat and fish according to the *Organisation for Economic Cooperation and Development*. While the Pythagoreans and other Greek philosophers made a case for vegetarianism, schools and traditions of philosophy advocating vegetarianism continue to exist in an unbroken tradition from ancient times in India. Prominent among such traditions is Jainism, but also the procedural traditions of Vedic orthodoxy, which at once legitimized animal sacrifices but yet claimed the superiority of a meat-free and violence-free lifestyle (*Manusmṛti* V.26–V.56). And without a doubt, the Bhakti traditions that sprout from this orthodoxy by and large take a strong stand against treating other animals as fitting receptacles of violence—values of *dayā* (compassion) and *ahiṃsā* (non-harm) are central to such traditions. But this is entailed by the wider Indian endorsement of the *Mahāvrata*-s, the objectivity we converge on when we disagree about knowledge (Chapter 6).

It is worth noting that because Hinduism is the microcosm of philosophy there is no *prima facie* reason for Hindus to agree on the question of moral standing. There are notable exceptions to the generalization that Hindus tend to favor treating animals as people and not as food. Many Hindus are not vegetarians, and in ancient times, the practice was not widely adopted or associated with what we now think of as Hindu Orthodoxy. The philosophers Śaṅkara and Rāmānuja, in their commentaries on the *Brahma Sūtra* (III.i.25)—a summary of the latter part of the Vedas—defend prescribed Vedic animal sacrifices—though their followers (especially Śrī Vaiṣṇava followers of Rāmānuja) are, as a rule, vegetarians. Kumārila in his Mīmāṃsā work, the *Ślokavārttika*, argues that naturalistic approaches to moral concepts are viciously circular (as "good" and a natural property such as "pleasure" are interchangeable according to Naturalism). Hence, we need to rely upon a non-natural source of moral intuition—*śruti*—for moral guidance, and *śruti* (which on this orthodox Hindu account is the Vedas) endorses the ritual slaughter and consumption of animals. If we fail to endorse *śruti* as the justification of moral action, we fall into absurd moral traps (for more, see Ranganathan 2016a).

In contrast to the Chinese or *W*estern traditions, vegetarianism is a widespread option endorsed by Hindus and Indians. Yet I shall not look for nor expect that there will be a foundational Hindu belief about moral standing. The tradition is too varied and diverse for such unanimity. Yet, in sharp contrast, we can generalize about the *W*est to a high degree, which owing to its foundational linguistic account of thought, is a tradition of remarkable homogeneity.

In his wide study of the moral status of animals in the *W*estern tradition, Gary Steiner begins by noting that the pre-Socratic Xenophanes is famous for observing that if horses could draw, their gods would look like horses, and if cattle did the same their gods would look like cattle. This is a criticism of the Greek practice of depicting the gods as human, and quite rightly noted by Steiner as an expression of anthropocentrism. For the Greeks, he notes, humans are somewhere between the animals and the gods. However, what is remarkable about this observation for us is that when Hindus draw pictures of their gods, they come in all sorts of forms, and humans are the minority presentation. Also strange in the Greek approach—which sets the tone for *W*estern imperialism—is that humans are somehow exempt from being counted as animals. We saw in previous chapters that the *W*est, and the linguistic account of thought, confuses thought with beliefs, and beliefs are true by virtue of attitude, irrespective of the proposition such attitudes are toward—a kind of ersatz fact that Śaṅkara calls *avidya* or nescience. Yoga, or disciplinarity, is our way to actual facts (not propositional attitudes, but true thoughts) and it is a fact that humans are animals—ask a biologist. The *W*est's denial of the animality of humans is remarkable for humans are animals and this denial constitutes *the basic delusion* of the *W*est. What is more remarkable is that if you call a *W*esterner an animal (try it, say to a *W*esterner: "you are an animal!") they take offense! Steiner identifies an underlying theme to the *W*est's tradition of anthropocentrism: "all and only human beings are worthy of moral consideration, because all and only human beings are rational and endowed with language." With this comes also the concomitant conclusion that only humans are capable of self-determination and moral responsibility (Steiner 2010: 1–2). We of course should not be surprised at Steiner's observations—they meet up with our review of trends in *W*estern theory. The *W*est as we have noted is the idea that language, or linguistic meaning, is thought, with an ancient Greek origin.

While an anthropocentric approach to thought as language may seem to prioritize and favor human interest (allowing us to count while others do not), this is exactly the view that gets us into trouble when humans try to understand those who do not share a language (Chapter 5). This is the basic assumption of Orthodox Indology (Chapters 2, 3, and 4), and in several chapters, we have seen how it leads to the conflation of belief and thought with linguistic meaning, and further it leads to interpretation as the primary mode of understanding (which is irrational). And, the idea that those who are different from us (lack our language) show themselves to be incompetent in the sphere of morals is exactly the view of Orthodox Indology with respect to the history of Indian philosophy. Indians, according to the Orthodox Indologist, show no native talent or inclination to moral reflection. (The implication of this, rarely noted, is that it seems to be a good thing that European powers took the time to colonize South Asia—for Europeans with interest in practical matters have to show all those brown folks what to do with themselves.) "India, the historical home to the largest conscientious push toward (ethical) vegetarianism, and the cultural home of the idea of karma as a basic explanation of practical rationality, has no robust or ancient tradition of moral philosophy." To believe that requires an inordinate amount of (make) belief (all believing is make-belief as beliefs are true by virtue of their constitutive attitude, namely the fiat of the believer). It is also to put Indians in the same position as non-human animals, from a *W*estern perspective. But this relegation of non-*W*estern and alien humans to the category of (non-linguistic) animals is the standard outcome of the *W*est given its linguistic account of thought: both are treated as beyond the pale of moral responsibility. As observed in Chapter 5, acrimony, chauvinistic nationalism, xenophobia, and a general paranoia of aliens, falls from the *W*est's approach to thought.

But perhaps there is another way to defend the prioritization of humans, that plays upon what we have in common, not what divides us (such as our differing languages). Spinoza gives voice to one such strategy: he argues that as the natures of humans and non-human animals are different, we ought not to morally consider non-human animals as their interests conflict with ours, and hence we should feel free to "use them at our pleasure" (Grey 2013).

An assumption underwriting Spinoza's argument is that if we share a nature, we share interests, and that if we do not share natures, we do not share interests. For if this is true, Spinoza is correct in being suspicious of beings with differing natures from him. However, this generalizes: men and women should view each other inimically as their biological natures are different, as should people of differing skin colors as their natures (the genes controlling their skin color) are different.

Yoga (*Sūtra*) and Sāṅkhya (*Kārikā*) both distinguish between nature (*prakṛti*), and persons (*puruṣa*). Nature is causality, and as far as something is natural, it is explained in terms of the causes. Persons, on the other hand, are only properly explained when we understand them by normative concepts (such as *DHARMA*) to respond appropriately in light of present challenges. On the Yoga account, all things with an interest in their own Lordliness are persons, and what it is to be a person is not the same as any natural capacity we might have: it is the normative idealization of us that accounts for when things go well for us as individuals.

The closely related Sāṅkhya tradition going back to Īśvarakṛṣṇa's *Sāṅkhya Kārikā* also draws a distinction between persons and nature. But on its account, anything that happens to a person is really something that happens to nature (SK 62–63). So persons play no role in the explanation of their life—they are a mere conscious function of the evolution of matter. In modern talk, persons are an emergent property of nature. These two positions of Yoga and Sāṅkhya are confused owing to the predilection of Orthodox Indologists to engage in interpretations (for more on this phenomenon, see Ranganathan 2016b) and the result is a conflation of philosophies that are different. But the two views are importantly different: on the Sāṅkhya account, you play no role in explaining your life, on the Yoga account, you explain your life when you are well and when things go badly it is the intercession of nature. The goal of Yoga, including and most centrally devotion to the Lord, is to transition us from a life explained naturally to one explained personally, where the normative ideals of unconservativism (*tapas*) and self-governance (*svādhyāya*) account for the life well-lived. This leads to our isolation (*kaivalya*) from external influence (YS IV.29–34).

For the *W*esterner following Spinoza, our life is natural, and hence *kaivalya* seems like an escape from life. But this is exactly what Yoga challenges. Death, starvation, and coercion from external forces are natural (*prakṛti*), but thriving, benefiting, and being free from the causes is not natural—it is personal (*puruṣa*) and it comes by a moral cleansing that allows us to transcend particular contexts and perspectives (*dharmamegha samādhi*) (YS IV.29). Life is only possible given the latter. Hence, your interests are not natural because they consist in negating natural influences. So *kaivalya* from nature is not the end of life, but the beginning of living as a free person. In so far as we can distinguish between external influence (nature) and our normative interests (persons) we can criticize the easy identification of nature with interests: the two come apart. Therefore, there is no need to engage in the paranoia that others who do not share our natures are a threat, and hence we need not agree with Spinoza. The yogi endorses diversity as consistent with a well-lived life: a diversity of natures is consistent with a unanimity of personal interests (Ranganathan 2017).

The Yoga account of personhood appears to be missing from the *W*est in so far as the philosophy of Yoga—the fourth moral theory of Bhakti we reviewed in Chapter 3—is not an option in the *W*estern tradition. As noted, the *W*est's linguistic account of thought entails that thought is *the meaning of what you say*, which you cannot deny without absurdity: hence, you believe whatever you think. But thinking according to Yoga is about controlling thought and not passively believing it, so Yoga is outside of the philosophical resources of the *W*est. A further reason for why Yoga will be foreign to the *W*est is that in the *W*est, thought, reflection and hence even the possibilities of reason and responsibility, have to do with language (Chapters 2 and 5). One of the peculiar implications of this approach to thought is that whether you think or not is a matter determined by linguistic ability, which is an attribute of nature. So thoughtfulness, which consists in appreciating abstract, causally inert objects (thoughts and concepts) depends upon a certain natural constitution, on this account. If moral standing has to do with such a capacity for thoughtfulness, moral standing is reduced to naturalistic, biological considerations in the *W*est. Hence, in a *W*esternized world, human life (even when a fetus, brain dead, or in deep pain) is thought to be valuable no matter what, but non-human life does not *prima facie* count: four legged animals can be eaten and vivisectioned but not humans: moral standing is reducible to biology in the *W*est.

One element in this story of the *W*est's account of moral standing that seems under-explained is why thoughtfulness should matter at all? When I am asleep, I am not very thoughtful but does that mean that I stop counting, morally? The connection between thoughtfulness and standing has to do with community membership. From the very beginning in the *W*est's tradition (evidenced in Plato and Aristotle's Virtue Ethics, up through Kant's Deontology and even Bentham's Utilitarianism) there is a connection between morality and community membership, such that morality is about getting along in your community. This *prima facie* requires thoughtfulness. As we have seen, Indian theories of dharma do not conflate community membership with dharma. But that is because Indians traditionally (prior to *W*esternization) did not conflate thought and language, which does bound communities. If thought is linguistic, then being a thoughtful being is about membership in one's linguistic community, and it is only in this case that moral standing even has any sense (as we saw in Chapter 5)! Hence, ironically, for the *W*esterner, to care about you is to colonize you, convert you, and make you part of their community. They cannot leave you alone: on their view, that is tantamount to denying you your standing.

The West: *self-governance and suffering*

In the *W*estern tradition, the acknowledgment that thinking is a matter determined by nature comes with certain further widely acknowledged entailments. Whether you count morally as the kind of thing who is thoughtful—the kind of thing that we should distinguish from the vast rubble of the universe that shows no capacity for self-governance or moral consideration—is a natural fact; and, moreover, is a *capacity*. There are two contrasting versions of the idea that moral status has to do with capacities from the *W*estern tradition: one Kantian, the other Benthamite.

The original thesis of the *W*est is that language is thought, reason and belief (*logos*). While Plato envisioned *logos* relating the philosopher to a realm of abstract objects—the actual meanings of what we say—Kant is famous for naturalizing this picture: the categories are built into the *a priori* structures of the human mind—making sense of this is the task of the first *Critique*. This sets up apparent problems for morality: if we are determined to be thinking things by virtue of this natural constitution, where is the room for freedom? Here Kant believes that the antinomy of freedom and determinism is resolved in the paradox of the free will—what is both free and determined (*Groundwork* 97–98). And the free will is what is constrained by the kinds of considerations that apply to humans as a category. In the abstract, he calls this the Categorical Imperative. It has several formulations, such as the Kingdom of Ends formulation (that we should choose laws that apply to us members of an ideal community), and the Principle of Humanity (treat other humans as an end, and not ever just as a means) (*Groundwork* 97–98). Moral laws are anthropocentric. They apply only to those things that can reason in the peculiar way that Kant can. Now, as the only things that have moral standing are those things that such laws apply to (the things that can be members of a Kingdom of Ends), non-human animals have no moral standing. We should be kind to them only in so far as being cruel to non-human animals would lead us to be cruel to other humans. But, this implies that if we could find a way to torture puppies without it affecting our treatment of humans, that would be fine (Kant 1996: 6:443; 1974: 5:298–303; Wood 1998: 194–195).

The essence of Kant's theory of moral standing and morality is self-governance: it is the capacity for self-governance that gives a being dignity. The lowest common denominator of such beings is humanity. Kant insists that we are always free to obey the abstract rules and reasons that apply to us as a category (second *Critique* 5:36–37). Yet Kant is famous for claiming that the goodness of the will—it being constrained and subsumed under the Categorical Imperative—has nothing to do with its efficacy, but merely with respect to an inner freedom of persons to accede to Categorical considerations (*Groundwork* 3). So while self-governance is central to his account of morality, it is possible to self-govern without actually governing oneself in the public world. We need only *believe* we govern ourselves as a matter of reverence for the moral law. This is easy to miss, as Kant makes a great fuss about the relationship between reverence or respect for the law (*achtung*) and duty: in the *Groundwork* he defines a duty as a requirement to act out of respect for the moral law. But what is reverence except a kind of propositional attitude where the agent reveres or respects the proposition (the Categorical Imperative). Self-governance looks like "Kant *reveres* the Categorical Imperative," and this is not really all that different from "Kant believes the Categorical Imperative." "Revere" as attitudes go is a bit more fancy, but in the same neighborhood as belief: in both cases we take the proposition to be true, and truth reveals its content (in this case, it is supposed to reveal humanity). Kant has swapped really governing oneself with having a certain propositional attitude toward a moral law as though that counts as free will. If anything, as we observed in our exploration on Subcontinent Dharma, believing undermines our freedom as it binds us to a proposition in a claim that is true by virtue of our attitude and not by virtue of the possibilities of disciplinary research.

Jeremy Bentham, the famous hedonic Utilitarian of the *W*estern tradition, departs from the standard story of the *W*est. In a famous footnote (17) to his 1823 *An Introduction to the Principles of Morals and Legislation* (*PML*), he compares human and non-human bondage and argues that the only relevant criterion of moral standing is the capacity of a being to suffer. While Kant is stereotypically *W*estern, Bentham's *W*esternization is more subtle: it consists in the reduction of standing to a natural capacity, but also to the idea that those who count are part of a moral community (*PML* ch. 1: IX)—both entailments of the standard *W*estern approach to moral standing.

There are many alarming features of Utilitarianism. For instance, if you believe that it is your duty to maximize happiness or minimize pain, you can be coerced into doing something bad on threat of having something worse happen. But stranger still, this Utilitarian account of moral standing disincentivizes transcending suffering, for to do so would be to undermine your moral standing. Then of course, there are the real though unusual cases of people who are congenitally insensitive to pain (*Congenital Insensitivity to Pain* Accessed 2017): they do not seem to be able to physically suffer. And there is the case of people who due to foolishness (hard drugs) or illness—or perhaps because as Buddhas they reached *nirvana*!—do not have room or capacity for psychological suffering. These folks can be injured, just as a rock or piece of furniture can be injured, but they cannot suffer, and hence, it seems that they do not count on Bentham's Utilitarian picture.

Suffering is a subjective criterion of standing, and all one needs to do to deprive someone of Bentham's standing is to undermine the capacity to suffer. But this is part of a bigger problem: both the Kantian and the Benthamite reduce moral standing to a capacity x (moral understanding and choice on Kant's account, the capacity to suffer on Bentham's account), and it would seem that all we have to do to deprive someone of any rights or any obligation on our part to take them seriously is to deprive them of x. So, once we have sufficiently injured someone so that they no longer are characterized by x, anything further we do to them would be alright! So, far from protecting someone from being diminished or marginalized, capacity accounts of moral standing render us vulnerable to someone willing to go far enough to deprive us of moral standing. Weirdest of all, a picture of moral standing that tied it to one's capacity to suffer *disincentivizes* the heroic struggle to overcome suffering, for it seems that to overcome it would be to render oneself morally worthless.

India: self-governance and duḥkha

Indian philosophers considered parallel theories, but without identifying the qualities that warrant standing with a capacity, thus avoiding the case of injury depriving one of standing. In the Indian tradition, many philosophers adopted Consequentialism (as we saw in Chapter 3). Buddhists are the most famous for having the most developed and systematic of such theories. On their account, we ought to minimize *duḥkha* (discomfort). But *duḥkha* is not a fact about you (for there may be no you on this account) but a trait of reality under certain circumstances. It can arise out of desire, as the Four Noble Truths entail, for desire undermines our capacity to see *dhamma*-s or dharmas (the constituents of reality) as *goods* that justify certain actions, and instead leads us to treat them as means or the right to some subjective end. However, some *dhamma*-s, such as anger, are wrong (*akusalā*) (*Aṅguttara Nikāya* I.189–190), which means that if we treated anger as a procedure, we would create more *duḥkha*. But if we treated it as an end that has to justify an appropriate response, then we can allow for Mindfulness to be what anger justifies, allowing it to play the role of a good, in a Consequentialist moral theory.

Jains, in the Indian tradition, held a self-governance position in morality, but for them the self that ought to govern itself is the *jīva*—living being—and the *jīva* in turn is primarily a character or soul, defined in part by infinite *vīrya* (virtue) (cf. Umasvati, *Tattvārthsūtra* viii 13). So this is not a special capacity, but rather a disposition that is part of the metaphysics of sentient individuals (of various degrees of *karmic* sophistication). While this virtuous disposition is innate, it can be hindered by karma (action). The Hero (the *Jina*) or Path Finder (*Tīrthaṅkara*) focuses on self-governance, and this consists in acting by way of one's own virtue, which paradoxically amounts to not acting, as one's virtue is not the same as an action. The Hero is hence unintrusive and benign (*Sūtrakṛtāṅga* I.xii.11–21). This allows others the room to exercise their self-governance (*Sūtrakṛtāṅga* I.ii.20–21).

There are of course other Indian approaches. The Brahmanical traditions of Vedānta and Mīmāṃsā that we reviewed earlier generally take the view that it is *prima facie* wrong to harm sentient beings, but that prescribed injury is permissible. Both the Vedānta and Mīmāṃsā approaches to dharma are procedural, which treats the requirement of non-human animals to self-govern as sufficient explanation for it being *prima facie* wrong to injure them. All things considered, this can be overridden by Vedic injunction. The Vedānta philosopher Madhva departs from Rāmānuja and Śaṅkara by reading the *Vedānta Sūtra* as not condoning animal sacrifices. On Madhva's view, individuals are *jīva*-s, and each has moral standing, but they differ in moral character, resulting in differing outcomes. One might adopt a Consequentialist variant, as the Nyāya philosophers apparently did: for them, there are several outcomes that moral theory should consider, including suffering, and one's standing has to do with one being a subject of such goods (cf. Chakrabarti 2017).

The objectivity of moral standing

I have contrasted two kinds of theories of moral standing. According to one group (Kant, Jains, Vedānta and Mīmāṃsā philosophers), moral standing is a function of something *intrinsic* to the thing with standing: in this camp, we find theories that base moral standing on intrinsic rights. But here, the intrinsic feature (perhaps that it warrants consideration) determines its standing, so standing here is a matter of self-determination by the thing in question. *Svādhyāya* as a technical term of the *Yoga Sūtra* is what I have translated as "self-governance": it is the proceduralization of one of the essential features of the Lord, namely being unafflicted. To deny that moral standing has to do with what is intrinsic is to deny that it is self-determined and this implies that it is extrinsic. Theories of standing that take the property to be extrinsic include those theories that reduce standing to the minimization of suffering or the maximization of happiness—states of affairs quite independent of the things with standing (Buddhists, Nyāya and Vaiśeṣika philosophers, Kaśmīrī Śaivas, Bentham, Mill—for more, see Chapter 3). To deny self-determination is determinative of standing is to be unconstrained by past self-determinations. *Tapas* as a technical term of the *Yoga Sūtra* names this activity of being unconstrained by one's past, doing something different, receptivity to the extrinsic, and I have translated it as "unconservativism." It is the proceduralization of the other essential trait of the Lord, namely that it is untouched by karma (past action, or choice), which is tantamount to being not-self-governed but also free from past determinations. To recap, the third essential practice of Yoga is *Īśvarapraṇidhāna*, or meditation on the Lord. As the Lord is analyzable into these two procedures of *tapas* and *svādhyāya, Īśvarapraṇidhāna* takes these two as its objects, and thereby accomplishes the goal of Yoga: *citta vṛtti nirodha*—critical thinking (Chapter 5).

As reviewed in past chapters, the three practices together, each treated as a procedural ideal, are presented in the Hindu tradition as Lakṣmī (*svādhyāya*), Viṣṇu (*tapas*), and Ādi Śeṣa (*Īśvarapraṇidhāna*) floating over an ocean of opaque, mental waves of the Milk Ocean—the same ocean that Devas and Asuras had to churn to prove they know how to reason and to disagree to procure the *amṛta* (Chapter 4)—their entire project was one of *citta vṛtti nirodha*. The ocean hence is this turbulence (*vṛtti*) of mind (*citta*) that Ādi Śeṣa, and all of us, rise above by devotion to our own unconservativism and self-governance. This allows us to be still (*nirodha*) in a dynamic world.

The goal of this philosophical investigation into Hinduism is to identify the Hindu resources that we can use to model a philosophical debate: the objectivity of the debate is cashed out in terms of what parties have to converge on while they disagree about the philosophical topic. In so far as the two opposite options of the debate on moral standing (one that emphasizes self-determination, and the other the extrinsic) follow from the essential traits of the Lord, or Lakṣmī (self-governance) and Viṣṇu (unconservativism), it is as though it is this couple that we converge on when we disagree about moral standing. The Lord, a unitary abstraction, entails these two disjuncts.

These two theoretical options exhaust the disagreement about standing, as the disagreement is reducible to the claim that standing has to do with an intrinsic determination (*svādhyāya*) or an extrinsic determination (*tapas*), including for instance the minimization of harm or maximization of happiness. When we ask the question of what accounts for moral standing, we are as though Ādi Śeṣa, floating above a natural world of mental turbulence, meditating on the Lord. What we converge on as this Ādi Śeṣa is the objectivity of the debate of moral standing: *UNCONSERVATIVISM* or *SELF-GOVERNANCE*.

As the central concept of moral standing is objective—something we can disagree about—it is not reducible to our perspective but what we can know from perspectives as such. Then, whether and to what extent one has standing is objective, and not a matter of perspective as the property of standing is objective. As it is objective, we can disagree about it: we can for instance disagree that someone with moral standing should be treated as such (if for instance they are an aggressor), so the objectivity of standing does not close moral controversy: it provides it an opportunity.

The extrinsic, the intrinsic, and people

Plants appear to have an interest in unconservativism (*tapas*), as transformation, growth and moving beyond their seedling past is part of what it is for them to thrive. However, they do not *prima facie* have an interest in self-governance: as rooted in the soil, plants thrive in friendly environments and it is obvious that plants do not thrive when yanked out of the soil and forced to self-govern or figure things out on their own. They are examples of *moral patients*. Then there are things whose thriving is best explained by their own self-governance, the determination of identity intrinsically. Objects of intrinsic value, defined as they are intrinsically by some defining characteristic, have such an interest: in order for them to maintain their own value, they have to have value by virtue of an intrinsic characteristic. If they do not, they are counterfeits. No surprise that Lakṣmī, the Goddess explicated as *svādhyāya*, is this Goddess of *artha*, a term that stands for "wealth" and prosperity, but also "value," "meaning," and "purpose." She is the essence of all things of intrinsic value.

However, some things have an interest in freedom from the past while determining their own values on their own terms: we could call these things *people* (*puruṣa*). A person is something that thrives given the freedom to be unconstrained by the past by determining themselves. When they lack such a freedom to determine themselves and thereby be unconservative, they become ill and diseased, which tends to undermine their interests in being unconservative and self-governing. In short, people have an interest in the Lord (unconservativism and self-governance), which is to say their own Lordliness. And this interest is objective: it is not about what they prefer, but rather what explains their thriving.

Moral considerations that are appropriate to persons go beyond what is appropriate for things that are merely alive. Your hair and finger nails, not to mention pathogens in bodies, are alive, but it is far from clear that they have any distinct interest in their own Lordliness, for it is not clear how they would thrive given that freedom. This is especially true of parasites, which thrive only when they take advantage of someone else's self-governance and cannot thrive on their own. Plants certainly have interests: unlike parasites, they do not harm their host, but like parasites, they do not thrive when given the challenge of self-governing on their own. They need a host, the Earth, to be the self-governing environment that allows them to thrive.

Death and killing undermine self-governance: so smashing an object of intrinsic value, or a person, undermines their standing. But pruning and harvesting plants and their products are consistent with their interest in extrinsic thriving, as they have no interest in self-governance (if they did, they would thrive given the challenge of self-governance, but plants die given such a challenge). Hence, it is not inconsistent with a plant's standing to eat them, or their parts, for we are not undermining an essential interest in self-governance they lack.

People, in contrast, are a bit like plants, and bit like valuable objects, and the way they manage the conflicting tension of unconservativism and self-governance is by allowing the one to facilitate the other. It is a marriage internal to the Lord. Putting people in display cases or fastening them to the ground generally undermines their health. Rather, by self-governance, people do something different, and that allows them to thrive. When they stop doing something different, they get into a rut, and that is a problem for their health.

Certain procedural generalities follow from these considerations. Eating most animals interferes with their interest in their own Lordliness, as does treating them as objects of amusement, or objects of experimentation. Plants on the other hand can be cultivated and can thrive, and imposing limits on them is not inconsistent with their interests. Consuming animal products does not necessarily undermine a person's interests in their own Lordliness. There is an important difference between harvesting the hair or consuming the milk of a consenting family member or member of one's community, and consuming these as a matter of coercion: in the one case, everyone's interest in unconservativism and self-governance is protected, while in the latter case, it is not.

Certain teleological entailments also follow from these considerations. Not only are most animals persons, so too is the Earth, in so far as she thrives given her own unconservativism and self-governance. But one could say the same for the planets, the moon, the stars, and our star: the Sun. But, and perhaps surprisingly, these considerations also entail that the Lord itself has moral standing, in so far as the objectivity of the basic concept of moral standing is a deductive entailment from the essential traits of the Lord. We are apparently obliged to consider the Lord in moral deliberation—which entails the objectivity of moral standing.

This approach to standing does not identify a person by a capacity. To have an interest in any of the elements of moral standing (whether unconservativism or self-governance) is not the same as having the capacity: one might be sick, injured, or trapped after all, and still have an interest in one's own Lordliness, or in *tapas* or *svādhyāya*. A person may be dead, and yet it is a fact about them that they would have thrived had their interest in Lordliness been protected.

If your personal identity hinges upon your standing, and your standing is an objective ideal, then the Hindu optimism for life after death is not unfounded. For what it is to be a person on this account is not to actually be self-governing and unconservative, but to have an interest in one's own unconservativism and self-governance. Either being dead constitutes a bad or misfortune relative to an interest in one's unconservativism and self-governance, in which case one continues to have moral standing, or death is no obstacle to one's unconservativism and self-governance, because in death, all that is left of us is this interest. In the former case, we can be understood as transmigrating (relative to the Lord), and in the latter case, we have merged with the Lord in Vaikuṇṭha (the land of moral standing)—the realm of Viṣṇu or the Great Self that Death speaks about in the *Kaṭha Upaniṣad*.

Finally, as the essential traits of the Lord entail the objectivity of the debate of moral standing, the Lord's standing is a deductive entailment from the Lord. Any deity that is Lordly would thereby entail their own standing. Lakṣmī and Viṣṇu, self-determination and unconservativism, together comprise the essential traits of the Lord, but individually, they also entail the objectivity of moral standing as any disjunct on their own can be added to another as a rule of inference. Hence, each entails the objectivity of moral standing: *UNCONSERVATIVISM* or *SELF-GOVERNANCE*. Together, they have an interest in each other. We too have an interest in their marriage: self-governance married to conservativism leads to the self-enforcement of past decisions, no matter how poorly informed; unconservativism married to affliction, would lead to a perpetual revolution that always results in pain. We do well when it is Viṣṇu and Lakṣmī who are together.

Objections

A representative Hindu account of standing is not an account of what Hindus believe: it is an account of what we converge on when we disagree about moral standing, using Hindu resources to model the debate. I do think that the account explains (entails) many common Hindu conclusions about what kinds of things have standing—like animals, and celestial objects. But nothing in this account depends upon a backdrop of unanimity among Hindus. Yet, in so far as very many common Hindu conclusions about standing follow from the objectivity of the debate, Hindus can demonstrate that their intuitions on these matters are not a matter of language, culture or tradition, but moral theory viewed macroscopically. The very opposite can be said for the standard *W*estern approaches, that are tied to its characteristic linguistic account of thought. In this case, it is all culture, history, and tradition.

I will consider five objections.

People's moral standing conflicts

If a person's moral standing has to do with their own interest in unconservativism and self-governance, it follows that any interference in personal dietary choices, or restrictions with respect to how they are to behave, impacts on their own standing. But then, it would seem that we would be prohibited from defending ourselves against other people. We might decide to endorse a right of self-defense, but this is arbitrary—it seems we have no grounds for protecting our own standing over that of anyone else's (a Jain view we have reviewed).

Those who identify moral standing as objective (what we can disagree about) do not have this problem: if moral standing is objective, then we can take sides in conflicts *objectively*: so long as we choose a side that is devoted to unconservativism and self-governance, then our endorsement is objective since it entails the objectivity of the debate of moral standing. So we can and should choose sides that protect an interest in unconservativism and self-governance in the face of tyranny that seeks to undermine this freedom in general. This is to choose what is in all of our interests.

The ontological argument

I noted that the objectivity of the Lord's moral standing follows as a matter of entailment from the Lord itself. From the very idea of the Lord, we hence deduce its moral objectivity. This sounds like Anselm's argument in the *Proslogium*. There Anselm argued that if we were to believe the proper definition of God, we could not deny God's existence for existence is one of the defining traits of God. The problem with this argument is not that it assumes that existence is a predicate (as my undergraduate metaphysics professor John Leslie said to us—if you doubt that existence is a predicate, think about an imaginary pot of money and a real one, and ask which you would prefer) but that it begs the question. It assumes what it tries to prove by starting out with a belief in God. (Anselm famously claims in his argument that he does not understand so that he may believe, but believes so that he may understand.) Anselm is interpreting God. Our observation is different. Whereas Anselm believes that existence defines God, we observe here that the objectivity of moral standing is a deductive entailment of the Lord, and hence the Lord's standing follows from the Lord, but we do not have to begin with belief to discern this entailment: indeed, one cannot reason logically by expecting premises to be what one believes (Chapter 4). But now we have come to a deductive demonstration of the moral considerability of the Lord that does not rest on faith. The conclusion follows whether or not one believes in the Lord as something defined by unconservativism and self-governance.

Entailment of the Lord's own standing is implausible

Here is the response to this objection: start with the conjunction, *UNCONSERVATIVISM* and *SELF-GOVERNANCE*, which is the Lord. Through (the deductive rule of) simplification, we can separate the conjuncts, and then by the logical rule of addition, we can add any disjunct to any proposition: so we merely recombine the two conjuncts as each other's disjuncts (*UNCONSERVATIVISM* or *SELF-GOVERNANCE*), and the derivation is valid. But the conclusion is the objectivity of the debate of moral standing. One further objection is that "Unconservativism" or "Self-Governance" are not propositions and hence we cannot employ them with rules of propositional logic. But a proposition is anything that can be true or false, and truth is what reveals its content. So meditating on self-governance reveals what it is like: intrinsic constraint, like Padma sitting on herself. Unconservativism reveals itself too: like Viṣṇu unconstrained by his various active-presentations, such as the disk.

Mental life matters

In his criticism of *W*estern approaches to taking (non-human) animals seriously, Steiner notes that many of the arguments turn on a supposed kinship of experience or mental existence of humans and non-human animals. But humans and non-humans are sufficiently different (Steiner 2010: 20). Following Thomas Nagel, Steiner claims that we really do not know what it is like to be a bat and yet, it would seem that in calling a bat a person, we are claiming to know this as something similar to what we experience. This objection is confused: the objectivity of moral standing does not have anything to do with subjective experiences. Rather, a bat is a person as it thrives given its own Lordliness.

But the Kantian might take this opportunity to complain that moral standing only belongs to those who are capable of earning it, and that has to do with one's cognitive abilities, and to acknowledge and reason about moral laws, which non-human animals cannot.

This complaint is question begging: it assumes that humans can reason about moral laws and others cannot. As we have seen in our investigation into thought (Chapter 5) and knowledge (Chapter 6) there is no good reason to believe that thinking and moral knowledge is restricted to humans: thought and knowledge are a function of disciplinarity, which most animals engage in. The only way to generate Kant's chauvinism is the *W*est or the linguistic account of thought, for then only linguistic beings apparently can think.

No empirical evidence of the self

One relatively standard objection to taking yourself seriously is that there is no empirical evidence for the self. We find this kind of argument in Hume, who may have very well derived it from Buddhists (Gopnik 2009). In *Questions of King Milinda*, we find the monk Nāgasena arguing that with respect to any object, all we find are dependently originating things, grouped together by a word that we apply given our own objectives and priorities. But then, we have no grounds for believing in the objectivity of the self. It is a kind of verbal delusion. This entails that there can be no Lord, or things characterized by moral standing as this would involve something that has the trait of standing as an enduring property. This argument is mistaken because it assumes that the ground of moral standing is empirical. Whether you have moral standing has to do with the kinds of interests you have that would explain a well-lived life for you. But these interests are objective (we can converge on them as we disagree about moral standing). If they were subjective, you could find them by introspection, but they are not and hence it is inappropriate to expect that the objectivity of your standing is something you can observe. Then, what it is to be the same person over time is also inappropriately taken to be something that one can observe: that is to treat it as subjective. You are the same person over time given the continuity of your own interest in Lordliness.

Conclusion

The concept of moral standing, *UNCONSERVATIVISM* or *SELF-GOVERNANCE*, is a deductive entailment of the Lord, but we get to it by following a disagreement between two opposing kinds of theories of moral standing: one bases standing on the extrinsic, the other on the intrinsic. Against the backdrop of Yoga/Bhakti, the Lord is a procedural abstraction, what we approximate when we perfect ourselves as persons. And this procedural abstraction is not defined by naturalistic concepts of biology or genetics: it is the procedural ideal of living well. A representative Hindu account of moral standing is the objectivity of the Lord's standing, and Hindus have resources to model this. A common Hindu conclusion that the Lord is internal to all people and that when we meet others, we are seeing an expression of this Lordliness, is a deductive entailment from an objective approach to moral standing. Common Hindu conclusions that people come in many biological shapes, including most animals, celestial bodies, the Earth, and that death does not put an end to personhood are also deductive entailments of an objective approach to moral standing. Perhaps surprisingly, the idea of the Lord as something that entails the objectivity of moral standing also follows from these considerations: the Lord reveals its own objectivity as something that counts. We get there not by faith, but by explication, validity and disagreement. In practical terms, this means that whether someone or something has moral standing is not about whether you can sympathize with them, or see yourself in them, but rather what explains their thriving. It just so happens, the same explains yours, but that emphasizes not our commonalities or shared experiences but our interests in our own quirkiness.

References

Chakrabarti, Kisor K. 2017. "Nyāya Consequentialism." In *The Bloomsbury Research Handbook of Indian Ethics*, edited by Shyam Ranganathan, 203–224. London: Bloomsbury Academic.

Congenital Insensitivity to Pain. US National Library of Medicine. https://ghr.nlm.nih.gov/condition/congenital-insensitivity-to-pain#resources, Accessed 2017.

Gopnik, Alison. 2009. "Could David Hume Have Known about Buddhism?: Charles François Dolu, the Royal College of La Flèche, and the Global Jesuit Intellectual Network." *Hume Studies* 35, no. 1: 5–28.

Grey, John. 2013. "'Use Them at Our Pleasure': Spinoza on Animal Ethics." *History of Philosophy Quarterly* 30, no. 4: 367–388.

Kant, Immanuel. 1956. *Groundwork of the Metaphysics of Morals*. Translated by H.J. Paton. New York: Harper Torchbooks. file:O:\OldArchive\FilingCabinet3\Kant\Groundwork\Groundwork.doc.

Kant, Immanuel. 1974. *Critique of Judgment*. Translated by J.H. Bernard. Hafner. Library of Classics. New York; London: Hafner Press, Collier Macmillan.

Kant, Immanuel. 1996. *The Metaphysics of Morals*. Translated by Mary J. Gregor. New York: Cambridge University Press.

Ranganathan, Shyam. 2016a. "Pūrva Mīmāṃsā: Non-Natural, Moral Realism (4.14)." In *Ethics 1*, edited by S. Ranganathan. E-PG Pathshala, University Grants Commission, Government of India. http://epgp.inflibnet.ac.in/ahl.php?csrno=27.

Ranganathan, Shyam. 2016b. "Review of David White Gordon's *The Yoga Sutra of Patanjali: A Biography*." *Philosophy East and West* 66, no. 3: 1043–1048.

Ranganathan, Shyam. 2017. "Patañjali's Yoga: Universal Ethics as the Formal Cause of Autonomy." In *The Bloomsbury Research Handbook of Indian Ethics*, edited by Shyam Ranganathan, 177–202. London: Bloomsbury Academic.

Steiner, G. 2010. *Anthropocentrism and Its Discontents: The Moral Status of Animals in the History of Western Philosophy*. Pittsburgh, PA: University of Pittsburgh Press.

Wood, Allen. 1998. "Kant on Duties Regarding Nonrational Nature." *Proceedings of the Aristotelian Society Supplement* 72: 189–210.

8 Metaphysics

Two truths

Introduction

In this chapter, we shall investigate the topic of a representative Hindu account of metaphysics, which is an account of what philosophers (and Hindus) converge on while they disagree about metaphysics, using Hindu resources. The practice I have employed to this point is to identify the relevant philosophical concept as what competing theories in that field have to converge on while they disagree about the topic. The following section identifies the disagreements of metaphysics as an objectivity that we converge on while we disagree about the topic. In the third section I shall identify the representative Hindu account of metaphysics, which accounts for the disagreements of metaphysics by way of two orders of truths (two kinds of facts), and more specifically, a Rāmānuja-esque, Viśiṣṭādvaita model of Brahman as itself being comprised of the two kinds of facts. As usual, my objective is not to describe what Hindus believe. Representative Hindu accounts of philosophical topics steer us clear of belief overall, and focus instead on thought as a creature of disciplinarity. Facts, as true thoughts, also bypass belief, and our representative Hindu account of the facts will further clarify why belief is not determinative of reality. Interpretation and programs of investigation that take belief as a starting point (like Orthodox Indology) are far removed from reality. Reality in turn is elucidated not by belief, but by disagreement.

The slippery fact of facts

Metaphysics is the philosophical investigation into reality. Attention to the topic has waned because of the *W*est. Recall that the *W*est is the linguistic account of thought with a European origin. If thought is linguistic—if *logos*—and if true thoughts are about reality, then it seems like coming to terms with reality is just a matter of figuring out what our words mean—and that is linguistics, not philosophy. The tradition beginning in large measure with Plato cements this approach: on Plato's account in the *Republic* via Socrates, it is the philosopher who figures out the significance of categories by way of *logos*, and is then in a position to impart doctrine to his community. Plato is often regarded as defending a realism about the meaning of our words: nominal expressions have as their meaning a kind of abstract object, the form or idea, for him. But, as it is merely the meaning of a word, and as words are anthropological phenomena, the tradition that Plato helps found tends toward skepticism. Taken to its extreme, we find the position defended by the now defunct tradition of Logical Positivism, which branded metaphysics as pure nonsense, or as meaningful as poetry (Ayer 1946). Ayer thought that philosophers could play an important role in what was really the purview of the linguist or lexicographer—in determining what our words mean, but it is unclear why, as philosophers should really give way to the scientist on his view. There were other, less faithful attempts at keeping Plato's dream alive. On Plato's account, reality is just what we mean. But what if our words fail to track reality—what if there is a reality beyond and we simply have the wrong language? In *Being and Time*, Heidegger entertains this worry: his was a project of constructive metaphysics where the point is to stipulate a correct linguistic orientation for linguistic beings, and it would seem that his approach has a chance in so far as he conceives of the *right* content of language as language users: humans, or what he called *dasein*-s.

But what is it to get our words right or wrong, when our words are just social artifacts, entirely of our own creation? Heidegger's own students picked up on this worry in more than one way. Hans Georg Gadamer, the lead figure of the interpretive tradition of the *W*est, identifies our words with tradition, noting that this historical starting point is always our starting point in understanding—but hence, differing traditions will have differing starting points. Jacques Derrida, focusing on of what Frege would have called sense and reference (*sign* and *signified*, to use Derrida's Saussurean terminology), noted that whenever we speak, we refer to something beyond, and the mode of presentation—or presence—of our language is a façade, which is always *deferring* (referring) to something else. To his credit, Derrida is aware of the identification of thought with language in the *W*est but moreover appreciates the threat this poses for objectivity—insights he attributes to Heidegger: if thought is linguistic meaning, nothing escapes linguistic meaning, which means that there is in the ultimate analysis no difference between a thing and how we talk about it. Yet, there is something more on his account: neither the sense (presence) nor absence (referent) but a difference (Derrida 1976: 22–23, 26).

In the Analytic tradition, similar concerns (that a linguistic approach to thought blurs the lines between artifice and reality) were faced head on. W.V.O. Quine, who in many ways is part of Ayer's Logical Positivist movement, notes that the usual distinctions drawn between the truth of what we say when there is something empirical at stake (the synthetic), and the truth of definitional claims (the analytic) is not cut and dry, and the two mutually inform each other. Our seemingly empirical claims about the way things are depend on our choices of how to define and delineate terminology and our definitions are informed by a general knowledge of the way the world is. But this implies that individual claims and words do not bring us to reality: rather, it is the totality of our language (science) that makes contact with experience and hence there is a blurring of the lines between speculative metaphysics and empirical science (Quine 1951). It does not follow from this that all schemes about the world are equally good: those approaches that show pragmatic advantages are superior. Thomas Kuhn, a philosopher of science, observes pragmatics is what survives relative to external challenges: it is hence hard to grade competing worldviews as they are naturally selected for their specific context and not against some absolute standard (cf. Kuhn 1970: 146). Therefore, we should doubt that we ever know some objective reality for the standard of knowledge is context-relative.

This skepticism about metaphysics opens the door to what is often termed "post-modernism"—doubts about the possibilities of reason, much vaunted in the modernist period. Nevertheless, it did not convince everyone, or very many people (except perhaps for literary critics!) because research and knowledge proceeds, and research is a matter of discovery, but, and importantly, research proceeds along disciplinary lines—not linguistic lines. There was faint recognition of this in the Analytic tradition, but usually by way of absurdity. For instance, Hillary Putnam appreciated that knowledge is made possible by researchers in differing disciplines, but as a *W*esterner, he committed to understanding thought by way of language, which meant that he had to assimilate disciplinary research to a "division of linguistic labor" (Putnam 1975: 145)—as though researchers in physics where actually specialized linguists. The *W*est and its peculiar approach to thought entails many absurdities—imperialism is just its most political absurdity. But here, we come to the epistemic absurdity that all disciplines are just a version of linguistics. They are not: disciplines are defined by their own practices. When researchers make a discovery they are not always or usually figuring out what our words mean: often there's no word for what is being discovered until it is discovered and named—and what takes us there are inquiry-based *uses* of words, not their meaning. Already philosophers of language have noted for some time, that we can use words to talk about objects, even if the meaning does not entail such an object (Donnellan 1966). In disciplinary research, this is the norm: we use our workaday resources to talk about matters that escape our cultural and linguistic past. Inquiry is thereby *unconservative*, and it is made possible by *self-governing* people who choose their own topics of investigation.

As we reviewed in Chapter 5, a representative Hindu account of thought explains the essence of thought as something essential to research. To think is to track objects (or subjects) from differing perspectives, and the discipline (yoga) is the common practice that we can engage in from multiple perspectives that allows us to compare, contrast, and collate our perspectives into a thought about a topic. This is not only an activity that most healthy critters such as ourselves do when we track objects and other persons in the public world: advanced disciplines such as philosophy or mathematics are especially formal disciplines, which require training in an activity that is unusual. But the basic pattern is the same. The objectivity of the thought is what we can disagree about, while true thoughts are transparent: they reveal to us what we can disagree about. In this state of clarity, the contents of our thoughts are known, and knowing is not the same as agreeing.

It is about understanding the objectivity of the thought itself. So for instance, in the case of mathematics, the objectivity of mathematical propositions is that we can disagree about them from differing perspectives. The true propositions, such as *2+2=4*, properly understood, reveal to us their derivability from a more basic system. To understand *2+2=4* is hence to know that it is derivable from more basic principles of number theory and arithmetic. This hence reveals to us the objectivity of *2+2=4*, what we can disagree about. In terms of a representative Hindu account of thought reviewed in Chapter 5, where the extension is the common use of competing semiotic resources with a common purpose, a full explication of the extension of *2+2=4*, would not only include descriptions of this claim, but derivations from more basic mathematical principles. Hence a disciplinary investigation into this thought would discover its internal resources that display its own objectivity. False mathematical propositions, such as *2+2=5* are not derivable from more basic systems and hence do not reveal themselves. (There could be systems relative to which *2+2=5* is derivable—here, it would be true. But given arithmetic, the same principles that allows the derivation of *2+2=4* would not help us here even if they are within the extension of *2+2=5*.) In philosophy, the objectivity of thinking in its various forms (thoughts, component concepts, theories, and their entailments) is facilitated by the discipline (crystallized in the method of explication) and what is true reveals to us this objectivity. We saw in Chapter 4 that the philosophical facts are synoptic of the disagreements. In the case of the empirical sciences, the discipline of science facilitates the objectivity of thinking by tracking empirical objects either directly or by their effects, and the truth reveals to us such objectivities—often in the form of empirical laws that explain observations from differing perspectives. The empirical thoughts are a collection of these dissenting perspectives, and the facts are the ones that are comprised by perspectives that reveal the content of disagreement. For instance, there are several differing descriptions of the night sky from differing perspectives: (a) “there is the evening star,” (b) “there is the morning star,” and (c) “there is Venus.” If these were competing extensional elements of an empirical thought, defined by a common empirical intension (to describe what is seen in the sky), then they would comprise an empirical fact, which reveals to us its own content of disagreement: Venus. The perspective that identifies Venus accurately as a planet in the sky, relative to the other two perspectives, is *dispositive*. The disciplinary commonality of the three represented perspectives leads us to identify this perspective as dispositive. We could imagine a false empirical thought, which adds to this extension (d) “that is a cup of coffee” said of an object on my desk. Here, the disciplinary exploration of the extension of this thought reveals no explanation of the disagreement. But instead of (d) we could also imagine (d_{fr}) “that blink in the sky is an illusion put their by God to test our faith.” I shall call this last extensional element a *free rider*: it sneaks into the line like Rāhu as though it is part of the group of perspectives that can disagree, but it cannot for it entails a rejection of the disciplinary considerations that would allow us to determine the objectivity of the disagreement. Free riders could never be dispositive. If we allowed for the thought with the extension (a), (b), (c), and (d_{fr}) to be explored, we could acknowledge that it is true by virtue of (c) (the acknowledgement of Venus in the sky) but this entails that (d_{fr}) is mistaken. But this generalizes: the acknowledgement of facts about objects entails a criticism of the undespositive perspectives that constitute a thought. In acknowledging that "evening star" tracks Venus, we at once acknowledge that it is responsive to the objectivity of Venus, but synoptically mistaken: Venus is not a star.

To move into a multicultural world, out of the nonsense of the *W*est, and to understand how thought is what we can investigate, disagree about, and debate from our differing perspectives, the role of discipline in facilitating thought is unavoidable (Chapter 5). To misunderstand thinking and to undermine its objectivity, we can certainly avoid the issue of disciplines: then a thought is just whatever we mean by what we say, but as this is nothing we can deny without absurdity, a thought is just whatever we believe, and this is made true by our attitude. Yoga, disciplinarity, challenges this: it is to control a proposition as something to be investigated, not something to be passively believed.

Yet, if metaphysics is about reality, what does it have to do with disciplinarity? Here, we can quote Frege: "'Facts, facts, facts' cries the scientist if he wants to bring home the necessity of a firm foundation for science. What is a fact? A fact is a thought that is true" (Frege 1988: 51). A fact is a thought, plus truth. Reality is the facts. Hence, to be out of touch with reality is to be out of touch with the facts. So, in so far as disciplines constitute thoughts and facilitate their truth, they reveal to us the facts. If we identify reality with the facts, and metaphysics with a philosophical investigation into reality, we can understand why metaphysical questions are different from ontological questions. A metaphysical question is an abstraction, and its answer is something true, or factual. Ontological questions have to do with the nature of things, which are usually neither true nor false. On this distinction, we can see that questions about what our words mean are at best ontological questions. Rather, when we disagree about metaphysics, we disagree about the facts. One possible answer to the metaphysical question of the nature of the facts is to say that they are material (materialism) or that they are mental (idealism): either way, we are making a claim about the facts, which if true is a kind of abstract, second order fact about facts.

We seem to lose our grip on metaphysics now, for it seems that for any question that we think is really a philosophical question about reality, it can be easily converted into a question about the truth of a certain thought, and then that matter is resolved by the relevant discipline, which may be but often is not philosophy. Therefore, metaphysics, a philosophical investigation into reality, gets converted into an investigation into the facts, then every discipline (from anthropology to zoology) has something to say about reality, and philosophy has no claim over the topic.

However, philosophy has a special claim to the topic of metaphysics for two reasons. First facts are true thoughts, and thoughts, and their components, namely concepts, are the topic of philosophical investigation. Second, the philosophical question about metaphysics arises because we can disagree about the first order facts. So even though the facts may be revealed by their respective disciplines, we can yet disagree about the category of facts as such, and this disagreement is philosophical as it is a disagreement about thoughts.

Philosophy can certainly help us discern the truth of philosophical claims, and this truth *reveals* the objectivity of what we can disagree about in philosophy. Yet there are many kinds of facts that we can disagree about and they are not philosophical: facts about how many grains of sand there are on a beach, the age of the universe, or the square root of 4. As we attempt to be philosophical about the facts, they slip out of our reach and become the topic of any and every discipline, except philosophy.

But stranger still, if facts are true thoughts, then in converging on the facts, we are converging on what is true. But whereas to converge on an object is to disagree about how it seems from various perspectives, to converge on the truth is to agree! Now facts are slippery for a different reason: in converging on the truth, we are not thereby converging on the objective as we agree, and yet facts are true thoughts, and thoughts are objective, in so far as we can disagree about them. So somehow, we land in a paradoxical place when we reach the truth by losing objectivity.

Truth, a diversion

Some progress might be had by reviewing the question of truth. If we can be philosophical about truth, then in being philosophical about thoughts also, we will have a way to grasp the facts. Our philosophical investigation into Hinduism began with a distinction between thoughts, truth, objects, subjects, *and* propositional attitude claims. One approach that is often taken to be a platitude is that truth consists in a *correspondence* between the way things are and how they are represented. It is a platitude if it models the notion of truth's revelatory properties, for most accounts of truth agree to the revelatory character of truth. It is criticized in its less vacuous form, for evoking the image of some separate thing that is our thought, which has to correspond to the way things are. The problem here is that it becomes rather unclear what this separate thing is. The early Wittgenstein, in his famous *Tractatus*, suggested that they were pictures, and in attempting to discern whether a thought was true, we compared the picture in our mind with the way things are, but this creates new problems: how do we know when the picture is accurate, and where this picture is residing? If we have some criterion that allows us to discern the identity of our pictures and the way things are, how do we know that the criterion corresponds to our pictures? If we invoke yet a new picture or criterion, we are in the territory of an infinite regress—a threat noted by Patañjali in the *Yoga Sūtra* (YS IV.21). It does not obviously help to understand the theory as suggesting that a thought is true just in case what it depicts obtains, for this leaves us with the problem of figuring out the correspondence between the two components. To avoid such problems, some philosophers have defended a more deflationary approach that treats truth as a metalinguistic device of assertion: so when we say some proposition is true, we are basically just asserting the proposition. Truth here too reveals its content, but in this case it is the asserted proposition and nothing more. This last theory has a strange implication, which I am surprised is not widely advertised: on this account, if I was to assert a valid argument it would thereby be sound, for truth here is just the assertion, and a sound argument is a valid argument with truth. Nevertheless, I cannot turn a valid argument into a sound argument merely by asserting it for if that is all it takes, then any time I entertain a valid argument by articulating it, it is thereby sound, and hence I could not ever articulate a merely valid argument without making it sound. Yet, validity comes apart from truth. The Peircean idea that truth is what we converge on at the end of inquiry is rather similar, but it adds that the condition under which assertion is 'true' is at the end of inquiry. The problem is that even at this point, what we converge on may be merely objective, and not true. If at this point we could not distinguish between the objective and the true, then our convergence on the validity of an argument would render it sound. But certainly we can converge on the validity of an argument without having to take it to be true. I am sure we could massage the view: at the end of inquiry, we might converge on an argument *being* valid, and that is true, but we can also merely converge on the validity of an argument at the end of inquiry. If truth is what we converge on at the end of inquiry, it is unclear how we maintain the distinction between the valid and the sound at the end of inquiry for what we converge on at this point is the truth.[1]

The more basic idea that truth is merely the property of a proposition that reveals its content helps us avoid much of these problems with a representative Hindu account of thought from Chapter 5. Thoughts are the common disciplinary employment of meaning, and the true thoughts reveal to us a content, synoptically, while the false fail to. Metaphorically, true thoughts correspond to their content, but literally, they do not. We require no criterion to compare pictures with reality, and we do not need to go down the path of an infinite regress. Rather, from that factive state (*prajñā*) we can discern the normative order that structures the facts (*Ṛta*). "It is different from observation and inference, for it relates to the essence of things" (YS I.47–49). In the case of facts about objects, the truth explains the disagreement in terms of an object, and in the case of facts about subjects, it brings our attention to the relevant subjects, and explains the subject's perspective, which we can also perceive from differing perspectives. Either way, truth protects the objectivity of a thought as something that tracks its content from differing perspectives. Truth is thereby a synopsis of disciplinary research and the discipline makes the synopsis of competing accounts from differing perspectives possible as the discipline constitutes the common axis to compare competing perspectives—a matter that we have already delved into in our exploration of a representative Hindu account of thought. False propositions (perhaps they come in degrees) fail to reveal the normative structure of what we can disagree about. They seem to have content, but from particular perspectives only (like beliefs!). So in the case of the truth, we know we have found it when the proposition depicts what we can disagree about from all relevant perspectives—unlike the false, it is reality.

While to converge on the truth is to agree, truth reveals the objectivity that makes such convergence possible. Therefore, thinking clearly about truth allows us to understand how we apparently regain an appreciation for objectivity after converging on the truth: if we understand *why* a thought is true, we understand its content objectively. When a thought is false, we cannot understand its content objectively: it depicts nothing we can disagree about. When we believe a false thought is true, we have left disciplinary research and are engaging in the indulgence of propositional attitudes, and their descriptions. Knowing, as per the representative Hindu account of knowledge, is not an attitude (as we saw in Chapter 6).

But now we can recognize philosophy in this picture: not merely as the discipline that helps us understand what a fact, a thought and the truth as such amounts to (as we have been doing) but what allows us to converge on the second order question: why are the facts, all of them, the facts? An answer to this question would be a candidate second order fact, and if it is true, it is a second order fact, and one that is philosophical. So it seems that there are two kinds of truths at play in metaphysics: the first order facts of disciplines, and the second order philosophical fact, about the first order facts. And yet, at the second level, we can disagree about how to characterize the first order facts: the second order of facts are themselves objective. And if the first order facts are all of them characterizable by a discipline, then the second order facts would have to do with yoga itself: disciplinarity itself, for it is in virtue of disciplinarity that the first order facts *are* the facts, even if they are facts of differing disciplines.

Viśiṣṭādvaita Brahman as a representative Hindu account of reality

Facts are true thoughts, and both truth and thought are facilitated by disciplinarity—we are taken to this conclusion via a representative Hindu account of thought. Metaphysical disagreements—philosophical disagreements about true thoughts—occur at a second order, where competing theories try to characterize all of the facts. Any accurate second order account would be a second order fact. Hence, there are two levels of truths. The first level characterizes the outcome of disciplinary research, while the second is synoptic. But what is essential to both levels is disciplinarity, as the facts, their thoughts, and their truth are reducible to disciplinarity. Disciplinarity in turn is made possible by the activation of our own unconservativism and self-governance: self-governance allows us to engage in the same practice, while unconservativism allows us to take up differing perspectives—disciplinarity is about engaging in the same practice from differing perspectives to triangulate on objects of inquiry. This is to undertake the project of controlling thought for investigation as opposed to believing it (YS I.2) Unconservativism and self-governance characterizes the procedural ideal of yoga, Īśvara or the Lord (YS I.24). It is instantiated in the first order facts, in so far as they are disciplinary, and when we disagree about the first order facts at the second level in metaphysics, we converge on our shared unconservativism and self-governance to contest the facts. Hence, the Lord is instantiated in the plurality of first order facts, but is what we converge on as a common procedural ideal at the second order.

Indian philosophers have long entertained a distinction between two kinds of facts, often called a distinction between two kinds of truths: first order or conventional truths, and second order or ultimate truth. This distinction between worldly (*saṁvṛti-satya*) or the ultimate (*paramārtha-satya*) is the philosophical distinction between the CONTINGENT or the NECESSARY—this is the objectivity of the concept REALITY, which we converge on when we disagree about reality. This way of cashing out the distinction between two truths is often attributed to the Buddhist tradition (Thakchoe 2011). But forms of the distinction are as old as the Vedas and it is simply the basic concept of metaphysics.

The early part of the Vedas, where we find an early description of a plurality of gods, identified them largely as forces of nature to be propitiated for the sake of beneficial consequences. This was a very early form of moral naturalism and Consequentialism where early Hindus theorized that in acting so as to appease the forces of nature, we are able to gain the outcomes we require and desire. One problem with this approach to moral reasoning is that it leaves the outcomes to luck: they remain outside our control and one of the signs of this lack of control is the need to appease not only the gods, but evil forces in the form of blood offerings to demons in sanctified sacrifices (*Aitaraya Brāhmaṇa* 2.1.7). Perhaps given a skepticism about the efficacy of appeasing the gods, and also because of an ethical concern for controlling outcomes, the tradition moves to the moral paradigm of the later Vedas in the *Upaniṣads*: a procedural ethics. The concern for controlling outcome is clearly on display in the *Kaṭha Upaniṣad*, where the God Death praises the boy Nachiketa (sent to his death prematurely) for not being bought off by trinkets and being concerned instead for control. Here Death teaches the boy an early articulation of the philosophy of Yoga: by controlling the senses by the intellect and via the mediation of the mind, we steer ourselves away from disaster and land in the realm of Viṣṇu (*Kaṭha Upaniṣad* I.2–3). This shift to control is accompanied elsewhere in the *Upaniṣads* with a concern for Brahman: the Great, Expansion, Development. To postulate Brahman as the basic reality is to treat luck as something that can be eliminated because reality is itself a process of growth: so taking control of our own life is not a matter of luck but a matter of reality. This is a pole-vault from the early teleology of the Vedas to the radical proceduralism of the later tradition, characterized by Yoga and Bhakti. In this move, we find an early articulation of the Two Truths doctrine: the lower truth is the plurality of natural forces that distract the senses, and the ultimate truth is the unifying Brahman. In the *Bṛhadāraṇyaka Upaniṣad* (IX.9) we find a dialectic where the various gods (the forces of nature) in the early Vedas are reduced to the one Brahman. It is moreover identified with *prāṇa* (breath)—which has obvious yogic implications. We learn in the *Yoga Sūtra* sometime later that controlling breath is about discarding boundaries between the inside and outside, but also importantly, it is something that one controls as part of one's own expansion (YS II). Breath is literally Brahman. What is metaphysically significant is that here we have a relatively early articulation of the idea that the basic first order facts of the world are reducible to a second order fact: Brahman.

Most ancient Indian philosophies have some account of what the basic facts are, and what the second order or metaphysically explanatory facts are. This helps philosophers do work. For instance, even in a tradition as distant from metaphysics as the Pūrva Mīmāṃsā, concerned as it is primarily with dharma, we find care devoted to questions of the reality of the gods. And while it is a first order fact that the gods are mentioned in the Vedas—and they are objective in so far as we can disagree about their importance—we find Pūrva Mīmāṃsā philosophers arguing that the gods are not real. For sure, they regard the Vedas as revealing the content of dharma, but to take the Vedas seriously does not commit oneself to having to take the reality of the gods seriously. But what is this except an argument that the second order facts about the Vedas do not entail any independent facts about the gods: they are merely literary devices in the text aimed at coaxing a moral form of life (*Nyāyaratnākara* of Pārthasārathi Miśra on Kumārila's *Ślokavārttika* 60).

We noted that the *Yoga Sūtra* and *Sāṅkhya Kārikā* hold that reality is comprised of two explanatory principles: *prakṛti* (nature) and *puruṣa* (person). But they differ as to their relationship. The Sāṅkhya view appears to be that both are part of the first order facts of the world, but the second order facts, which we understand with intellectual clarity, are that the personal facts are reducible to the natural facts (SK 62–63). Yoga in contrast denies this reduction. Rather, the natural facts should be treated as eliminable via a moral transformation that protects our personal boundaries (*kaivalya*) in a public world (YS IV.29–34). The *Vaiśeṣika Sūtra*, known for its ontological realism, begins (I.i.2) with an account of basic categories to which contingent facts are reducible, and this reduction of the contingent to an exhaustive categorization is a second order, metaphysical account of the first order facts.

Two truths are basic to metaphysical explanation. However, not every philosophy emphasizes the distinction. Nāgārjuna, often regarded as a second Buddha, is famous for a theory about the distinction. Nāgārjuna distinguishes between conventional truth and ultimate truth. Nāgārjuna deconstructively shows in his *Mūlamadhyamakakārikā* that while *prima facie*, it seems that any object of inquiry is definable by a *svabhāva*—essence—close inspection reveals that it is empty of such traits. This is because a deeper insight into reality reveals that an object becomes as though a placeholder for relationships, and the traits that we thought defined an object become absorbed into the shifting constellation of *relata*. Ultimately, nothing has *svabhāva*, which literally means 'own-being,' which for him is autonomy. So the ultimate truth is that everything is empty. This means that nothing is reducible to necessary and sufficient traits, and all things are filled with possibilities. For Nāgārjuna as a Buddhist this is an entailment of Dependent Origination: the idea that at base, everything is relational and there are no primary explanations.

In his day, Nāgārjuna observed that many people misunderstood the argument. It was and continues to be a common straw-man claim that Nāgārjuna's philosophy of Emptiness is the doctrine of Nihilism—that nothing is real and that nothing matters. He provided a counter argument. The ethical teachings of the Buddha depend upon a distinction between two truths. Trying to understand Emptiness without Buddhist moral teaching is like trying to hold a snake dangerously. If we deny Emptiness, we have to understand everything as defined by an *svabhāva* (an essence, or its autonomy) and then there can be no change—and yet, things change. Emptiness is not Moral Nihilism: it is the appreciation of our responsibility to the future as something open ended—possibilities for which we are responsible (*Mūlamadhyamakakārikā* XXIV).

Nāgārjuna's argument is so easily caricatured, yet insightful and cutting. It raises the problem of accounting for the dynamism of reality in a world defined by essences, and one where we can be responsible for our selves, given the essential nature of reality. It has a response to Parmenidean paradoxes, where the essential nature of reality seems to rule out change. The problem with this theory, as a model of the objectivity of metaphysics, is that it does not explain how the facts are controversial, and hence it has no explanation for the objectivity of the facts. According to Nāgārjuna, we have to buy into the essence of the first order truths that include the dictates of Buddhist morality in order to understand the second order truth: Emptiness. If I have to believe the first order facts in order to understand the second order facts, then I have replaced thinking about facts, with belief, and I have thereby rendered the objectivity of the first order facts inexplicable for they are nothing I can disagree about if I understand the second order facts. The problem here is that the second order fact (Emptiness) does not explain how the first order facts are controversial, and thereby objective. It rather replaces the certitude of the first order facts including the conventions of Buddhist morality with an underdetermined second order fact. The second order fact, Emptiness, is also not objective if there is no sense to us disagreeing about Emptiness: from all perspectives, it is empty.

On the yogic model of two truths that I accounted for at the start of this section, we treat both levels of facts as controversial: the second order disagreement about how to characterize all the first order facts shows that the first order facts are not at all settled, even though they are the outcome of disciplinary research. Second, in so far as we can disagree at all about second order, metaphysical theories about the facts, the second order is controversial: the Lord is what we happen upon when we acknowledge the objectivity of the second level. The Lord, unconservativism and self-governance, unlike Emptiness, is something we can disagree about in so far as it entails its own objectivity: the disjunct of unconservativism or self-governance. Hence, as we disagree about the facts, it may seem to us that we or our opponents are indulging either in self-governance or unconservativism as we dispute the facts.

The Hindu philosopher who describes the yogic approach to two truths is the Vedānta philosopher Rāmānuja. For Rāmānuja, Brahman indicates an ultimate person—the Lord—but it can also be analyzed into a body and self: the body is constituted by all the facts (all reality) and each is a species or mode (*prakāra*) or expression of the Lord, which relates to its constituents as its higher Self (*Vedārthasaṅgraha* §117). We ourselves are each a fact of Brahman's Body, and our essence is the Lord.

While a Vedānta philosopher, he explicitly identified the Lord with Viṣṇu and Lakṣmī: while not conventionally noted, these two deities personify unconservativism and self-governance, the essential traits of the Lord as described in the *Yoga Sūtra*. Proceduralized, these are *tapas* and *svādhyāya*, which along with *Īśvarapraṇidhāna* make up the essential practices of yoga. By parity, Viṣṇu and Lakṣmī sitting on Ādi Śeṣa (*Īśvarapraṇidhāna*), who floats over a wavy ocean, forms a central motif in the Bhakti tradition of which Rāmānuja is a part. This coincidence of the philosophy of Yoga and the philosophy of Bhakti in Rāmānuja seems surprising until we appreciate that the moral theory defended in the *Yoga Sūtra* is Bhakti, and "Yoga" is another way of talking about the same theory. When we talk about bhakti (devotion) we emphasize the procedural ideal of practice that we emulate, and when we talk about yoga, we talk about the practice defined by the procedural ideal. Morally, these are the same theories. (Of course, Hindus can and often identify different deities as the object of their veneration, and this very activity of choosing or discovering one's own ideal is described in the YS as part of the function of self-governance, see YS II.44.)

For us what is certainly useful in Rāmānuja's vision of Brahman is that his model of reality is what we converge on when we allow for the objectivity of the facts, as something that can be disputed both at the first and the second level. For in appreciating that the first order facts are creatures of disciplinarity and thereby instantiate the Lord, we recognize that they are creatures of dispute and disagreement, with Lordliness as an organizing principle, and at the second level we appreciate that it is a common Lordliness that we converge on when we are free to dispute the facts. The facts are as though a little *Ādi Śeṣa*, a creature of disciplinarity, revealing the Lord—rising above the turbulence of mental content. But just as Ādi Śeṣa does not converge on one person but a disjunct, which we can disagree about, at the second level we converge on the objectivity of the Lord: *UNCONSERVATIVISM* or *SELF-GOVERNANCE*.

There are of course other versions of Vedānta, and by no means is Rāmānuja's model the only picture of what Brahman looks like. Ādi Śaṅkara, the famous Advaitan, promotes a reductive monism: the controversies about the facts on his account arise from a superimposition of the Self on to objects of knowing, creating a phenomenal world (preamble, *Vedānta Sūtra Bhāṣya*). Advaita Vedānta so understood is a suitable diagnosis of the ailments of the *W*est, as the *W*est consists in the imposition of the subjectivity of believers on to propositions that create beliefs via the linguistic account of thought, which form the basis for interpreting everything. The *W*esternized world is a world of *avidya* (nescience) brought about by this superimposition. While a cool critical tool it is unclear how Śaṅkara's model helps us understand how the facts themselves are controversial. On Śaṅkara's account, the first order facts are not facts but beliefs, which we cannot disagree with as they are true by virtue of their constitutive attitude—rather, we need to disengage this superimposition by self-knowledge. The second order fact (the Self) is a fact, but properly understood there is no room for disagreement: it is merely the Subjectivity (the Self of all) that makes possible the delusion of the ordinary worldview, and the power of that Self to create such an ersatz reality is its *māyā* (illusion), which is the same as nature (*prakṛti*) (*Vedānta Sūtra Bhāṣya* III.ii.14).

Madhva, in his *Mahābhāratatātparyanirṇaya*, in contrast holds that all things in reality are constrained by an essential character, except Brahman, which he identifies with Viṣṇu. The underdetermining essence of Brahman makes possible a world of controversy where we see things, defined essentially, as though they are merely contingent for Brahman moves what is essentially frozen by essence. But the ultimate truth is that nothing changes—not really. Brahman, the unconservative (Viṣṇu), hence allows for the self-governance of everything else—including the essence of self-governance, Lakṣmī (*Mahābhāratatātparyanirṇaya* I.70–103). This model answers Parmenidean worries about the reality of change against the backdrop of reality that never changes. Parmenides, the pre-Socratic, was reported to have held that reality cannot change, for if it did, it would stop being real. Madhva's solution to this type of worry is to add into the mix of the facts, which cannot change, one thing (Brahman) that does—in this respect, it is like Nāgārjuna's Emptiness. Yet, to understand things and Brahman is to understand their essence, which leaves no room for disagreement.

The yogic model we find in Rāmānuja is different, for to understand it is not to agree on the facts: it is rather to understand the facts as in flux and contestable, held together by procedural ideals that are themselves objective and contestable. Reality is what we know from our perspective, but it is not reducible to our perspective.

Just to be clear, the idea that Rāmānuja's model of Brahman is a representative Hindu account of reality does not require that Hindus believe it, nor does it entail that they do—my presentation may not even be what Rāmānuja believed, and that is fine. Rather, it models what we converge on while we disagree about metaphysics. The representative Hindu model of metaphysics entails a kind of robust realism. The facts are not the same as what we believe. Even when we believe we know what the facts are, we may have grounds to revise our assessment. The facts are different from our beliefs. The facts are rather determined by disciplinary considerations—not our beliefs. We can be surprised by the facts.

On the ineffability of the facts

A common gloss on the distinction between the two varieties of truth is that it articulates a distinction between what is effable and what is ineffable—the conventional truths are effable while the ultimate truths are not. Similarly, one might suppose that the conventional truths are conceptual, and the ultimate truths are not. Does a representative Hindu account of metaphysics take us to these conclusions? The question is worth raising as it seems that in many Jain, Buddhist and Hindu traditions, the distinction between the two truths does take us here. Certainly, as we saw with Nāgārjuna's handling of the distinction, the ultimate truth is empty, and lacks *svabhāva*. Yet, concepts apparently have *svabhāva*. Moreover to talk of "emptiness" is a way of signaling that the ultimate truths cannot be expressed linguistically.

To probe this we need to first acknowledge that the ineffability of the ultimate truth and it being non-conceptual are not the same claim—unless one assumes the linguistic account of thought. On the assumption of the linguistic account of thought, concepts are linguistic meanings, and hence if language cannot articulate a certain idea, then we would have to conclude that the matter is non-conceptual. If we adopt a disciplinary approach to thought, which facilitates and constitutes a representative Hindu approach to thought (Chapter 5), we see that the issue of linguistic effability and conceptual content are distinct. The ultimate facts, and thoughts themselves, are not expressible by language, but that is because the thought and the facts are constituted by the disciplinary employment of language. Thinking and the facts are hence not what we encode as linguistic meaning: they are rather the normative structure of our public interactions, which permit objectivity. One implication of a representative Hindu approach to thought is hence that thinking is not a matter of having attitudes towards thoughts: it is rather about engaging publicly in inquiry, and the inquiry facilitates the triangulation and isolation of objects, which we can see from differing perspectives. So thinking is hence not a particularly human affair: it is what animals such as ourselves, or the Earth, do when they track objects in public space.

But our topic here is not merely thought, but the facts—the true thoughts. And this injects into the discussion the question of truth: how do we figure out what thoughts are true? And, it would seem the moment we have a view about the truth of a thought, we now have a propositional attitude of belief. This requires some capacity to represent thoughts, and hence something like language is required. But the Earth and my dog (Jyoti, a Border Collie) apparently do not speak language. So apparently, they would not be able to know what the facts are. But if they do not know what the facts are, then they cannot apparently converge on the facts while disagreeing.

In Chapter 6, on a representative Hindu account of epistemology, we observed that the objectivity of knowledge—what we converge on as we disagree about knowledge—is cashed out in terms of the *Mahāvrata*-s: five ostensibly political values that procedurally facilitate the objectivity of knowledge. By adopting a non-harmful approach to competing perspectives, we come to the truth, and the truth reveals to us not only a world where we do not deprive other perspectives of what is theirs, we do not hoard or clutter our own perspective, but we are in apposition to understand and learn (*brahmacarya*) by respecting personal boundaries. Coming to understand that a thought is true (the facts) is hence an immersion in the ethics of knowing. So the determination of truth on a representative Hindu model of knowledge does not require language or representation: it is facilitated by a preserving approach to a diversity of perspectives. Thus, in so far as the Earth, or Jyoti (the Border Collie) do not harm what they can inspect, they are in a position to have the truth reveal the content of their thoughts. None of this requires agreement. It is the exploration of disagreement.

Our topic here is on metaphysics. So our topic is not about how we can determine what the facts are (that is an epistemic question) but rather, we are concerned with accounting for the objectivity of the facts: we are trying to answer the question of what they are like. A disciplinary approach to thought that constitutes a representative Hindu approach to the topic (what Hindus and all of us converge on as we disagree about thought) entails that disciplinarity constitutes thoughts, and the essence of disciplinarity is the Lord. And hence, in so far as we converge on the facts as we disagree about them, we converge on our shared Lordliness—our freedom and interest in not collapsing our perspectives, in maintaining our autonomy while relating to each other ethically. All of this is a condition of thought and hence the facts. This does not require language: it rather requires that our interest as agents is elucidated by considerations of disciplinarity that are external to us but also subsume us. Hence, as the Earth, and animals in general, converge on what they can take divergent perspectives on without having to agree (assume the same perspective), they converge on a common Lordliness.

The lessons of a representative Hindu account of metaphysics

Is this mysticism? If mysticism is what transcends reason, this is not mysticism. Our careful journey of querying differing topics of philosophy, including logic, gets us here. If mysticism is what transcends language, then yes it is mysticism, but the facts transcend language and that does not render them beyond our capacity for understanding or inquiry. To converge on the Lord is to give up on belief, and attitude, as the proxy for reason and knowing, and to instead engage in disciplined inquiry that facilitates disagreement, thinking, and the possibility of true thoughts. But this is not to converge on beliefs, but the procedural ideal of personal freedom, to be unconstrained by the past, and to control our future.

A metaphysical take-home from these considerations is that the metaphysical essentials, which make disagreement about the facts possible, paradoxically have something in common. What we have in common is this interest in our own individuality—our own Lordliness.

Another metaphysical take-home is that this distinction between the conventional and the absolute—the contingent and the necessary—cannot be divorced from ethical considerations. We saw this beginning with our investigation into a representative Hindu account of logic: even making sense of validity requires a diversity of perspectives that can converge on the force of a third-party perspective without giving in. Attempts to divorce the ethical from the logical lead to absurdities of trying to make sense of reason in terms not of a diversity of perspectives, but of truths and principles, which in turn is incompatible with validity which comes apart from truth. In acknowledging that a representative Hindu account of metaphysics elucidates the topic in relationship to moral considerations, we find a theme in Indian philosophy. As noted, Buddhists such as Nāgārjuna draw a strong connection between ethical considerations and the Two Truths. Jains, for their part, also base their idea of the absolute description of persons on the moral analysis of the individual as an intrinsically virtuous thing, clouded and confused by action. The ultimate truth reveals us as this virtue, but also thereby free not to be determined by action. In contrast, the conventional view is that we are agents, defined by past choices. The difference is that getting to a representative Hindu account of metaphysics and the Two Truths is not about identifying the true or accurate account of these matters, but rather identifying what arises from the freedom to disagree. We get at the truth, the ultimate truth, but this truth is objective, and not partial. Surely Hindus could come to believe it, and many do, and that would be fine, so long as no one confused their belief in this account, with the account. The ultimate truth of the Lord is ultimately true, not because we believe it, but because when we attempt to dispute it, we converge on our freedom to be unconservative, to part with others, while determining for our selves, as a matter of self-governance, what we wish to affirm. But then we are as though Ādi Śeṣa, converging on Viṣṇu and Lakṣmī, on that sea of turbulence, where the gods were granted the opportunity to redeem themselves.

Contesting the facts, and the freedom to do so, seems like a verbal matter. But it is not. As we saw in our representative Hindu account of moral standing, persons are things distinguished by an interest in both essential traits of the Lord, and hence persons have an interest in their own unconservativism and self-governance. But when such agents move in a public world (humans, elephants, planets), they operate with an understanding that is relative to their perspective, and this understanding is made possible by their own non-harm of other things in the environment, which alethically reveals a diversity of perspectives. This revelation is *prima facie* a contestation of the facts, for each perspective will take an opposing view to the facts as others see it from their oppositional perspective. The objectivity of this contestation is the Lord of Yoga.

Objections

I shall consider two objections.

Argument is biased

The claim that the essence of the first order facts is disciplinarity, or that all the facts at the ground level are facts of disciplines, is a substantive claim but one relied upon for an analysis of the facts. It derives from Chapter 5, where it was argued that thoughts are creatures of disciplinarity. While it may have been defended, it is still a controversial position and to assume it is to assume a position that is partial, and not what we converge on when we disagree. This argument is mistaken: the only way to make sense of controversy and the room to disagree is by understanding thoughts via disciplinarity for thought so understood is perpetually distinguished from our beliefs and attitudes: it is what we converge on when we disagree about thought. This was the point of the representative Hindu account of thought, which models what we converge on when we disagree about thought. If it is a bias, it is one that is inclusive of all biases. Then, it is objective, as it is something we can see from differing disagreeing perspectives.

This is a weird view of reality

In this investigation, we have moved initially from methodological contrasts between interpretation and explication, to successive accounts of representative

Hindu accounts of philosophical topics (ethics, logic, philosophy of thought, epistemology, moral standing, now metaphysics) and oddly the cumulative result is substantive. But this takes us to a place where the facts are as though personal (animated by or instantiating the Lord) and at a second metaphysical level, an ultimate personal abstraction, with moral standing, is what we converge on. It is weird, and it requires some type of mystical outlook. That is the objection. Yet, we got to this by accounting for disagreement, not shared beliefs. The account constitutes an explanation of the centrality of disciplinary research to our understanding of the facts. It is not mystical for it does not entail that anything escapes reason. It might be weird relative to common beliefs, but knowledge from disciplinary sources upsets common beliefs. Hence, a philosophical account of the objectivity of metaphysics will upset common beliefs, which is just as well as beliefs are pseudo thoughts.

What might be especially troubling to the positivistically inclined is the implication that the facts as instantiating the Lord have moral standing, as moral standing follows from the Lord (Chapter 7). Then, in taking reality seriously, it seems we have to be morally responsible to and considerate of the facts. My response to this is threefold. First, moral realism, and the idea that the facts have moral attributes is common in the Indian tradition, where many orientations hold that facts have to do with dharma. But it is also a very common position in the *W*est—it is only strange for positivists. But it is not such a strange position: in so far as moral patients, objects of intrinsic value, and people comprise the facts, they are the kinds of things that dharma has to accommodate. Second, if we are open to disagreement, then the kinds of things that can disagree have to be taken seriously (Chapter 6), and then we are in the realm of morality. So for this reason too, moral considerations are never far from the facts as facts are only facts by way of disagreement, and disagreement is personal. Third, facts as true thoughts have an interest in their own Lordliness as creatures of disciplinarity, and this entails that reality is personal and instantiates personhood. This option is quite distinct from the usual theories that reality is mental (idealism) or physical or material (physicalism or materialism) and for this reason may seem strange. But we get there by being open to research as a disciplinary exercise and hence we should be quite comfortable with it as people who support research. To acknowledge that reality is personal is to acknowledge that it is something that we are responsible to and for: it is to transcend thinking about reality in terms of beliefs and to move to the facts.

Conclusion

In this chapter we examined the idea of a representative Hindu account of metaphysics. This is what Hindus, as philosophers, converge on while they disagree about metaphysics. What makes this modeling Hindu is that we use Hindu resources to model the disagreements in question. Our investigation of metaphysics took us to the facts, which are true thoughts, and thoughts, as per a representative Hindu account of thought, are the common use of resources in service of some inquiry: the inquiries themselves differ according to such practices, and each is a discipline, or yoga. The essence of disciplinarity is unconservativism and self-governance (the Lord) for this allows us to engage in the same practice from differing perspectives. So all the first order facts instantiate the Lord. The metaphysical question of what the essence of the facts are takes us to a second order disagreement about the first order facts, and at this level we converge on our own Lordliness, which characterizes the second order disagreement about what metaphysical theory to adopt. Rāmānuja's Viśiṣṭādvaita Vedānta is a traditional Hindu resource that incorporates these two levels of metaphysical explanation by way of a procedural ideal of Bhakti (Yoga)—devotion to the Lord—and hence functions as a representative Hindu account of metaphysics. We get to this model of metaphysics not by agreement, or beliefs, but by accounting for disagreement.

Note

1 For more on truth, see Wright (1992), Glanzberg (2014), and Dowden and Swartz (Accessed 2015). The topic of Indian accounts of truth has been discussed in the literature, but often with some confusion, where truth is conflated with *pramāṇa* (justification) (Mohanty 1980; Chakrabarti 1984). The confusion is understandable: if thought is an exercise in disciplinarity, then truth will be revealed by *pramāṇa*.

References

Ayer, A.J. 1946. *Language Truth and Logic*. New York: Dover Publications.

Chakrabarti, Kisor Kumar. 1984. "Some Remarks on Indian Theories of Truth." *Journal of Indian Philosophy* 12, no. 4: 339–355.

Derrida, Jacques. 1976. *Of Grammatology*. 1st American edn. Baltimore, MD: Johns Hopkins University Press.

Donnellan, Keith S. 1966. "Reference and Definite Descriptions." *Philosophical Review* 75 (1966): 281–304.

Dowden, Bradley, and Norman Swartz. Accessed 2015. "Truth." In *Internet Encyclopedia of Philosophy*, edited by James Fieser. :www.iep.utm.edu/truth/.

Frege, Gottlob. 1988. "Thoughts." In *Propositions and Attitudes*, edited by Nathan U. Salmon and Scott Soames, translated by P. Geach and R.H. Stoothoff, 33–55. Oxford; New York: Oxford University Press.

Glanzberg, Michael. 2014. *Truth*. In *Stanford Encyclopedia of Philosophy*, edited by Edward Zalta. Fall 2014 Edition. http://plato.stanford.edu/archives/fall2014/entries/truth/.

Kuhn, Thomas S. 1970. *The Structure of Scientific Revolutions*. 2nd edn. Chicago, IL: University of Chicago Press.

Madhva/Ānandatīrtha. 1993. *Mahābhāratatātparyanirṇaya*. Translated by K.T. Pandurang, edited by K.T. Pandurang. Vol. 1. Chirtanur: Srīman Madhva Siddhantonnanhini Sabha.

Miśra, Pārthasārathi. 1978. *Nyāyaratnākara (Commentary on Kumārila's Ślokavārttika)*, edited by Swami Dvarikadasa Sastri. Prachyabharati Series 10. Varanasi: Tara Publications.

Mohanty, J.N. 1980. "Indian Theories of Truth: Thoughts on Their Common Framework." *Philosophy East and West* 30, no. 4: 439–451.

Putnam, Hilary. 1975. "The Meaning of Meaning." *Minnesota Studies in the Philosophy of Science* 7: 131–193.

Quine, Willard Van Orman. 1951. "Two Dogmas of Empiricism." *Philosophical Review* 60, no. 1: 20–43.

Thakchoe, Sonam. 2011. "The Theory of Two Truths in India." In *Stanford Encyclopedia of Philosophy*, edited by Uri Nodelman and Edward Zalta. Summer 2011 Edition. http://plato.stanford.edu/entries/twotruths-india/.

Wright, Crispin. 1992. *Truth and Objectivity*. Cambridge, MA: Harvard University Press.

9 The politics of the Milk Ocean

Mokṣa

Introduction

In this chapter, I will pursue the question of a representative Hindu account of politics, which is what we have to converge on while we disagree about politics or political philosophy. What makes the modeling Hindu is that we shall use Hindu resources to model the objectivity of the disagreement. The topic of this chapter is very much like the topic of Chapter 5. In Chapter 5, we pursued the question of thought: what is it? There I argued that a representative Hindu approach to thought departs from the standard approach to thought from the European tradition, which identifies thought with linguistic meaning. A representative Hindu approach to thought in contrast treats thought as the common disciplinary (yogic) use of meaningful devices in service of an inquiry. This is to treat thought as an object. But if we treat thought as something we are engaged in, thinking is the disciplinarity of diverse perspectives in the public world. Either way, thought or thinking does not depend on language: barks and chirps could count as well as sentences for modeling thought, and engaged disciplined activity that tracks objects in a common public world whether by dog, human, the Goddess Earth, or the Sun is thinking. The argument in favor of this model is not that it constitutes the right perspective on thought: rather, it is what we converge on as we disagree about thought. We pursued these implications through Chapter 6 on epistemology, Chapter 7 on moral standing, but also Chapter 8 on metaphysics. Now as we return to the topic of politics, informed as it is by representative Hindu findings in these various areas of inquiry, we see that a representative Hindu account of politics would not only have to accommodate a great amount of human diversity in the form of diversity of perspectives, it will also be non-speciesist. Hence a representative Hindu account would have to account for how people can get along as they disagree on various topics, and the category of personhood as a result of the representative Hindu account of thought is not restricted to human beings. It ranges over anything that has a joint interest in their unconservativism and self-governance (Chapter 7). Hence, it is fitting to return to this topic after having explored the divergence between conventional anthropocentric approaches to philosophical topics, and representative Hindu approaches.

In Chapter 5, I addressed the objection that on this account, a perspective being geographically western meant that it was *ipso facto* imperialistic. The proper response to this concern is that the question of the imperialism of a perspective is a function of the assumed model of thought. If we assume the model of thought characteristic of the *W*est (the intellectual tradition), then any perspective becomes imperialistic for the (linguistically encoded) perspective is equated with the content of thought. If we adopt yoga, disciplinarity, then we engage a *prāyaścitta*—expiation. Disciplinarity allows us to attenuate the bias of all perspectives by treating it as a contribution to our understanding of objectivity. This approach to thought is the representative Hindu approach to thought: what we have to converge on as we disagree about thought. So the same *darśana* (perspective) can function imperialistically or yogically as a contribution to research and it is a matter of what background account of thought is assumed. In the *W*estern tradition, the topic is not usually broached and hence the linguistic account of thought is assumed. We do not have to assume any account of thought: we need only identify what we converge on as we disagree about thought: that is a disciplinary account of thought. So in short, disciplinarity is a choice but an objective finding. The linguistic account of thought is not objective, but what is inherited as a matter of tradition.

This is the corollary of the observations of Chapters 2 and 3, that whether we see a philosophy as contributing to our appreciation of the objectivity of ethics, *THE RIGHT OR THE GOOD*, or as a religion has to do with whether we adopt explication or interpretation. If we adopt explication, all we find is moral theory. Religion is what we find if we adopt the *W*est, and its linguistic account of thought that entails interpretation. Anything non-western that is underivable from western beliefs is thereby treated as religion. On this approach, everyone's thought as such is psychologized, and conflated with belief. But for the *W*esterner, beliefs of a *W*estern origin appear in their consciousness without any special introduction: they seem as though the *sui generis*, indubitable propositions of reason while everything from the outside that cannot be explained by these self-evident beliefs has to be understood by way of tradition and other empirical sources. The self-evidence here is of course an illusion: all belief is true by way of the attitude of the believer, so in so far as *W*estern beliefs are believed, they will seem self-evident and indubitable, so long as they are believed.

As the *W*est is wedded to interpretation, it is wedded to an account of explanation that renders disagreement unintelligible. Hence, in identifying non-western perspectives as religion, the point is not to criticize non-western contributions to thought, but to rather put them beyond the point of controversy. Of course, some authors in this tradition (Comte, Marx and Engels, but earlier Hume) have criticized religious beliefs and this is easy to do if the *W*esterner takes their own beliefs as the contents of reason. But as beliefs are true by virtue of the attitude of the believer, it is a far more natural outcome of the *W*est for everyone to merely accept the difference between the secularism of Europe and religious belief as something to be described and studied social scientifically. Hence, religious studies is largely an enterprise in the social sciences.

All of this brings into doubt ordinary distinctions between the secular and religious, for if religion is a kind of racialization of perspectives with a European self defining the "secular" orientation and everything that deviates from it is religion, then secularism is a kind of racism that institutionalizes the European as the universal self. Thinking clearly about a representative Hindu account of politics will help us out of this quagmire: there are two different versions of Secularism, and what we need is Secularism_1 (philosophy, free thinking), which is Hinduism, and what we need to reject is Secularism_2, which is the *W*est and its definition of religion as what deviates from the secular (itself). In the next section we shall review the supposed non-existent history of Indian political philosophy but also the standard approach to secularism in the *W*est. In the third section, I shall identify Secularism_1 as what Hindus and we converge on when we are free to disagree in general and about politics in particular. Its objectivity is *mokṣa*: freedom. Secularism_1 is not a mere elaboration of familiar political theories from the *W*estern tradition. It is a radical openness to disagreement, which opens up disagreement to persons who can disagree. A Secularism_1 politics is hence inclusive beyond what is customary in the *W*est, and philosophy constitutes its public means of interaction. It includes the interactions of humans, other animals, and the Earth as participants in politics. In the fourth section, I will consider some objections before concluding.

Political philosophy and India

The term "politics" comes from the Greek *polis*, which means 'city,' but philosophically the term has come to denote the part of philosophical concern that has to do with power in general, and the legitimate use of force in particular. The distinction is crucial: a highway robber may have the power to force you to part with your money but not the authority to do so, as perhaps a state has when it levies a tax. We can see this concern for legitimacy in the implementation of power in the works of the major political philosophers of the *W*est, such as Plato, Hobbes, Locke, Rousseau, Mill, Marx, and more. Feminist philosophy is an exploration of political philosophy, as is critical philosophy of race, without these inquiries having to talk about the state or city: they are contributions to political philosophy because they confront questions of power.

Interpreters informed by the *W*est begin their inquiry into Indian political theory (or ethics) by believing they know what political philosophy (or ethics) is (something European) and then they try to figure out whether Indians said the same thing as Europeans. For Indians to have political philosophy (or ethics), for a *W*esterner, Indians have to either say the same thing as Europeans or nothing at all. Hinduism is a microcosm of philosophy on every issue, with the logical options of philosophy constituting the options of Hinduism. So too with ethics (Chapter 3): as Hinduism contains within it the four basic options of moral theory, it surpasses the basic options of the *W*estern tradition, which lacks any defenders of Bhakti: the moral theory that defines the right action by a procedural ideal, the Lord, and the good as the perfection of the practice of the right. Bhakti, as noted in Chapter 3, as defended by Patañjali in the *Yoga Sūtra*, provides an ancient origin for the politics of direct action and civil disobedience with the goal of getting opponents to renounce their hostility via discipline, rooted in the practice of *ahiṃsā* or non-harm (YS II.33–35). The goal is one's own autonomy (*kaivalya*) and the means is one's devotion to the regulative ideal (Īśvara, the Lord), which the *Yoga Sūtra* analyzes (via *Īśvarapraṇidhāna*) into the procedural ideals of *tapas* and *svādhyāya*, unconservativism and self-governance. As noted (Chapter 3), this project was highly influential on M.K. Gandhi, who was highly influential on the American civil rights leader, Martin Luther King. Patañjali's Yoga constitutes a bedrock of progressive activism the world over, rooted in *ahiṃsā*, geared toward inclusive and radical social change. The moral and political orientation of those who choose to defy the powers that be, not via martyrdom, but civil disobedience, have their roots not in the Virtue Theory, Consequentialism, or Deontology of the *W*est, but Patañjali's Yoga. But we can generalize: all the moral theories of the Indian and Hindu tradition have something to say about the legitimate exercise of power and hence they all have to do with political philosophy: find the Indian dharma theories about *THE RIGHT OR THE GOOD* and one will have found Indian political philosophy too.

A non-*W*esternized exploration of Indian philosophy including Indian political philosophy will part ways with even the most sympathetic of *W*esternized treatments. One example of such an account claims that the highpoint of Hindu political theory was developed during the nineteenth and twentieth centuries as a response to British imperialism: the best Hindu political philosophy features nationalism on this account. Examples of these prominent political philosophers are Swami Vivekananda, Aurobindo Ghose, Rabindranath Tagore, and Gandhi—who mixed their common religious ideas and traditional philosophy with modernist concerns (Dalton 2011). Such a narrative ignores the wealth of moral philosophy from the tradition that was always political and chooses Indian responses to the *W*est that emulate its models of nationalism as a political climax.

Aside from a profound ignorance of Indian moral philosophy, one reason that we continue to fail to appreciate the contributions of Indian philosophers to moral and political questions is the image of political philosophy as something that must always be preoccupied with the state, and much Indian moral and political philosophy is not preoccupied with the state. This is what makes the Indian political philosophy of Yoga, with its idealization of *kaivalya* (autonomy) useful: it provides an alternative political frame to counter the totalizing and hegemonic vision of collectivist political theories that characterize the *W*est starting with Plato. Yet Indian and Hindu sources have written about state politics too. Indeed, there are two differing and opposing traditions of note. One we find in works such as Kautilya's *Arthaśāstra* and the *nītiśāstra*-s. These are works written explicitly with the king and ruler in mind, and while they do not deny dharma, they often provide prudential council for sovereigns, which is not often couched as a position on dharma. Political council is treated positivistically: as a matter of judicious expedience. The other tradition is steeped in a very robust moral realism: we find this in the epics, such as the *Rāmāyaṇa* and the *Mahābhārata*. Political questions here are questions of dharma, and often the dharma of the king. The statist political ideas of Hindu and Indian philosophers fall within a continuum between the positivistic and the moral realist—and often lead to differing views about just war (Roy 2007). If we broaden our focus to all Indian philosophy, there are Jain and Buddhist contributions that fall within this spectrum too—including the *Ratnāvalī*, attributed to Nāgārjuna, a Buddhist two-truths philosopher.

In contrast to comprehensive forms of Hinduism, we have been pursuing a representative Hinduism: what Hindus can converge on while they philosophically disagree. It requires no commitment to substantive theses as it eschews interpretation (explanation in terms of what you take to be true). It models the objective: what we converge on when we are free to disagree. What makes the account 'Hindu' is that we use Indian resources to model these disagreements, but the objectivity so modeled is not ethnic: it is simply what we stumble on when we disagree across philosophical topics. In the case of political philosophy, what we converge on while we disagree about the appropriate use of force is the freedom to disagree about power—this is continuous with the Churning of the Milk Ocean. Its fruit is the *amṛta*, distributed by unconservativism (Viṣṇu).

Secularism$_1$ and Secularism$_2$

Religion is what lies beyond the explanatory resources of the *W*est: it is what aliens apparently endorse and practice, but what cannot be derived from native European beliefs. Religion depends upon interpretation, for if we deny interpretation and endorse explication, all we find is philosophy, including moral philosophy, and at no point is there an opportunity to distinguish religion from the secular: it is all secular when we adopt explication. Then our mode of explanation (explication) and what we explain (perspectives that entail theories that explain their controversial claims) participate in open philosophical disagreement and the freedom to think. Secularism as free thought (Holyoake 1896: 51) is what we get when we adopt explication. But if we adopt the *W*est and its imperialist narrative of interpretation, then not only is religion distinguished from the secular—which is defined as European thought—but even people who are called religious can and often do adopt *W*esternization as a means of formulating their identity in opposition to the west (yes, small "w" geographic west). So instead of adopting philosophy as the means of social interaction, they endorse the conflation of thought and belief and choose to associate only with those who share their beliefs, and not those they disagree with. Anti-western nationalist agendas are made possible by this subtle adoption of the *W*est. But as an act of political resistance to the powers of the *W*est it is futile, as the very conflation of thought and belief has as its unifying political past the *W*est.

Call the first and original approach to secularism, Secularism$_1$, and the second, more common approach, Secularism$_2$. According to the first, secularism is free thought. Hinduism as the microcosm of philosophy is Secularism$_1$. According to the second, secularism is the non-religious.[1] This is the *W*est.

If a state like India adopts Secularism$_2$, then philosophy (in the form of representative Hinduism) is excluded from public debate (as it is a religion), and what we have instead is a clash of comprehensive doctrines, some Hindu, some Hindu nationalist, some Liberal or Marxist, often irrationally and violently. But if Secularism$_2$ is generated by the *W*est, it is imperialism and interpretation: we have reason to reject it not merely because its bias undermines our intellectual freedom, but also because it is irrational—and these come to the same thing.

Secularism$_2$ and ***W*estern** *political theory*

Philosophers who endorse Secularism$_2$ have a challenge: how do we reconcile the religious with Secularism$_2$, which is the *W*est? There are three notable responses.

Conservativism

The first is to affirm a religion, and to relegate philosophy to the role of handmaiden to theology *at best*. This is a totalizing and imperialist stance for what was defined as alien to European philosophy—religion—becomes the official position, which means that there can be no significant or worthy alternatives—inside or outside the community. So while at first, the affirmation of religion as the official culturally encoded position appears at odds with the *W*est, it is actually a way to save the *W*estern orientation from the threat of an outside it creates. It simply makes the outside view (religion, or what is uninterpretable by the *W*est) the inside view while clearly marking it as religious. This saves the European frame as the means of defining the status quo. Theocracies and religious nationalisms are *W*estern, even when we do not associate the religions with Europe. And, certainly, conservatives who attempt to encode religious law (as religious law) into public policy exemplify this impulse.

Far left

A second option is to deny the legitimacy of religion as furnishing the content of thought and to affirm a radical Secularism$_2$. But then we have a new problem: how do we legitimize Secularism$_2$, especially as its content is European philosophy, a mere tradition of philosophy? In order to get Secularism$_2$ off the ground we need the *W*est and its interpretive approach to thought that conflates thought and belief. Yet philosophy on this model seems at once subversive as it entertains many beliefs, but also vacuous as it appears a restatement and reorganization of beliefs. And beliefs, as we noted in Chapters 1 and 4, are true by virtue of the attitude of the believer. Here science can play a role. Science is a yoga, but it is a contrary yoga to philosophy. The way we get religious identity off the ground is by interpretation, which is anti-philosophical. So by affirming science as the default yoga (which makes no room for philosophy), one can continue to endorse an anti-philosophical method of explanation—interpretation that gives rise to religious identity—but one can further demonstrate the irrationality of religion in so far as it is not derivable from the legitimating discipline: empirical science. Secularism is hence still the non-religious, where religion continues to be defined by its inexplicability by European belief systems, but this time both religion and philosophy get lumped in the category as what falls beyond the secular. The most straightforward articulation of this position on Secularism$_2$ can be found in Marx and Engels' writings.[2]

Marx argued that human history is characterized by the oppression of class struggle, and that this can only end when the largest contemporary class—the workers—take control and outlaw the opposing class: the capitalists, who create capital (investments) by employing wage-laborers and keeping the profits. Marx's thought is an important resource for Indians who criticize caste hierarchy and discrimination (Ghandy 2011): on this Indian account, caste is yet another form of Marx's class struggle. It has also inspired outright Maoist insurrections in many parts of India.[3]

Liberalism

Liberalism is a third option, which endorses Secularism$_2$, but unlike the previous two positions that endorse or criticize religion, Liberalism ignores religion. The point of a liberal society is to provide a context for people to pursue their own conception of the *Good* with others. Liberalism is a comprehensive doctrine and constitutes the basic beliefs of a liberal society. Mill's comprehensive vision of a society where all were free to pursue their own conception of the *Good* is supported in part by a hard lesson learned by the British on the colonial front, but also through the corresponding insight that if further such problems of rebellion are to be avoided:

> it must be through far wider political conceptions than merely English or European practice can supply, and through a much more profound study of Indian experience, and of the conditions of Indian government, than either English politicians, or those who supply the English public with opinions, have hitherto shown any willingness to undertake.

What colonial administrators of India, such as Mill, would have observed is that Indians are happy disagreeing with each other while they pursue their own theory of *the Right or the Good* together—this would be obvious even as he regarded them as "semi-barbarous" (cf. Mill 1861: 573–579). But whereas a representative Hindu approach requires no basic or shared value (just disagreement), the Millian *W*esternization entails that this pursuit of *the Right or the Good* as one sees it is a basic value that underwrites the social fabric of some community. So while Mill's liberalism was learned from the experience of Hinduism and India, it is a *W*esternization of a representative Hindu approach to morality that entails that only some people could be trusted to pursue the good as individuals, and everyone else is to be treated as racially immature and in need of a benevolent dictator (*On Liberty* I.10). These are the people for whom the pursuit of the good as one sees it is a basic value: in short, the mature societies endorse Comprehensive Liberalism. Certainly, the racism is annoying, but a greater philosophical problem is accounting for the basis of a Comprehensive Liberalism: how is it not just another conception of the *Good* that people can and should be free to pursue or get rid of? If we were truly open to pursuing our own conception of the *Good*, to determine what makes us happy, it seems that we should be free to endorse anti-liberal policies. But this would undermine the liberal character of a liberal society.

John Rawls' *Political Liberalism* is an effort to avoid this problem: if we have to buy Comprehensive Liberalism then it would seem like we have not actually solved the problem of how we can get along with each other while we pursue our own conception of the Good. On Rawls' later solution, a liberal society can be founded on a "overlapping consensus" of competing comprehensive doctrines and its liberality arises out of common values internal to each comprehensive doctrine (Rawls 1996: 15)—just as Kant's philosophy of religion holds that there is a common core moral theory across religions. This appears to undermine some of the dogmatism of Secularism$_2$ seen in the conservative and far left options, for it does not restrict public discourse to a chosen religion (conservativism) nor does it rule out the participation of religious people from public discourse (as we find in the far left). But it is not so different from Mill's solution, for here too there has to be a commitment to liberal values in order for a liberal society to provide its members the freedom to pursue their own conception of the Good. So illiberal people could not participate in such a social context in so far as their comprehensive doctrines do not share the basic values of a liberal society. But then, we seem to be back to a theme that arises from the *W*est and Secularism$_2$ positions:

- There has to be some shared commitment to values, or beliefs, that underwrite society, and those who disagree cannot participate in society.

Mokṣa and power

The thread of inquiry that has been pursued in this book is about accounting for Hinduism, not as an artifact of the *W*est, but objectively. Hinduism so understood is the microcosm of philosophy with a South Asian twist. Modeling Hinduism is hence about modeling the disagreements of philosophy, using Indian resources. What we find when we are truly open to disagreement is that the usual barriers to entry to participate in the facts, to be counted as knowing, thinking, and even reasonable, fall out of the way. In the *W*est, barriers to entry have to do with community membership but also species: being a person is about being human, and moreover you have to be the right kind of human (a member of the self-chosen community) in order to be counted as thinking and relating to others. The actual values of a society that define what it is to be the right kind of human specify our specific roles in society, and these are true as a matter of definition, culturally encoded analytical truths (Chapter 5). Dissent is unimaginable in so far as one attempts to dissent from the basic values encoded in one's culture: that is to try to pull the ground from under one's feet. But when we try to model reason, thinking, knowing, morally counting, and the facts, as something objective—that we can disagree about—the values that appear as the objective content of our disagreements are the values of Yoga. These constitute our representative Hindu response to the various areas of philosophy but then they also set up the foundation for a representative Hindu account of the proper deployment of power. The objectivity of power, what we converge on as we disagree, has to be something consistent with our freedom to disagree, and hence this power is *mokṣa*—freedom from limitations that constrain our contribution to an understanding of objectivity, but also freedom in the classical sense, from having to be limited by our past choices (karma). This freedom is unconservativism, or *tapas*. But the condition of this freedom is our own self-governance (*svādhyāya*). These two characteristics of the Lord, on Yoga's account, hence constitute the substance of political power. The Lord is hence our representative Hindu account of politics. But we already saw that this procedural abstraction was something we converged on time and again when we attempted to understand what was involved in disagreeing.

We should not be surprised if the standard gloss on the concept of *MOKṢA* as it is found in the Indian tradition is Orientalist, and depicts it as a concern for freedom that is apolitical. The *W*est and its methodology of interpretation disappears all moral disagreement between the *W*est and non-*W*esterners in proportion to their divergence (cf. Ariel Accessed 2017) and hence the differences between accounts of *mokṣa* that differ in relationship to differing accounts of dharma (morality, or *THE RIGHT OR THE GOOD*) simply vanish from standard *W*esternized accounts of Indian and Hindu philosophy. But we should also not take such an account seriously in so far as it is founded on interpretation, which violates validity.

Secularism$_1$ via a representative Hinduism (S1RH) shows us that it is a myth that we require common values, shared beliefs, or a common purpose to get along. We simply need to be open to disagreeing about everything, and what we come to is a stability that constitutes the symbiotic diversity of the common world. Disagreement constitutes the unity of a thought (Chapter 5) and the facts (Chapter 8). If we really know how to disagree, we really know how to get along. Political problems are not a function of disagreement, but rather the anti-social Asuras, who want it their way, and no way else. Those who disagree want things their way, but they appreciate the role that others play as valued opponents in churning the ocean that hides the nectar of immortality.

A S1RH association would be 'religious' only because it is Hindu, but it would eschew the idea that there is an official doctrine that has to be linguistically and culturally encoded. It would hence be anti-nationalist. And whereas a conservative state would attempt to ground knowledge on tradition or ethnic identity, a S1RH association would be grounded on the facts as a product of disciplinary research.

A S1RH association would promote inquiry over ideology, research over belief, and it would also surpass the social goals of a far left political association: in order to facilitate radical and open disagreement, it would have to ensure that everyone was free to disagree, which means that no one would be condemned to a role in life that was inimical to their interests as unconservative self-governing dissenters.

In other words, their needs, especially as cashed out by the *Mahāvrata*-s (the five values of the objectivity of knowledge, reviewed in Chapter 6) would need to be fulfilled. But as the Lord, as the substance of a politics of disagreement, is a non-speciesist criterion of moral standing (Chapter 7), the objectivity of politics is blind to natural or social distinctions. So one's biology could not be used as a criterion of one's rights. The politics of the Lord would hence be inclusive, but there would be no special priority granted to humans. This entails a commitment to the radical health and resilience of all concerned, and all concerned includes beings beyond humanity that can take oppositional views in a disagreement about force. What they converge on is peace.

Not only is belief on the chopping block, but so is community as a basic unit of explanation. The *W*est entails that communities are the basic unity of ethical and political explanation in so far as the thinkable is linguistic and languages define community membership (Chapter 5). A representative Hindu approach to politics, the politics of Lordliness, emphasizes the individual—*kaivalya*—to be free from the coercive imposition of context. A representative Hindu politics would undermine nationalism as it undermines the idea that what we have in common is community membership. What we have in common is the Lord, namely a procedural ideal that explains what it is for us to thrive. A requirement of protecting our own Lordliness is that we transform the public world into someplace safe for Lordliness. But as Lordliness is an abstraction, it is nothing proprietary. Hence, to understand the Lord (to be devoted to the Lord) is to be devoted to the conditions of thriving that are universal in the strict sense, as an abstraction that is unproprietary. Other people are hence important contributors to our own possibility of Lordliness, as their reality as thriving individuals contributes to a world that is characterized not only by Lordliness but also the resulting objectivity of politics: *mokṣa*.

As noted in many of the preceding chapters, thinking, inquiry, and knowledge are not reducible to language and humans have no special claim to being thinking or knowing individuals. Even reason is about appreciating the force of a third party, without having to give in, and cautious, respectful animals show their reason all the time as they maintain safe boundaries and distances from others.

A S1RH association would approximate some of the social means of liberalism, namely the support for everyone to endorse or adopt whatever comprehensive option they choose as part of their contribution to the lasting peace of perpetual disagreement. It would be more liberal than most liberal theories as there would be no *a priori* limitation on what comprehensive doctrine one can endorse or employ to contribute to the social goal of disagreement. Liberal theories as species of the *W*est identify thought with belief and hence have problems accommodating disagreement, for no one can disagree with a belief made true by attitude. Then it seems like the only beliefs that are permissible are those that are liberal and open. However, when we move to S1RH, thought is untied from belief and the stability of social interaction is not explained by a common perspective, but a cooperative venture of yoga.

It is useful to close this section by reflecting on the Constitution of India's article 51-A (g,h,i), that falls under the heading "Fundamental Duties":

- It shall be the duty of every citizen of India to protect and improve the natural environment including forests, lakes, rivers and wildlife and to have compassion for living creatures;
- to develop the scientific temper, humanism and the spirit of inquiry and reform;
- to safeguard public property and to abjure violence.

It seems to occur in an area of the constitution that is unenforceable (Burns 2016) but nevertheless, it is quite unique with few comparisons in its specification of environmental protection and compassion for living creatures. In it we see some reflection of a representative Hindu account of politics, but also a sign of the *W*est, in so far as the exhortation to science is paired with humanism. Humanism is a value that makes sense given the linguistic account of thought, and falls by the way when we want to understand disagreement. Our disciplinary approach to thought and knowledge that makes disagreement a positive contribution in contrast entails an interest in the environment, compassion for living creatures, but also disciplined inquiry of all sorts. But this requires taking a diversity of perspectives seriously, including and especially the Earth's. A politics of the Lord moves away from identifying our interests in contingencies such as caste, race, sex, and biology in general, to the power that is a function of our thriving: *mokṣa*. The thriving of persons is not biological: it is moral. It has to do with a person's inculcation of their own unconservativism and self-governance.

One of the implications of a politics that is a function of disciplined inquiry is that it is anti-imperialist and anti-colonial. As a result, no person who participates in a politics of freedom has to put up with having their own unconservativism or self-governance impeded. So for humans worried about having to give up their requirements for invading colonies of ants, not to worry. The politics of freedom is not the politics of martyrdom. Such a politics would be a function of an active resistance of the tyranny that arises from the attempt of some parties to impose their perspective on others (interpretation). Correlatively, it would be a politics that is a function of disciplinarity. It is hence a politics based on knowledge of the facts—not belief and tradition. It is hence the ideal foundation for prosperity.

Objections

I shall consider three objections in this section.

Religious people cannot participate

Secularism$_1$ would seem to make it difficult for people with religious identities to participate, for religious people would ostensibly want to identify with their religion or beliefs, and yet these are not recognized by $Secularism_1$. This may not be a problem for Hindus who traditionally did not count themselves as Hindus but as members of comprehensive philosophical communities. But for most others, religious identity, and their beliefs are important. The $Secularism_1$ response is that disagreement that makes room for people of divergent comprehensive philosophical commitments is only possible if we adopt $Secularism_1$. $Secularism_2$ conflates thought with belief and only makes room for an official position—and it is a matter of luck whether one's comprehensive commitments are consistent with the official position. The only guaranteed freedom for religious folks to participate in the public world is $Secularism_1$.

What about the end of **saṃsāra***?*

Conventional views on *mokṣa* for Jain, Buddhist and Hindu philosophers describe it as a state that arises at the end of cycles of birth and death (*saṃsāra*). *Mokṣa* as a political value has nothing to do with how Indians thought about *mokṣa*. The proper response to this objection is to note that traditional views are typically based on a story about past action and choice (karma) no longer having any influence on a person. When we disagree about politics, even our past decision to adopt a political position no longer binds us. It would be the end of being coerced in a whirlpool (*saṃsāra*) of life. To ignore the political aspects of *mokṣa* takes work.

The reluctance to see the obvious political implications of *mokṣa* arises not only from ignoring politics and its relevance to Indian philosophy, but also interpretation that assumes commonly held beliefs as a constraint on the intelligibility of something like *mokṣa*, such as the idea that *mokṣa* is an entirely mysterious affair beyond secular matters. As a philosophical idea, however, it is easy to identify as coextensive with complete political freedom. The other cause of Orientalist treatments of *mokṣa* is the *W*est's commitment to communitarianism, which we noted in Chapter 5: if ethical and political questions are about community membership (that which is semantically encoded in the common language), Indian views about ethics and politics that do not countenance the community will seem 'otherworldly.' But that is once again interpretation at play.

Belief is important for taking victims seriously

One of the basic conditions of appreciating disagreement is that disagreement is possible when we are speaking about thought, and becomes rather impossible when we are speaking of belief, for reasons that have been reviewed over and again in previous chapters: belief is an attitude towards a proposition and a belief is true in virtue of that attitude. Disagreeing with a belief is not possible when we understand that a person believes a proposition, but if we try, we are in the realm of conflict. For then we are apparently denying another person's self-determined attitude towards a proposition. Xenophobia and paranoia rest on this conflation of thought and belief, for outsiders who do not share our beliefs appear as though to deny them and thereby threaten us—an irrationality based on the conflation of thought and belief. Yet belief is important. An important aspect of truth and reconciliation, as we find in the cases of colonized peoples, but also women speaking up against sexual harassment, is the importance of victims being believed. A failure to believe victims of oppression and violence simply furthers their oppression and violence it seems. But then, we need to protect belief and value it. Our disciplinary approach to thought and reason that forms the conditions of an objective approach to politics as freedom apparently gives equal footing to perpetrators and victims, as though everyone's perspective is equally important to understanding the controversies at stake, but this too serves to discredit victims.

The response to this objection is in two parts. First, if a belief is a propositional attitude that some thought is true, it is true in virtue of the attitude of the believer. If I believe a victim, then the truth of my belief has to do with my attitude, not with what the victim has to contribute to our understanding of the facts. The problem is not merely that in believing someone, we may be trusting someone whose claims are false. Believing someone is not really a way to take them seriously: it is a way for ourselves to have a self-congratulatory attitude towards the people in question. Second, what victims of abuse and oppression deserve and need is not to be believed, but to have their perspectives considered as dispositive. A dispositive perspective (Chapter 8) elucidates the topic of disagreement, and hence settles that a proposition is true. Thoughts without dispositive perspectives are false. Oppressors in contrast, who impose their perspective on others (mentally or physically) are practitioners of interpretation. They have various beliefs they wish others to assent to as a means of cementing their power. To understand a disagreement that they are involved in is to understand them as free riders (Rāhus), who cannot have a dispositive vantage, for they not only want to participate in the disagreement but deny the disciplinarity that makes a disagreement possible and hence a dispositive vantage possible. So in taking complainants seriously, we do not have to believe them, assume that their narratives are true, nor treat them on par with oppressors. On the one hand, we know that their narratives are accurate if they can elucidate the controversy. With respect to the accused, we know their narrative is inaccurate if they adopt the policy of free-ridership. Finally, the only way to bring to light the facts, not merely beliefs, is an open, disciplined approach to thinking that actively discourages interpretation and takes a diversity of perspectives, *prima facie* seriously. This is not only how we begin to address historical wrongs, it is also the way to prevent them from happening in the first place. Otherwise, we operate in an environment of belief, where questions of guilt and innocence are reduced to whose beliefs end up constituting the public narrative.

Conclusion

Representative Hinduism does not describe what Hindus believe, but it tracks what is objective about Hinduism. In the case of politics, concerned as it is with the appropriate use of power, what is objective about a representative Hindu approach to politics—the one that arises from a full, unconstrained disagreement about politics—is freedom: *mokṣa*. *Mokṣa*, freedom, is conventionally treated not as a political value but as a 'spiritual' or sometimes 'soteriological' value, but usually by the same tradition that interprets Indian and Hindu philosophy with the result that it is bereft of deep or serious moral philosophy. Explicated, Hindu philosophy contains a wealth of moral theory (all the logically basic options of ethics) and each theory has something to say about freedom. When we bring the wealth of moral theory back into light, and we appreciate the close relationship that exists between Indian theories of dharma (reviewed in Chapter 3) and freedom, it stops seeming so implausible to look at *mokṣa* as a political value as theories of dharma are political. Indeed, given that political philosophy is concerned with the legitimate employment of power, *mokṣa* is a political value as it constitutes a normative limit to power's coercive influence—what we converge on when we can disagree about politics. This freedom is possible given Hinduism, which is a version of Secularism_1—unconstrained freedom to philosophically disagree. It constitutes a valuable alternative to Secularism_2: the *W*est, which treats European origin beliefs as the content of public reason and anything that deviates, religion. Secularism_1 founded on explication is rational as explication is rational: Secularism_2 founded on interpretation is irrational as interpretation is irrational.

Notes

1 For recent investigations into Secularism^2 as it pertains to South Asia, see Adcock (2013) and de Roover (2016).
2 See, for instance, Marx and Engel's various comments on religion and philosophy (Marx and Engels 1957).
3 For an account of the relationship between classical Marxist philosophy and its Maoist version, see Moufawad-Paul (2016).

References

Adcock, C.S. 2013. *The Limits of Tolerance: Indian Secularism and the Politics of Religious Freedom*. Oxford: Oxford University Press.

Ariel, Glucklich. Accessed 2017. "Mokṣa." In *Oxford Bibliographies Online*. Oxford: Oxford University Press. www.oxfordbibliographies.com/document/obo-9780195399318/obo-9780195399318-0036.xml.

Burns, Kyle. 2016. "Constitutions and the Environment: Comparative Approaches to Environmental Protection and the Struggle to Translate Rights into Enforcement." *Harvard Environmental Law Review*, November 14. http://harvardelr.com/2016/11/14/constitutions-the-environment-comparative-approaches-to-environmental-protection-and-the-struggle-to-translate-rights-into-enforcement/.

Dalton, Dennis. 2011. "Hindu Political Philosophy." In *The Oxford Handbook of the History of Political Philosophy*, 18–82. Oxford: Oxford University Press.

de Roover, J. 2016. *Europe, India, and the Limits of Secularism*. Oxford: Oxford University Press.

Ghandy, Anuradha. 2011. *Scripting the Change: Selected Writings of Anuradha Ghandy*. New Delhi: Daanish Books.

Holyoake, G.J. 1896. *The Origin and Nature of Secularism*. London: Watts and Co.

Marx, Karl, and Friedrich Engels (eds.). 1957. *Marx and Engels on Religion*. Moscow: Progress Publishers. www.marxists.org/archive/marx/works/subject/religion/.

Mill, John Stuart. 1861. "Considerations on Representative Government." In *The Collected Works of John Stuart Mill*, Volume 19: *Essays on Politics and Society Part 2*, edited by John M. Robson. :http://oll.libertyfund.org/titles/234, Accessed Fall 2014.

Moufawad-Paul, J. 2016. *Continuity and Rupture: Philosophy in the Maoist Terrain*. Alresford, Hants: John Hunt Publishing.

Rawls, John. 1996. *Political Liberalism*. In *John Dewey Essays in Philosophy*, No. 4. New York: Columbia University Press.

Roy, Kaushik. 2007. "Just and Unjust War in Hindu Philosophy." *Journal of Military Ethics* 6, no. 3: 232–245.

10 Conclusion

Introduction

This short concluding chapter is a summary that ties up the leading ideas of this book. Our focus in this book is Hinduism, the religion, and especially representative Hinduism: what Hindus and we converge on when we freely disagree on philosophy, using Hindu resources to model the disagreement. In the next section, I will review the findings of the various chapters. In the third section, I will summarize the argument. In the fourth, I will consider some objections. In the fifth section I conclude.

Review

Chapter 1 (Introduction)

Our philosophical investigation into Hinduism is not an investigation into ideas or philosophies that are Hindu. Rather our investigation is into the religion on the whole. Hinduism presents challenges for this type of investigation, as it is a class not a kind. Kinds are defined by traits that are instantiated by their members. The class definition of Hinduism—South Asian, no common founder—underdetermines its members. The philosophical options of Hinduism are the philosophical options of philosophy itself. The only way that we can intelligently speak about Hinduism is to identify what Hindus have to converge on while they disagree about various philosophical topics: this is objective as objectivity is what we converge on while we disagree. Such identifications would count as *representative* Hinduisms.

A common obstacle to this is the usual assumption that Hinduism is not merely philosophy: it is also social practice, festivals, and the like. But this is to assume that disagreements and differences about such matters are not also philosophical differences. Social practice is simply the topic of the moral and political disagreements of Hindus.

The alternative, to identify a *comprehensive* doctrine shared by Hindus, is implausible given the logic of the category of Hinduism. In order to appreciate the possibilities of representative Hinduism, we have to be clear about philosophy:

philosophy is the discipline where we disagree about thoughts, bundles of thoughts (perspectives), their entailed explanations (theories), and parts of thoughts themselves (concepts). Philosophy is objective because it tracks what we can disagree about, and is constitutionally different from psychology, which tracks attitudes such as beliefs. A belief, like other propositional attitude claims, ties a proposition *p* to an attitude, such as, 'I believe that *p*.' Such claims are true by virtue of the attitude they describe, and this is independent of the imbedded proposition. Philosophy is concerned with such propositions, not attitudes. A cursory review of the options of Hinduism show that they are the options of philosophy (including atheism and materialism), and the only way to distinguish the religious from the secular is to identify European beliefs as the content of secular reason, and anything that deviates from this as religion. Hinduism is hence a religion, though it is the microcosm of philosophy itself. This methodology of marginalizing philosophy, including philosophy that is non-European, as religion is the methodology of the *W*est. The *W*est *prima facie* is the method of interpretation with a European origin. To interpret is to explain by way of what one takes to be true. Interpretation is an outcome of the *W*est—the linguistic account of thought with a European and Greek origin, summarized in the Greek idea of *logos* (that conflates thought, reason, opinion, and words). Interpretation arises from the linguistic account of thought for in identifying thought as the meaning of what one says, one cannot deny one's thought without denying its meaning, which is to claim that one's thought is meaningless: absurd. Hence, to avoid the absurdity, one has to believe every thought one entertains and hence explanation by way of thought is explanation by way of belief: interpretation. But then, anything that deviates from one's beliefs seems irrational and inexplicable, and hence given the *W*estern origins of this theory of thought, *W*estern beliefs are employed as interpretive principles and then everything non-western seems mysterious, however socially entrenched: this is what gets called religion in our world.

Chapter 2 (Interpretation and explication)

In the second chapter, we review the explanatory methodology of philosophy that is explication (explanation by way of validity) and interpretation (explanation by way of beliefs). Explication allows us to appreciate how Indians disagreed about a single concept of dharma, THE RIGHT OR THE GOOD, and interpretation proliferates meanings of "dharma" as uses of the term depart from the outlook of the interpreter. Orthodox Indology, rooted in linguistics, employs interpretation, and supports the colonialist narrative that Indians were uninterested in moral and practical problems, but is also an elaboration of the *W*est's narrative that anything that deviates from a European outlook is inexplicable.

Hinduism is a religion for the same reason that anything is a religion: it is not derivable from the doxastic resources of the *W*est. And yet it is unique among most religions. While most are kind categories where essential definitions of the category are shared by its members, the class definition of Hinduism (South Asian, no common founder) underdetermines its members. The only way for Hindus to understand the options of Hinduism is to adopt explication: what holds Hinduism together are its philosophical disagreements, which are open-ended.

Chapter 3 (Ethics)

The means and goal of imperialism and colonialism is to depict colonized and imperialized people as constitutionally incapable of being rational about practical matters. Physical violence can accomplish this, but so can depicting an entire intellectual tradition as bereft of any serious moral theorizing. With the *W*est's interpretation, we end up with the myth of India as this tradition of mysticism, lacking moral philosophy. But if we explicate Indian and Hindu perspectives, we find that it contains the full range of basic, logical options in moral theory, beyond what we find in the *W*estern tradition. In addition to the teleological theories of Virtue Ethics, Consequentialism, and the one procedural ethics of Deontology, it also contains a radical procedural ethics: Bhakti/Yoga—the logical opposite of Virtue Ethics, and a traditional source of criticism of teleological theories. Major deities of Hinduism, such as Śiva and Pārvatī, are associated with and explicatable as ideals of teleological theories. Ādi Śeṣa (approximating the Lord), Viṣṇu (unconservativism), and Lakṣmī (self-governance) are reducible to procedural ideals of Bhakti/Yoga. While virtually every other religion is associated with a founding or basic moral theory (Theistic religions with Virtue Ethics, for instance), Hindus have no basic moral theory but the moral options of Hinduism traverse the options of moral theory. The very term "dharma" hence serves as a representative Hindu account of ethics: *THE RIGHT OR THE GOOD*. While it is implausible that Hinduism is an ancient dharma, if by that we mean a continuous singular doctrine, Hinduism is the *sanātana dharma*, if by that we mean moral philosophy.

Chapter 4 (Logic)

In the case of logic, we contrasted the views of famous logicians from the *W*estern tradition with the myth of the Churning of the Milk Ocean. The standard accounts of logic in the *W*estern tradition rely upon the conflation of truth with thought by way of the conflation of thought and what you take to be true: belief. This leads to *psychologism*, but it also problematizes validity: logical inference as what follows from a proposition if it were true. In contrast, the story of the Churning of the Milk Ocean, where Viṣṇu allows the gods to prove themselves, provides a model for thinking about logic that protects validity. Reason is the force of a third-party perspective that we do not have to give in to, and the objectivity of this is non-empirical transitivity: the churning on the back of Viṣṇu as the turtle. Here we see that what it is to be a god is to be able to disagree. Demons do not know how to disagree. Chief among such demons is Rāhu: the demon that pretends to be a God. This is the demon of description: when propositional attitudes are described, the result is something we cannot disagree with for to converge on their self-fulfilling truth is to agree. The only solution is to change one's attitude, and oppose the conflation of the attitude (Ketu) with a description of a thought (Rāhu)—as Viṣṇu unconservatively hurls his disk at Rāhu, slicing Ketu from Rāhu. Explication is the churning of the ocean: it is the way of the gods. Interpretation is the Rāhuvian imitation of reasoning. This story constitutes the representative Hindu account of reason. Along the way, we review the distinction between interpretation and explication, and explicate what is involved in being a philosopher and reading philosophy.

Chapter 5 (Thought)

According to the linguistic account of thought, thought is the meaning of what you say, and to endorse this theory of thought is to believe the meaning of what you say as your thought. But as thought and the meaning of what you say are the same thing on this account, for every thought you have, you believe it—to deny a thought is to deny that it has the meaning of what you say, which is absurd. The alternative is to distinguish thinking from believing by a project of controlling mentality, and not passively believing it: this allows the distinction between the meaning of what one says (one's belief) and one's thought—the latter is the disciplinary use one makes of mental representation or thought. This is Yoga: *yogas citta vṛtti nirodha.* Sentences, words, and meaningful acts (barks, chirps) can express the same thought if they share a disciplinary purpose. Enter Subcontinent Dharma: every nation here is defined by its own theory of dharma, and "dharma" is simply defined in every nation's language by its national theory of dharma. Can people on Subcontinent Dharma have a cross-linguistic discussion about dharma? Only if they embrace Yoga. If cultures stick to the linguistic account of thought, the result is chauvinism, xenophobia, imperialism and war externally, and totalitarianism within every culture, where saying something critical of the defining theory of dharma is a threat to the fragile egos of believers. Yoga is the representative Hindu account of thought.

Chapter 6 (Knowledge)

Standard accounts of knowledge in the *W*estern tradition treat it as a kind of propositional attitude, especially belief: this results in classical Gettier problems. A move to a yogic account of thought allows us to avoid these problems, but retain the insight that knowledge (*jñāna*) has to do with *pramāṇa* (justification) and truth (*satya*). The disagreements of epistemology converge on the question of *THE JUSTIFIED OR THE TRUE*. Four theories are possible: two are juristic, two alethic. As in the case of ethics, the Indian tradition in the form of Yoga presents a unique option. It is a foundationalist theory of truth: accordingly, justification leads to the truth. And this is possible if justification is disciplinary research. A model for thinking about the objectivity of knowledge is the Great Vows, widely endorsed in Indian philosophy. Accordingly, when we put aside harm via justification we are led to the truth: a respectful world that protects personal boundaries. This is the representative Hindu account of knowledge, which is to say, what we converge on when we disagree about knowledge. Knowledge so understood, like thought, is not peculiarly human and something disciplined beings can engage.

Chapter 7 (Moral standing)

Indians and Hindus endorse a wide account of moral standing that cuts across species lines, and extends to astronomical bodies, such as the Earth and the Sun. In contrast, the dominant approach to the topic in the *W*est has been to identify moral standing with language use, which effectively disqualifies most non-linguistic animals. In the *W*estern and Indian traditions, the basic disagreements on moral standing split along one line: either self-determination or unconservativism—to be unconstrained by past self-determination—is central to standing. This disjunctive concept of *SELF-GOVERNANCE* or *UNCONSERVATIVISM*—the objectivity of the debate about moral standing—is entailed by the concept of the Lord we find in the Yoga tradition—idealized as Viṣṇu and Lakṣmī in the literary tradition of philosophies associated with Yoga. This allows us to distinguish between the objective requirements of objects of intrinsic worth (that have an interest in self-governance), moral patients such as plants (that have an interest in unconservativism), and people (that have an interest in both). The representative Hindu account of moral standing is derivable from the objectivity of the disagreements of moral standing. The usual anthropocentric accounts from the *W*est are based on the quirky tradition of the *W*est and its linguistic account of thought.

Chapter 8 (Metaphysics)

Thinking clearly about reality leads us to the facts. The facts at the first level are all of them constituted by disciplines as facts are true thoughts, and thoughts themselves are creatures of disciplinarity. Truth, unlike objectivity, is what we agree upon when we converge on it. But if the truth of thoughts is something objective, then it consists in revealing the disciplinary structure of disagreement, which is the content of thought. False thoughts reveal nothing. This apparently entails that the first order facts as creatures of disciplinarity instantiate the essence of disciplinarity: the Lord, unconservativism and self-governance. At the second level, we can entertain opposing metaphysical theories of the facts: the accurate second order theory would explain why the first order facts are the facts, and it would also be a kind of fact itself. But at this level, when we disagree, we converge on our own Lordliness to contest the facts, but this Lordliness is not individual but something we share with all who are in a position to disagree about the facts. The representative Hindu model of metaphysics that entails this picture is Rāmānuja's Viśiṣṭādvaita.

Chapter 9 (Politics)

We can contrast two models of secularism. According to Secularism_1, the secular is a freedom to disagree, philosophically. According to Secularism_2, secularism is the non-religious. Politics, for its part, is a disagreement about the legitimate exercise of power. But the objectivity of this disagreement is *mokṣa*: freedom. A representative Hindu politics is Secularism$_1$: it is a politics of *mokṣa*. But as Secularism$_1$ is based on a representative Hindu account of thought, it is anti-speciesist and inclusive. A representative Hindu politics would be not only for humans, but for people, who as seen in Chapter 7, come in all sorts of shapes and forms. It locates dignity not in the false need of people to be believed, but to be treated as presumptively dispositive.

Representative Hinduism

In every chapter, we have contrasted alternatives, identified the crux of the disagreement as the objectivity of the topic, and identified a Hindu resource to model this. Representative Hinduism is simply a representation of what we converge on when we disagree about philosophy, using Hindu resources to model the disagreement. This is the only responsible way to generalize about Hinduism because Hinduism is a philosophical disagreement that is unconstrained by its class definition of *South Asian, no common founder*. While I have identified some Indian models as such representations, there could be others, and nothing that I have written here precludes this. But what will stay the same is the objectivity of the debates, for this is what we as philosophers converge on while we disagree.

In making our way to a responsible generalization of Hinduism as its philosophical disagreements, we had to part ways with the *W*est. We had to acknowledge the *W*est as part of the explanation of why Hinduism was ever identified as a religion: everything that is a religion is a religion because it falls outside of the European resources of the *W*est. For the same token, we could not look to the *W*est and its tradition of theorizing to elucidate the disagreements of philosophy, which is our means of representing Hinduism responsibly. This is because the methodology of philosophy—explication—is contrary to the methodology of the *W*est: interpretation. Hinduism as the microcosm of philosophy with a South Asian flavor falls outside of the *W*est not merely because of its geographic difference, but also because it is only elucidated by explication and this is un-*W*estern.

The essence of explication is not explanation by way of what one takes to be true (interpretation). It is explanation by way of validity—what follows *if* the premises are true. Validity (entailment) departs from interpretation for interpretation has to start with the truth, but validity does not. This means that when we employ validity to understand, we do not have to agree about what is true: we start with a perspective, understand how it entails a theory that entails its controversial claims, and then we understand the objectivity of the debate—the basic concepts—as what competing theories converge on when they disagree. When we explicate Hinduism, there are never any grounds for demarcating any of its options as "religious"—that distinction arises if we take the *W*est's interpretation as the backdrop.

As Hinduism is a giant tradition of philosophical disagreement, it can and should critically assess the *W*est as a philosophical failure, and in so doing allow Hindus and people to be free of having to understand everything from a *W*estern perspective. Indeed, they can free themselves from the disease of having to identify with a perspective at all: when we do philosophy, we do not need one, as far as we are forever concerned with what can be understood from the third-person vantage. Having always to identify with a perspective is to endorse interpretation: to have to explain everything by way of one's beliefs undermines one's own freedom as a person to be unconservative and self-governing.

None of this entails that we cannot come to conclusions having engaged in a philosophical investigation, but the credible conclusions are going to take the facts as the comprehension of inquiry, and the facts as true thoughts reveal to us the normative structure of disciplined disagreement. This is not the same as belief, and our beliefs may always be surprised by the normative structure of disagreement. Moreover, in deciding to identify the true as comprehending the outcome of an investigation, we reject interpretation, which begins with what we take to be true. Hindus who follow this thread will find themselves free of the burden of having to confess a faith. Most everyone else will expect some type of story from the Hindu as to what it is they believe. Hindus can and should resist this: it is unnecessary for them to be Hindu. Hindus can hence be role models for how we can get along in a post-*W*estern world, where disciplinarity and not belief is the foundation of social interaction.

Objections

I shall respond to four objections to the study overall.

Not enough philology, not enough ethnography

One objection that follows from the *W*esternization of the study of things Indian is the expectation that a rigorous account of something as broad as Hinduism would be based either on a philological inventory of texts, or an ethnographic survey of Indian beliefs—or something in between, namely a survey of what great and influential Hindus wrote. A philosophical investigation into Hinduism has to some extent bothered with what influential Hindus have written but only in so far as they fill details of philosophical disagreements. However, this seems unrigorous: as though to generalize about Hinduism, we need to engage in an induction, and we need a representative sample base of Hindu texts or beliefs, or influential figures, and this investigation may be faulted for not being a survey of popular Hindu figures and their writings.

This worry is mistaken. The only generalizations we need to model Hinduism are generalizations about philosophical disagreements, for Hinduism is intelligible only via explication and its disagreements, but we get to that not by social science but via explication and philosophy. This is because the scope of disagreement is logical (*p* and not *p* are its boundaries) and not psychological, social, or historical. Hence, philology and a social scientific survey of prominent Hindu opinions are not relevant to a philosophical investigation into Hinduism at the level of generality we need in order to say something about Hinduism the religion as such. If anything, trying to ground one's account of Hinduism in ethnographic and philological sources produces a veneer of objectivity that is illusory. It seems objective as it relies upon data as consequences of disciplinary inquiry, but the disagreements of Hinduism are not reducible to specific positions of specific Hindus, nor are they even reducible to a survey of such positions. It is reducible to disjunctions such as *THE RIGHT OR THE GOOD*, which we learn about explicating a wide range of philosophy.

Hindus really do agree on a lot

As a rejoinder, one might claim that there is indeed a large amount of consensus and agreement about Hinduism among Hindus, and hence we need to study their artifacts and texts, and beliefs to determine the commonalities of Hinduism. In short, because there is so much commonality, a proper account of Hinduism should represent the commonalities. This is an invalid deduction. If the category of Hinduism is a class, then nothing about similarities among the tokens of Hinduism entail anything about Hinduism. And then there is the inconvenience of the agreements: Hindus often agree about action (karma) as practically important, but so do Jains and Buddhists, not to mention almost everyone. Here, the agreement is too wide. We could *stipulate* what Hindus have to agree to—something narrower and unique to Hindus (like a belief in the gods, or caste)—which is a common ploy, but this overlooks the dissenting options within Hinduism. But, and more importantly, the impetus to such stipulations are interpretive: they are explanations of Hinduism based on what we take to be true, and interpretation is irrational.

This study is too substantive

Peculiar outcomes of this investigation into Hinduism are substantive theses of philosophy but the starting point is the disagreements of philosophy internal to Hinduism. Hence, it seems like the results are wrong conclusions from the premises: from the mass of disagreement, no particular option in philosophy follows for anything and everything follows from a contradiction (the options of the disagreement). And yet, this investigation has proceeded as though in coming to terms with the disagreement, we can settle some philosophical debates, like the nature of thought and truth. So something is amiss. Given the grounding notion of objectivity as what we can disagree about, and truth as what reveals the content of thought, then in coming to terms with the disagreements, we are learning about the objective, and are hence coming to know, which involves true thinking. We are elevated as gods as we learn to disagree, and from such an elevated position, controversies become the contents of the facts and these facts can help us move on from a controversy. It is not an invalid inference nor is it a synthesis of opposing positions; it is rather a discovery of (new) philosophical facts by way of reason that begin with the disagreements, which are contradictions, and hence false. Arguments that always go from the false to the true are always valid!

The study relied upon untestable hypotheses: it is really an interpretation

This is a rehash of an objection addressed in Chapter 2, but it is worth repeating because people who endorse interpretation have difficulty shaking the conviction that any explanation is interpretive and it will seem to them that my frequent reference to the *W*est is a kind of interpretive bias. If my argument were truly interpretive, I would have to believe the *W*est as true and then explain only what is derivable from it, and everything else as mysterious. Alternatively, I would have to believe explication and only explain what is a derivation from that and everything else as mysterious. But as an explicator I endeavored to make *explicit* both methodologies (interpretation and explication) and contrast their logical implications—implications that are not necessarily true but objective. One of the ways this was expressed was via a contrast between the *W*est and a representative Hinduism.

The motivation for an obsessive indulgence in interpretation is a naïve view that there is no alternative. But to endorse interpretation as the default mode of explanation is to choose not to see it as something we can disagree about. This is not a fact: it is a choice that seems like a fact given the *W*est and the conflation of thought, belief, and language. That is *māyā*.

Conclusion

To talk responsibly about Hinduism is to come to terms with philosophy as something that was branded a religion, for the same reason anything is a religion: it falls outside of the interpretive resources of the *W*est. Or, put another way, as Hinduism as a category entails no common comprehensive doctrine, the only way to responsibly represent it is to represent it via its philosophical disagreements, which are philosophical disagreements as such. Whereas most religions are kinds—categories whose definition is instantiated by its members as members—*HINDUISM* is a class. The options of Hinduism are not any one specific theory but the disagreements of philosophy. Hinduism is the microcosm of philosophy with a South Asian twist. When Hindus disagree, they disagree about what philosophy all should adopt, and hence it is the microcosm of the metaphilosophical project: a philosophical disagreement about philosophies. As philosophical disagreements are not ethnic, representative Hinduism can serve as a model for what a philosophical world looks like.

Index

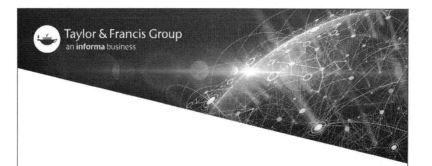

Made in the USA
Las Vegas, NV
26 June 2021

25486727R00133